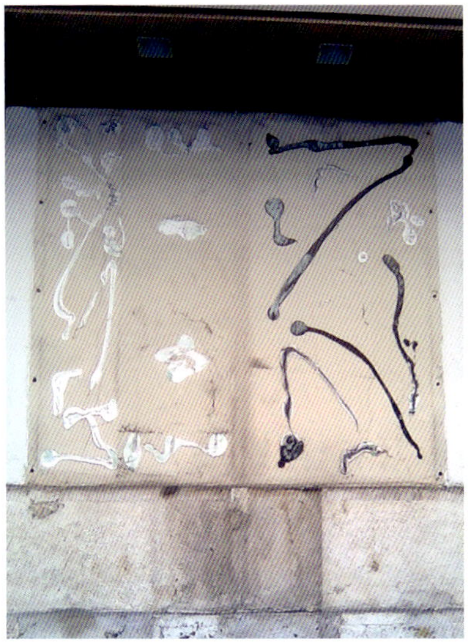

VERLAG FÜR MODERNE KUNST

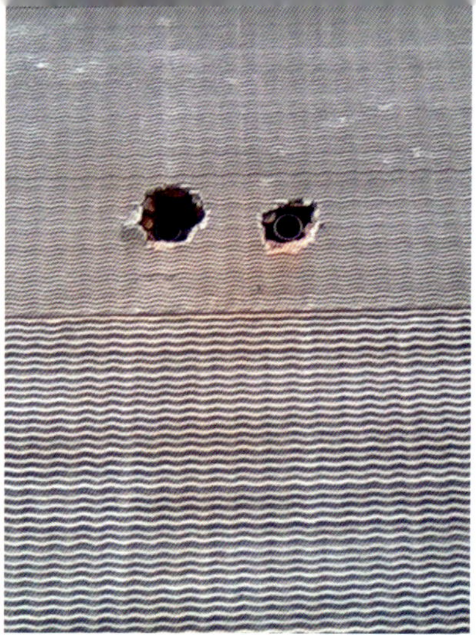

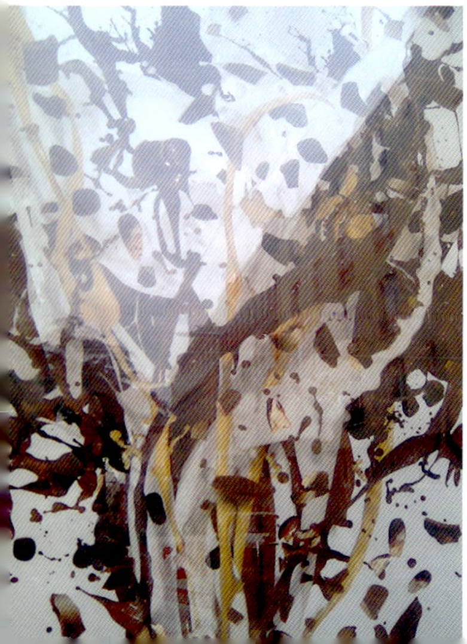

Manuel Gorkiewicz

Therapy

Make-Up Works

Voluptuous U-Turns on the Street of Style, Beauty, and Greed

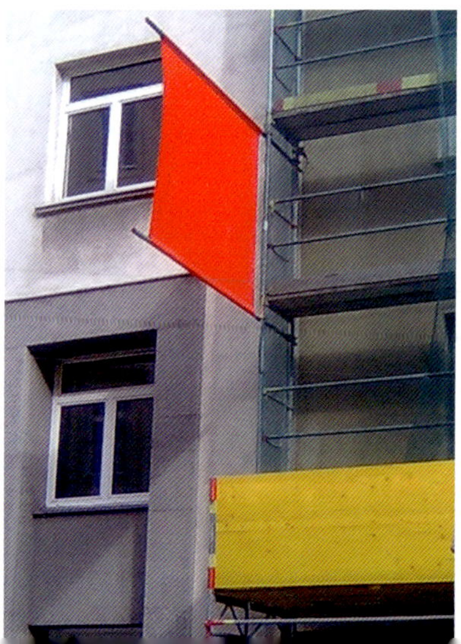

Manuel Gorkiewicz

Contents

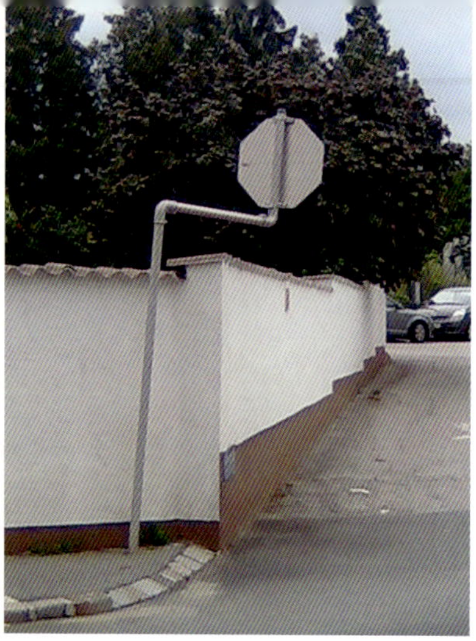

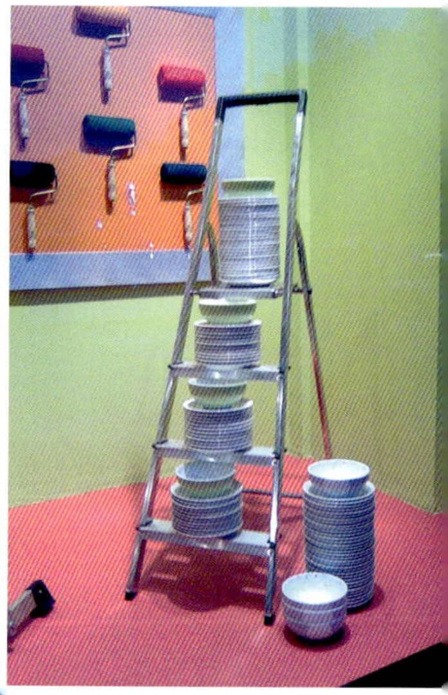

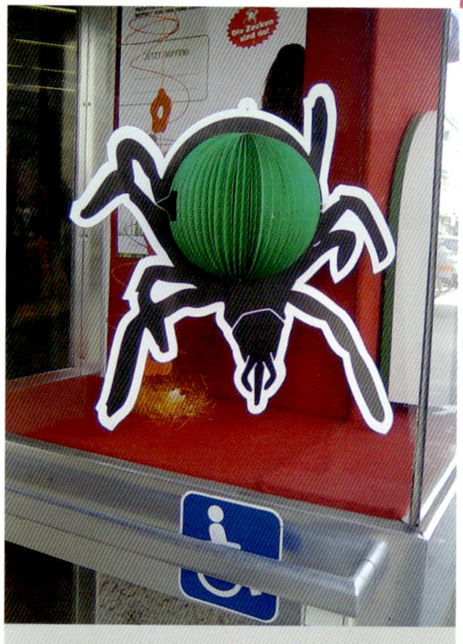
Die Zecken sind da!
JETZT IMPFEN!

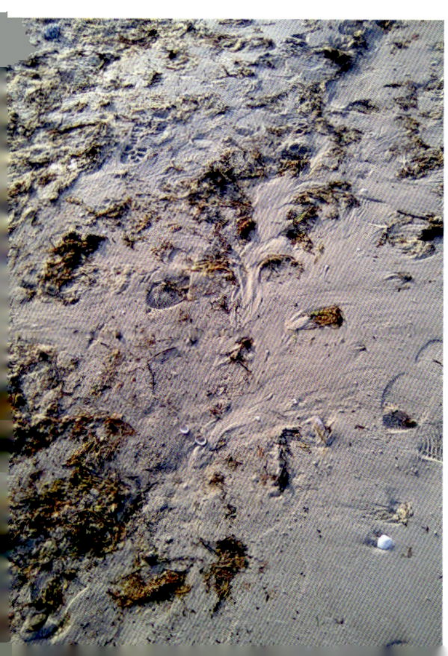

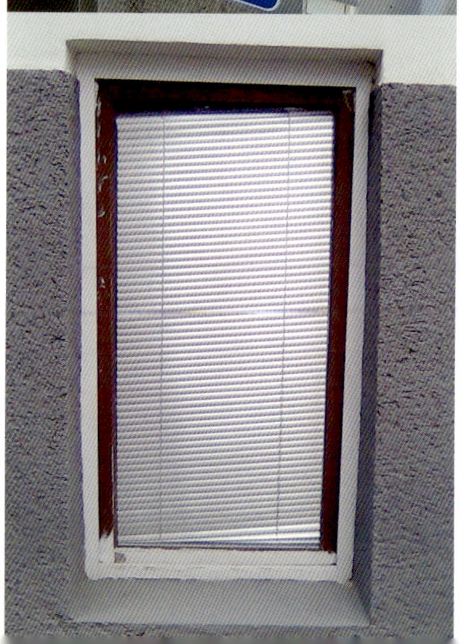

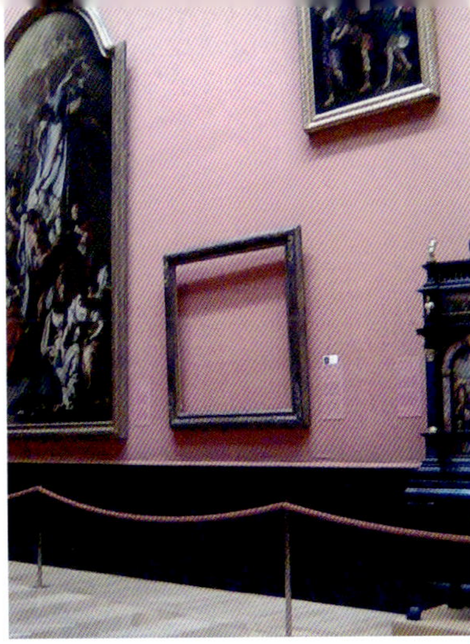

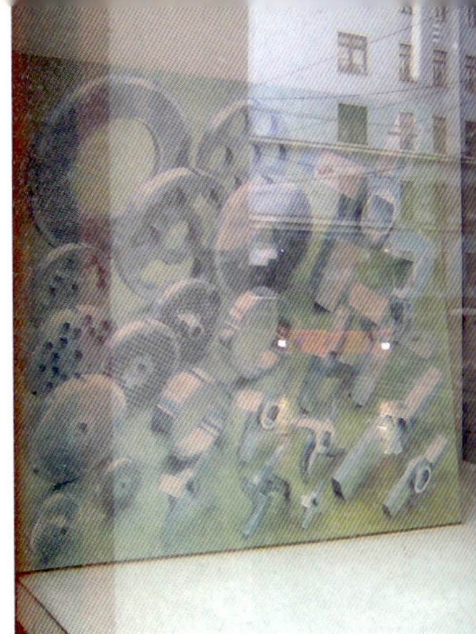

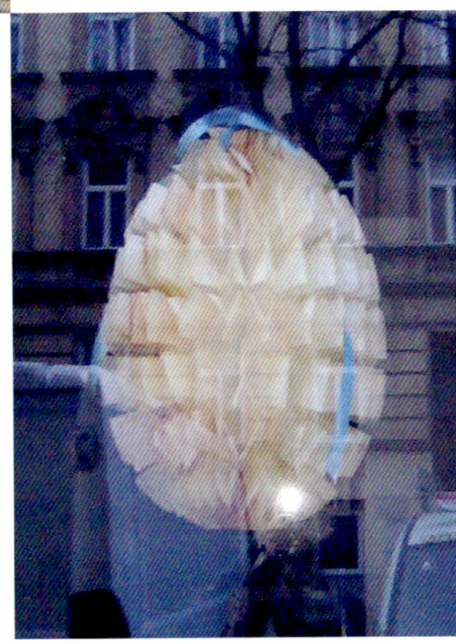

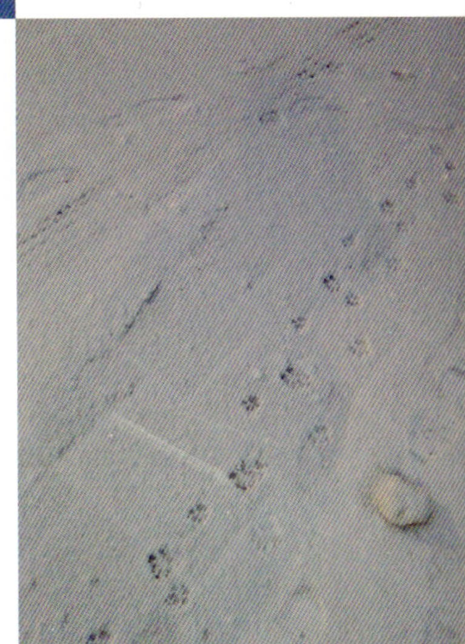

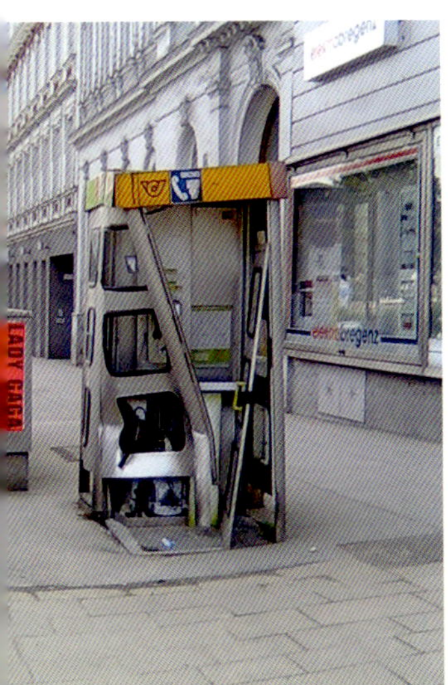

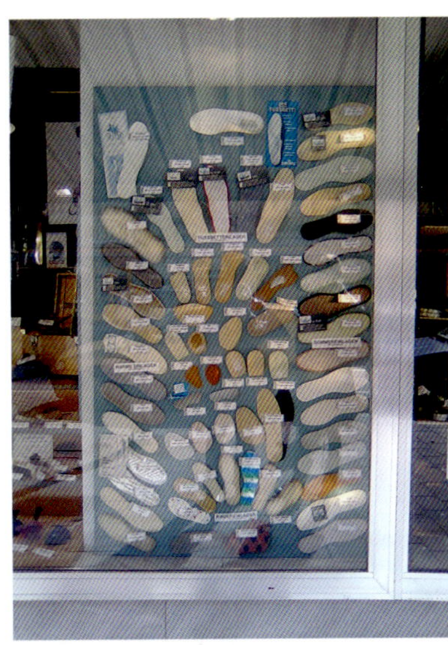

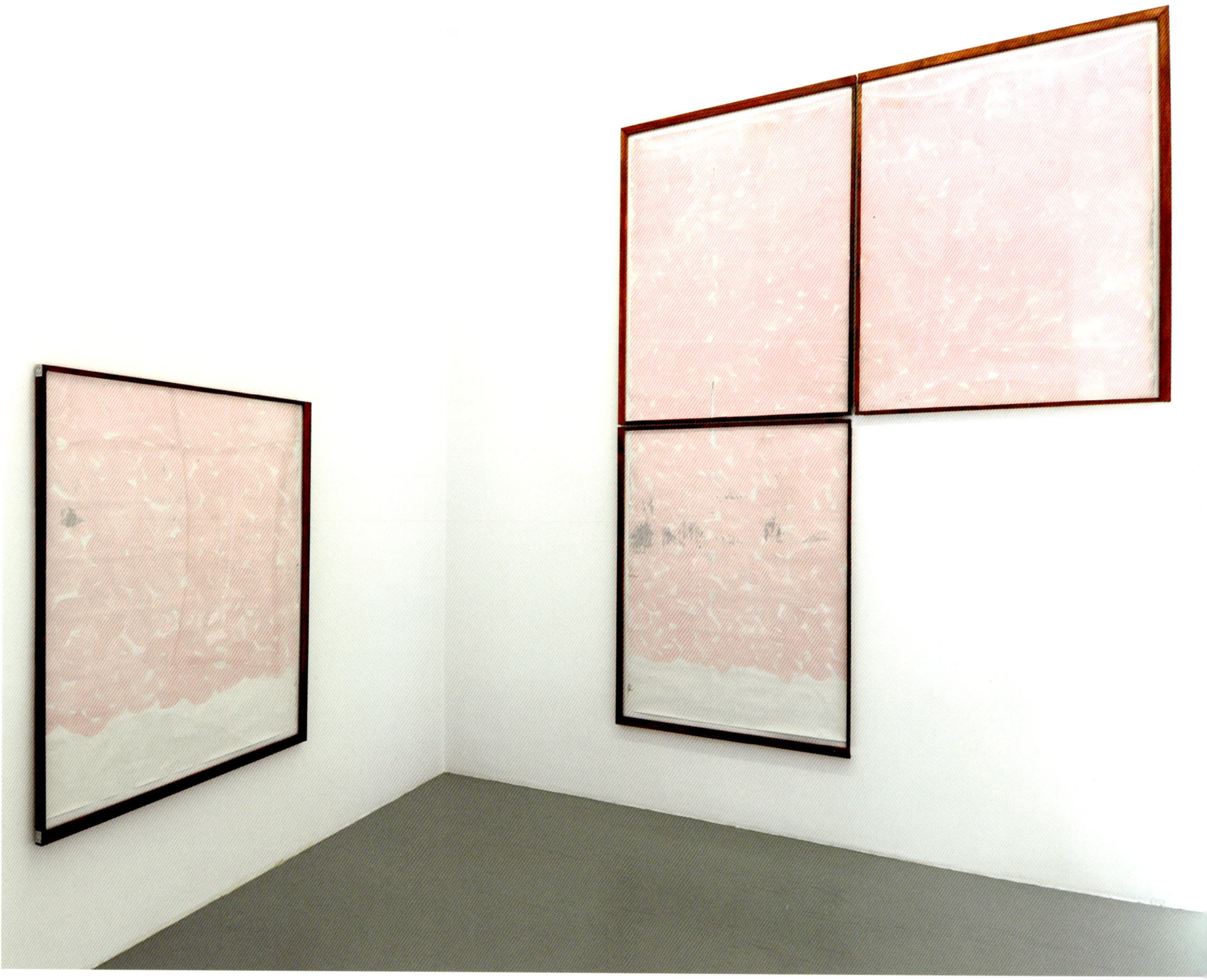

Galerie Mezzanin, Vienna, 2009

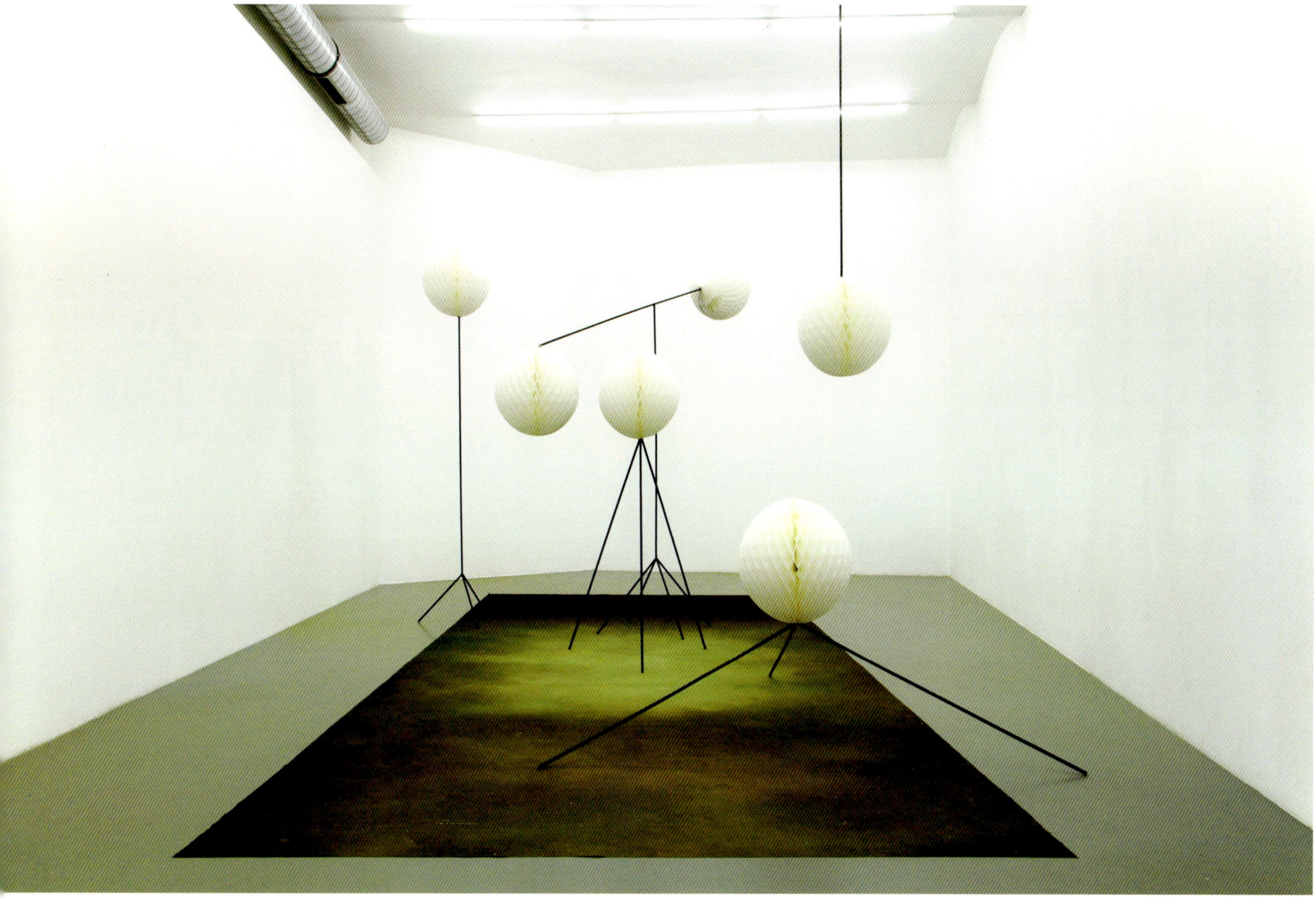

floor: Untitled, 670 x 290 cm, acrylic on canvas, 2009
from left to right: Untitled (Diego), 70 x 70 x 300 cm, iron, paper, 2009
Untitled (Maria & Sabel), 290 x 290 x 300 cm, iron, paper, 2009
Untitled (Margarita), 110 x 110 x 200 cm, iron, paper, 2009
Untitled (Perro), 260 x 260 x 110 cm, iron, paper, 2009
Untitled (Mari), 60 x 60 x 300 cm, iron, paper, 2009

left page: Untitled, each: 170 x 145 cm, acrylic on paper, 2009
next page: Untitled, 245 x 400 cm, acrylic on canvas, 2009

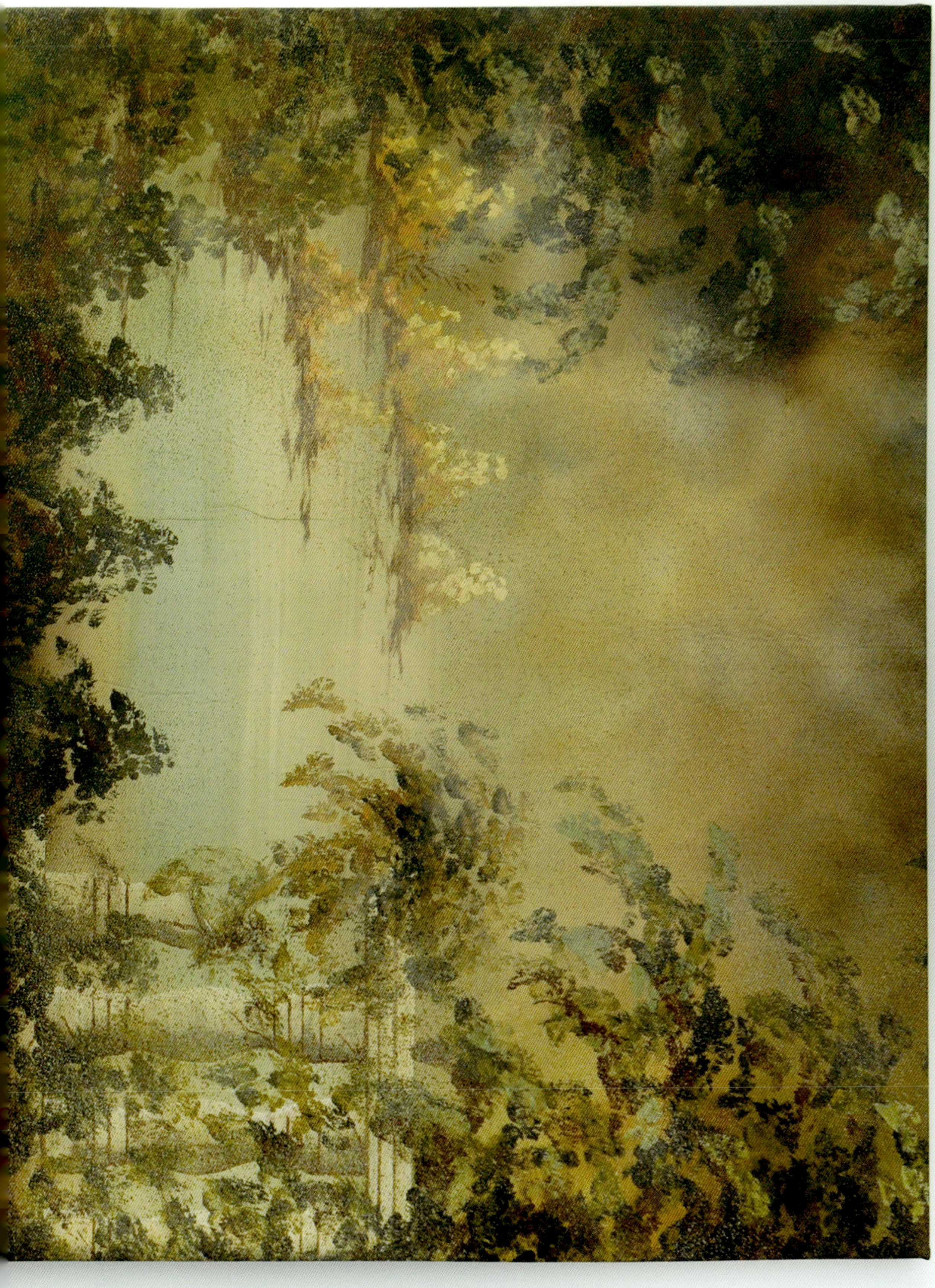

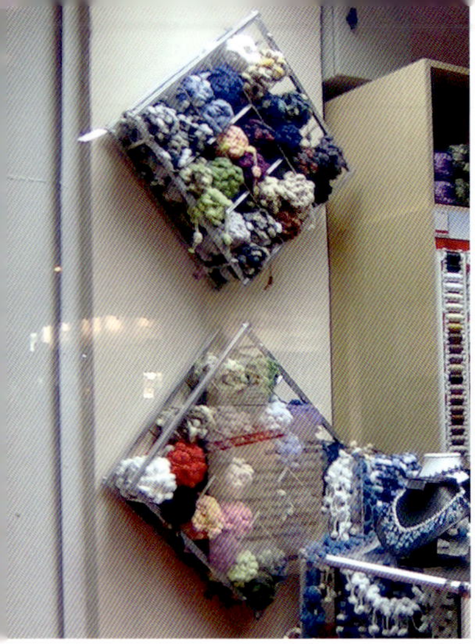

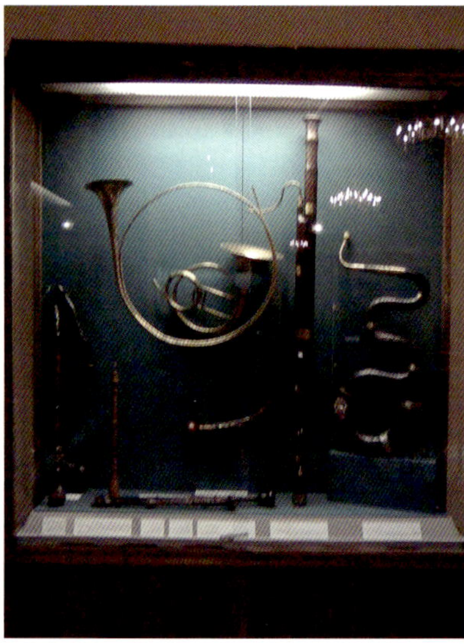

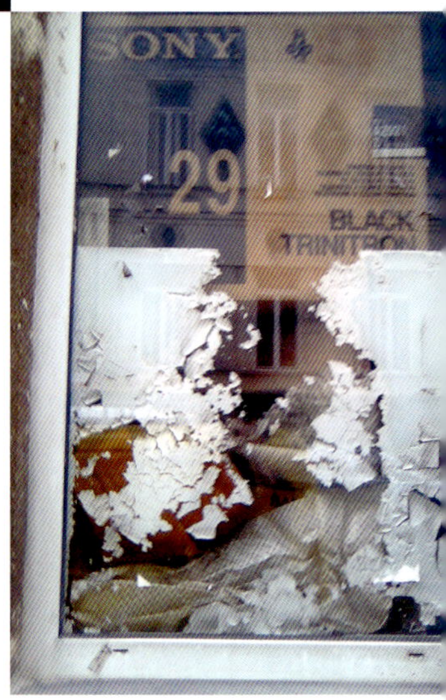
SONY
29
BLACK
TRINITRON

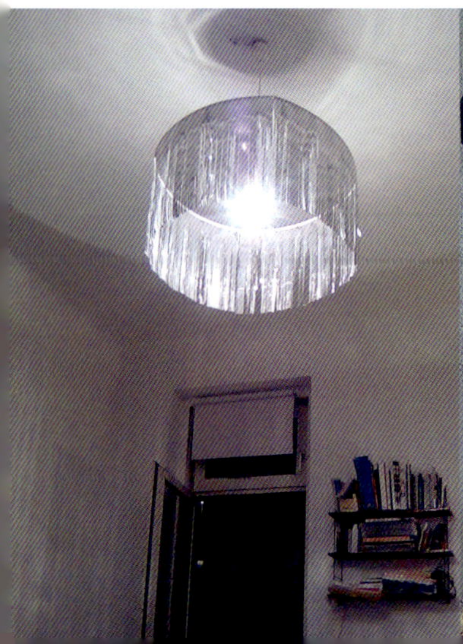

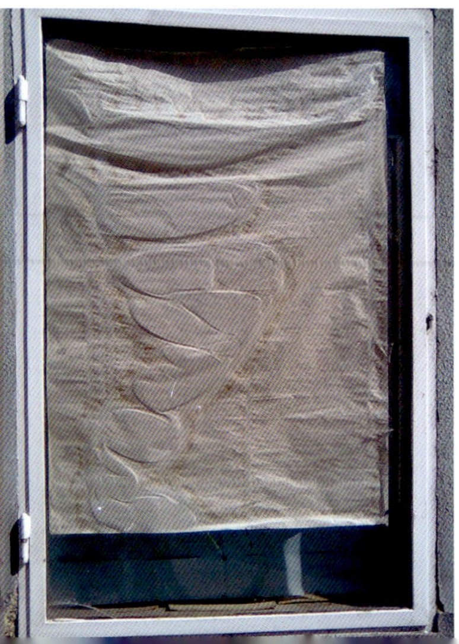

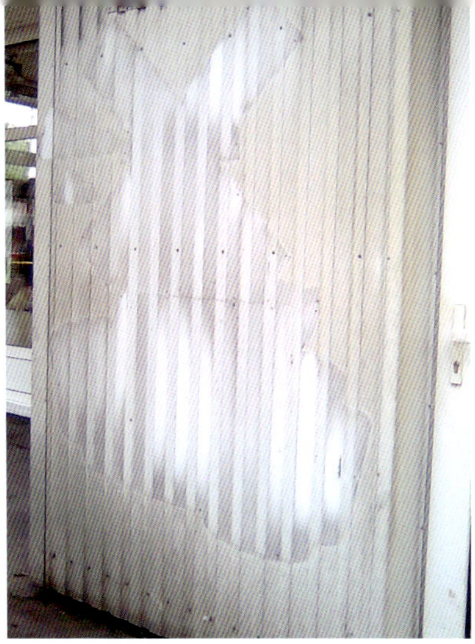

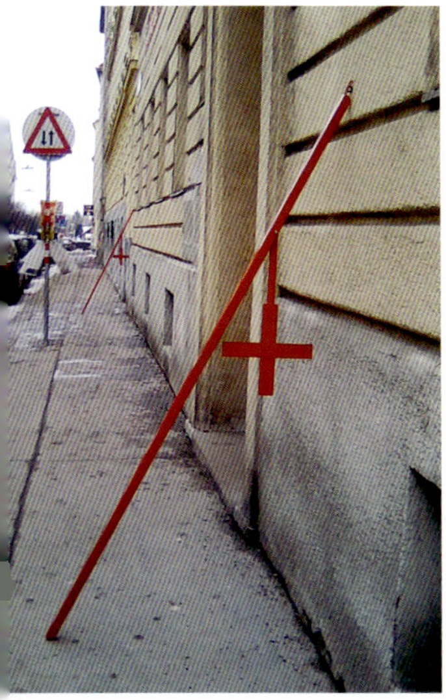

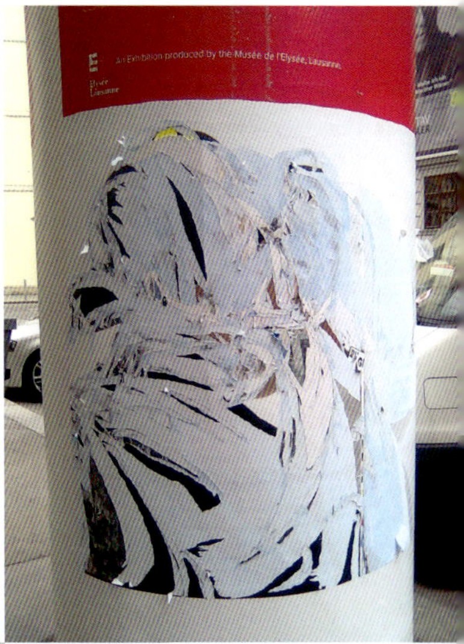
An Exhibition produced by the Musée de l'Elysée, Lausanne.
Elysée
Lausanne

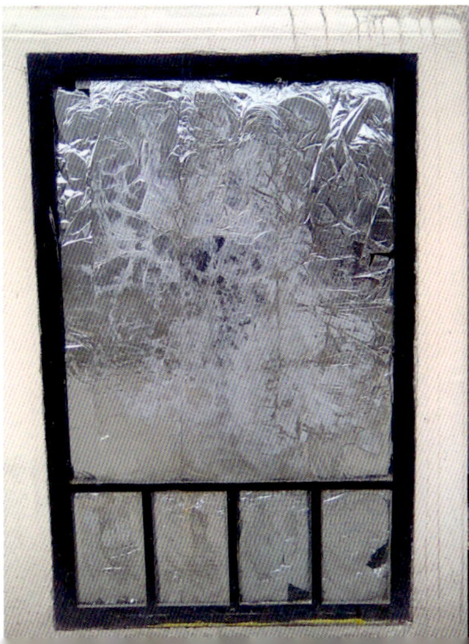

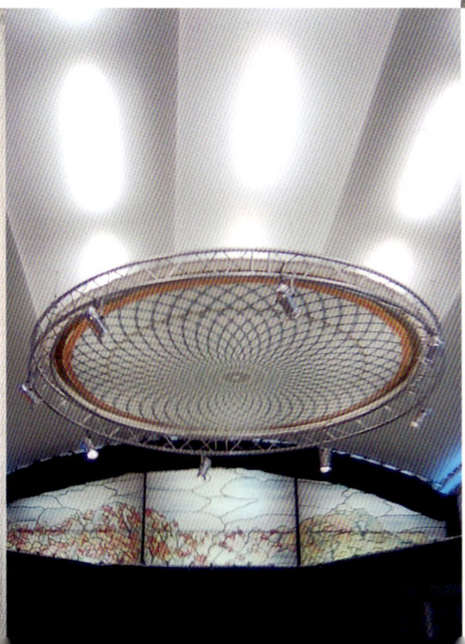

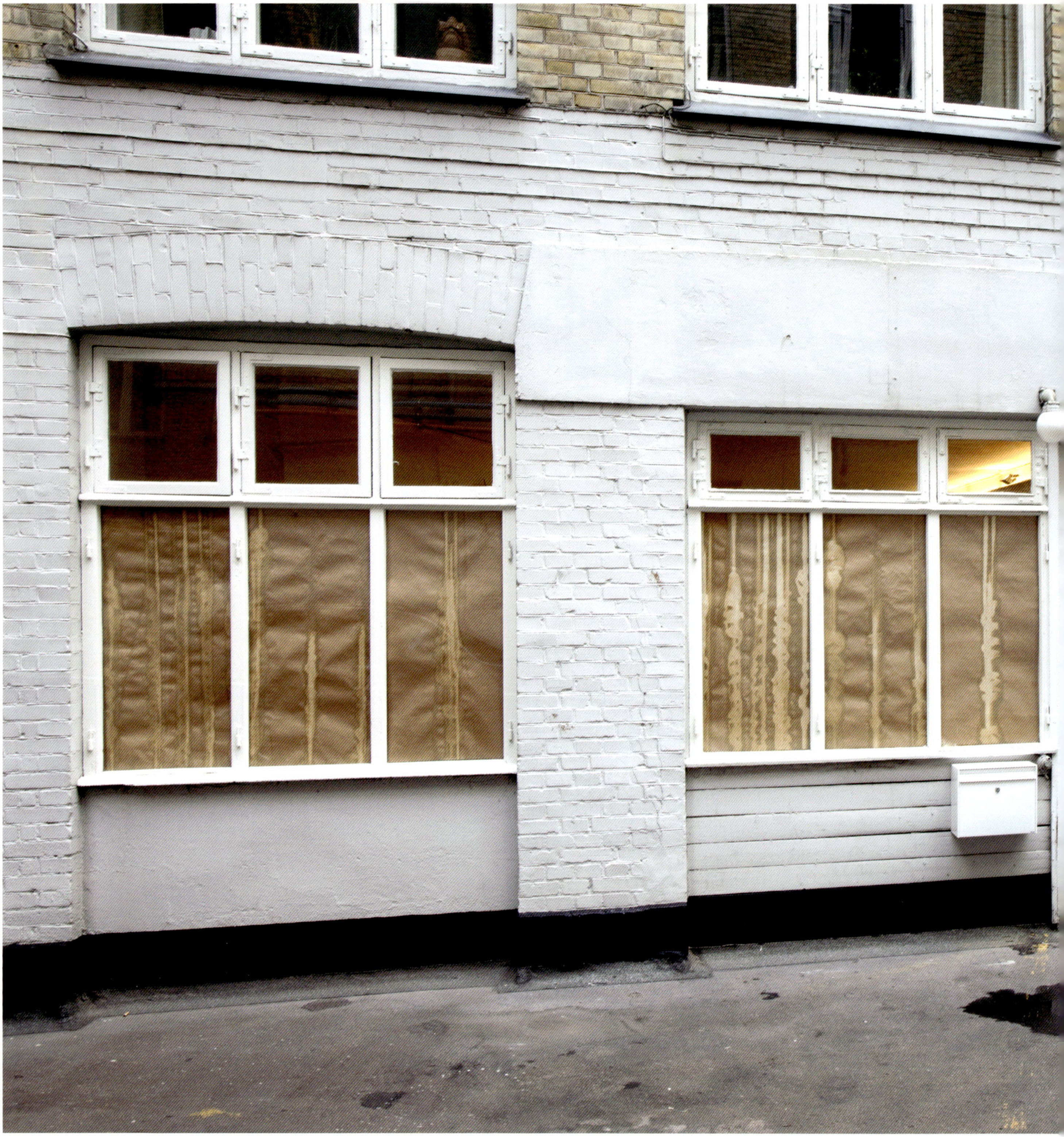

"Regarding Branches of Shops and Trees"
Antonia Low and Manuel Gorkiewicz
skulpturiDK, Copenhagen, 2009

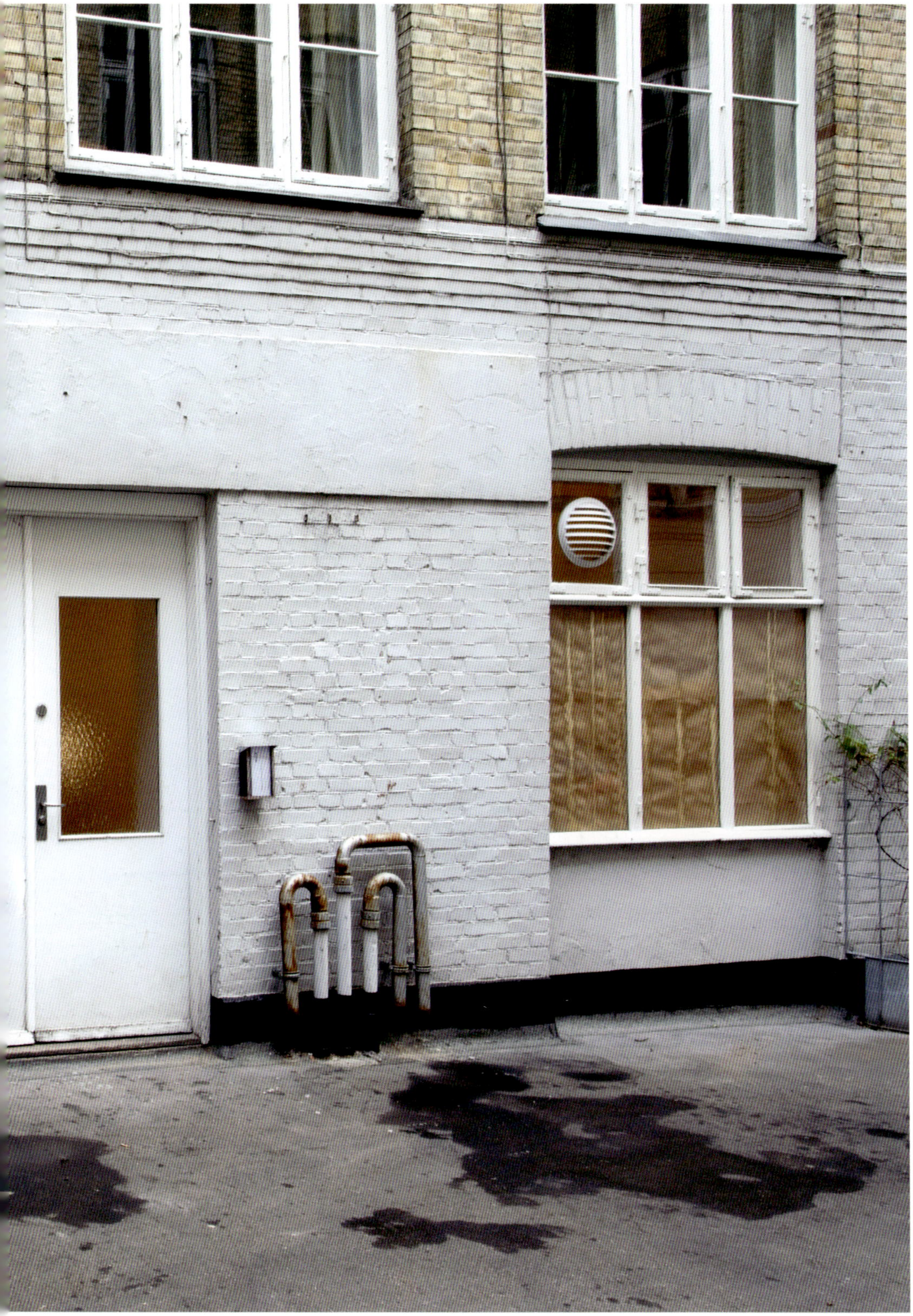

Untitled, chlorine on paper, 2009

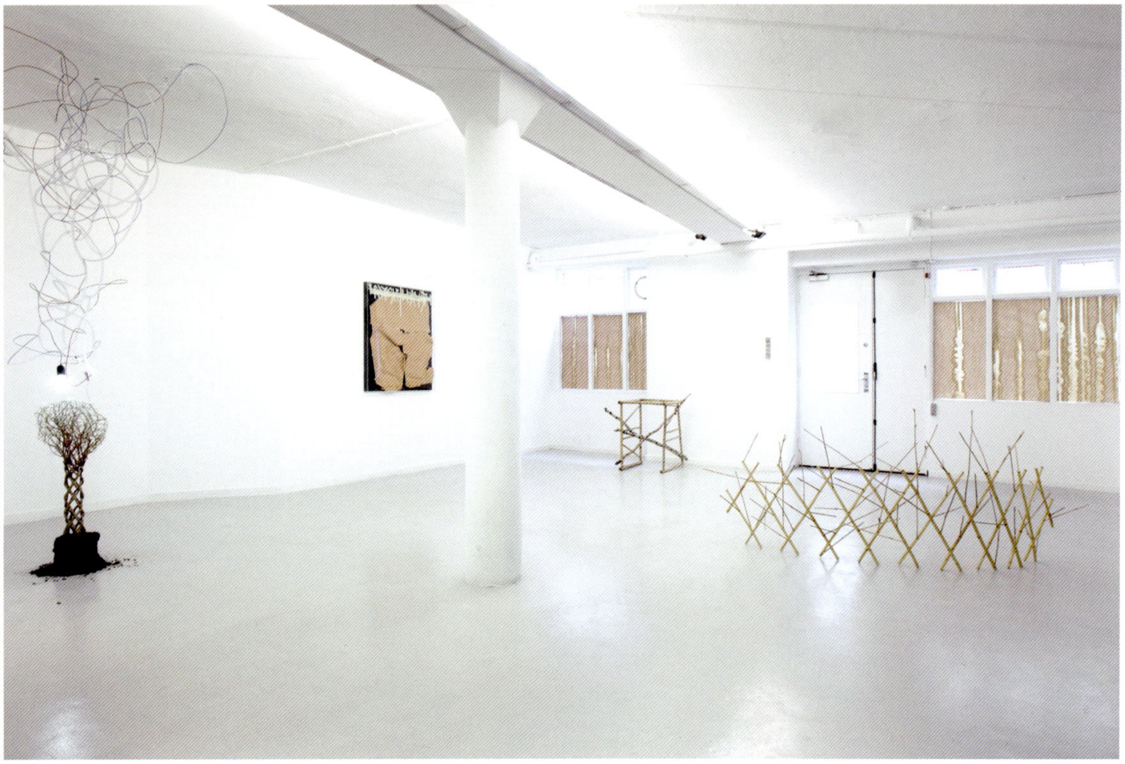

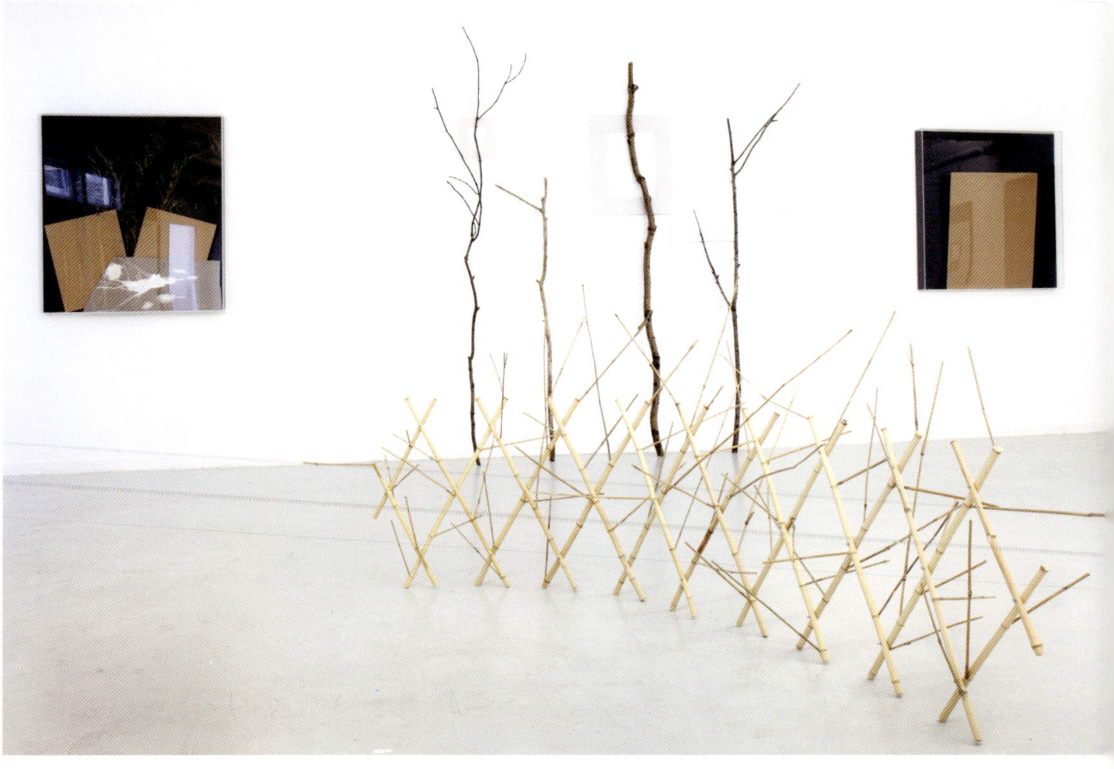

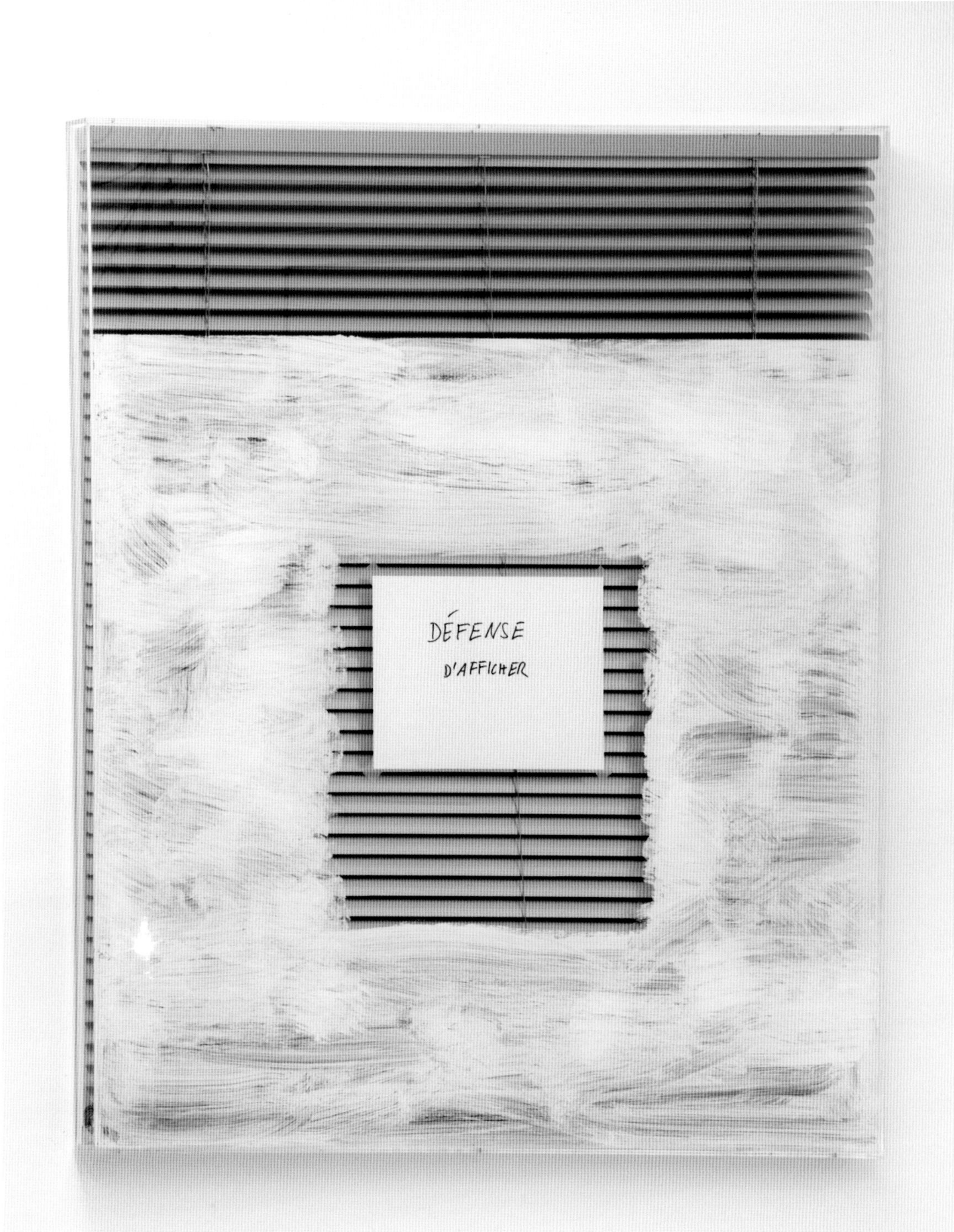

top left:
Untitled, 110 x 100 x 5 cm, wood, plexiglass, paper, tape, 2009
bottom left:
Untitled, 110 x 100 x 5 cm, wood, plexiglass, acrylic on paper, bamboo, 2009
Untitled, 100 x 100 x 10 cm, wood, plexiglass, cardboard, 2009
this page:
Untitled, 110 x 100 x 5 cm, wood, plexiglass, acrylic on paper, jalousie, 2009

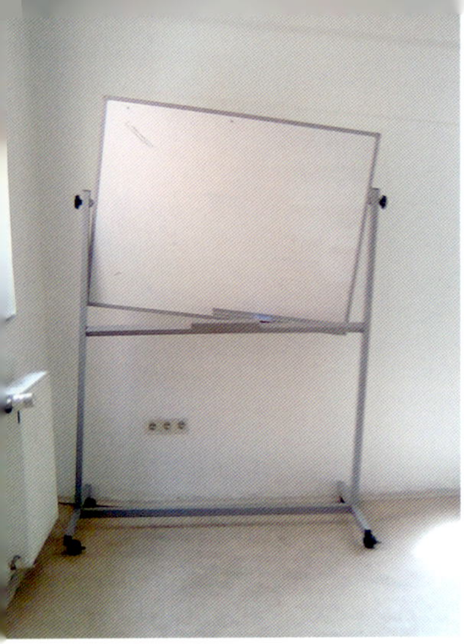

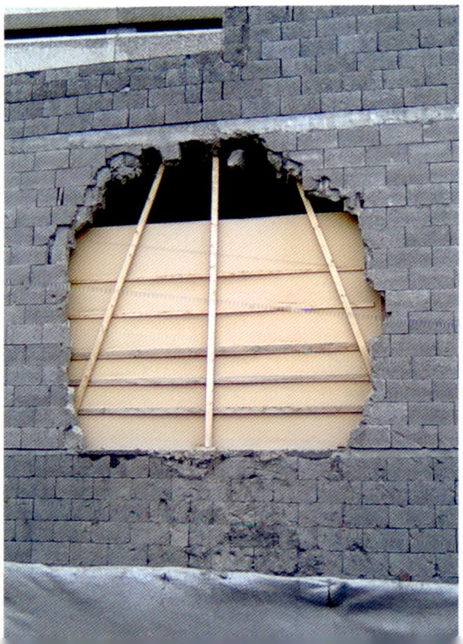

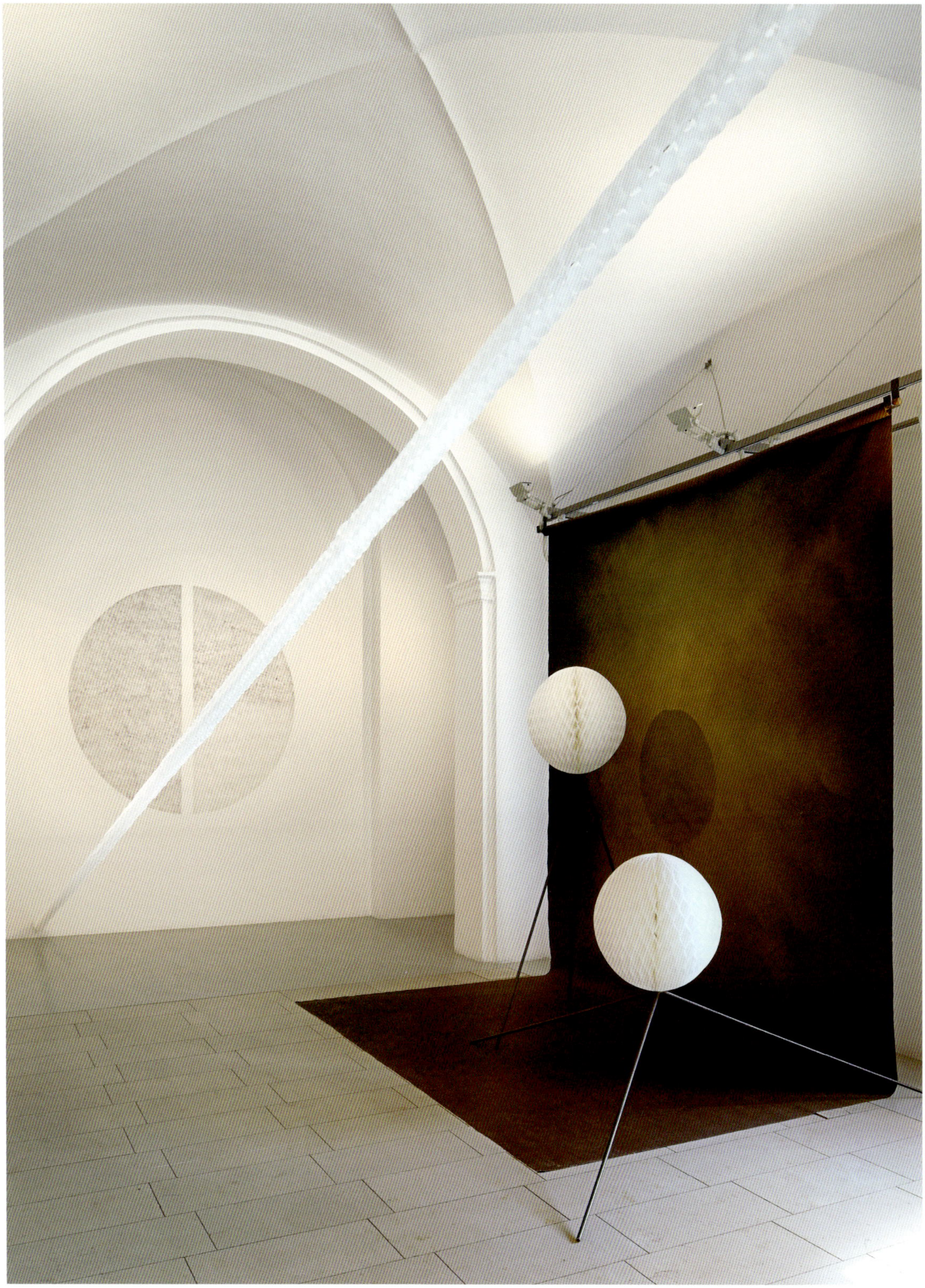

Austrian Cultural Forum Prague, 2010

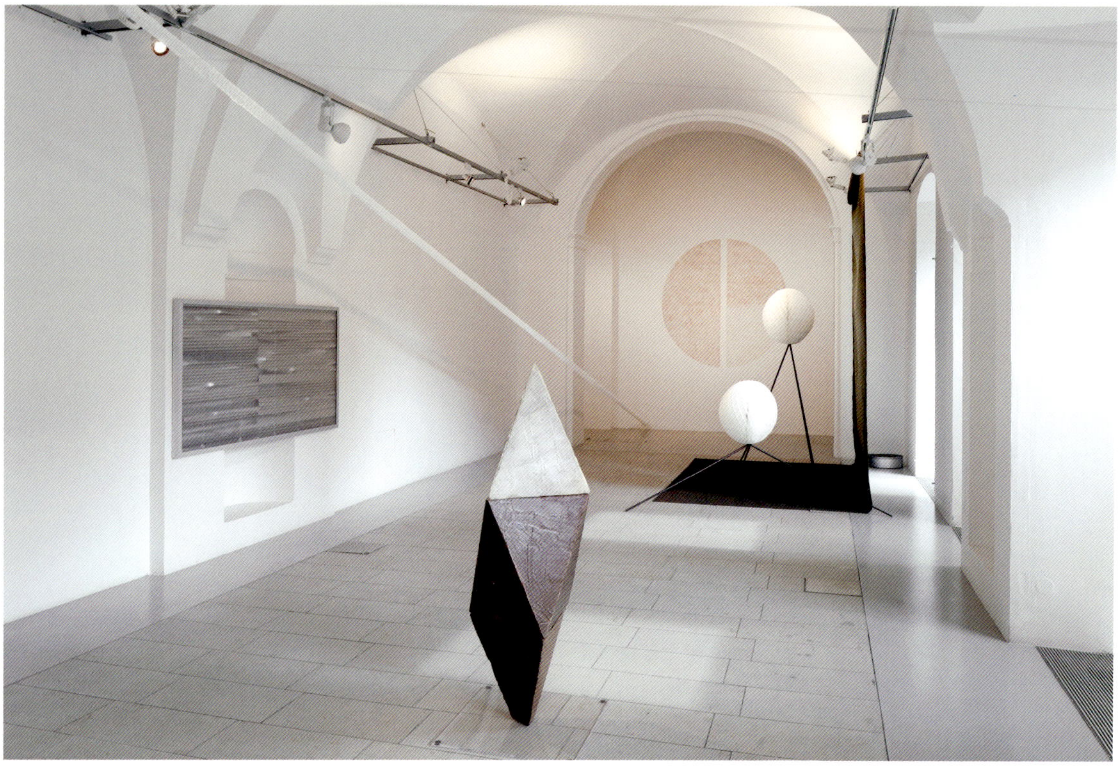

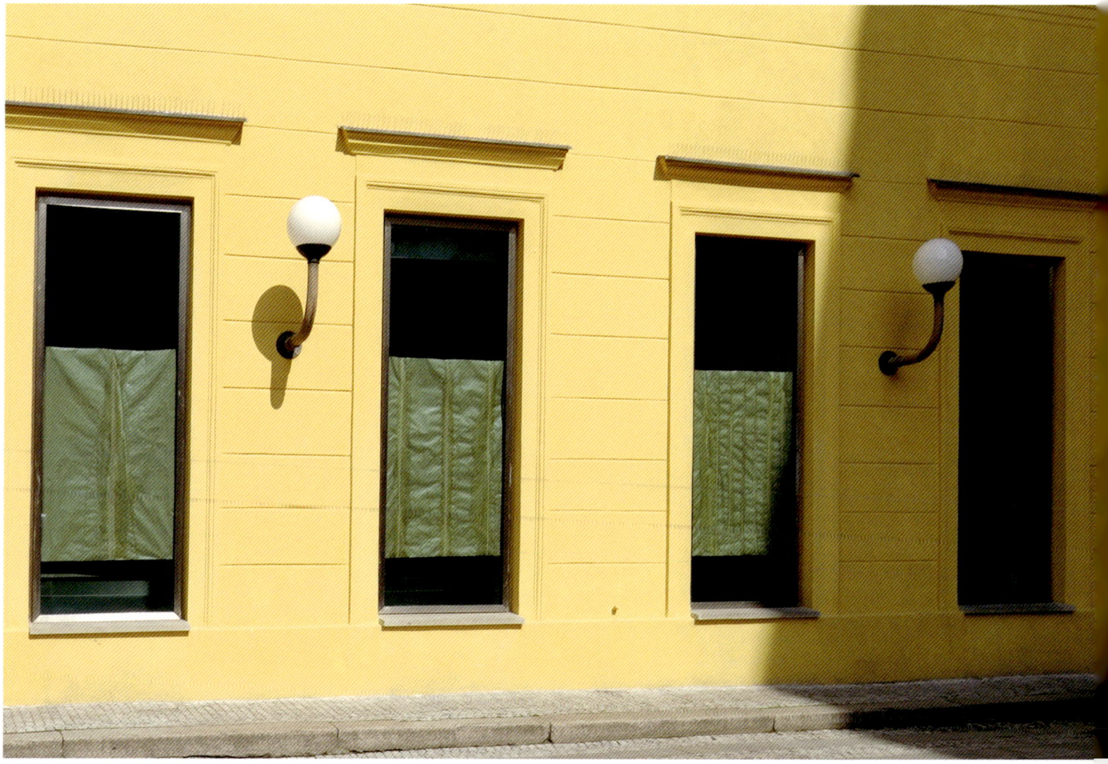

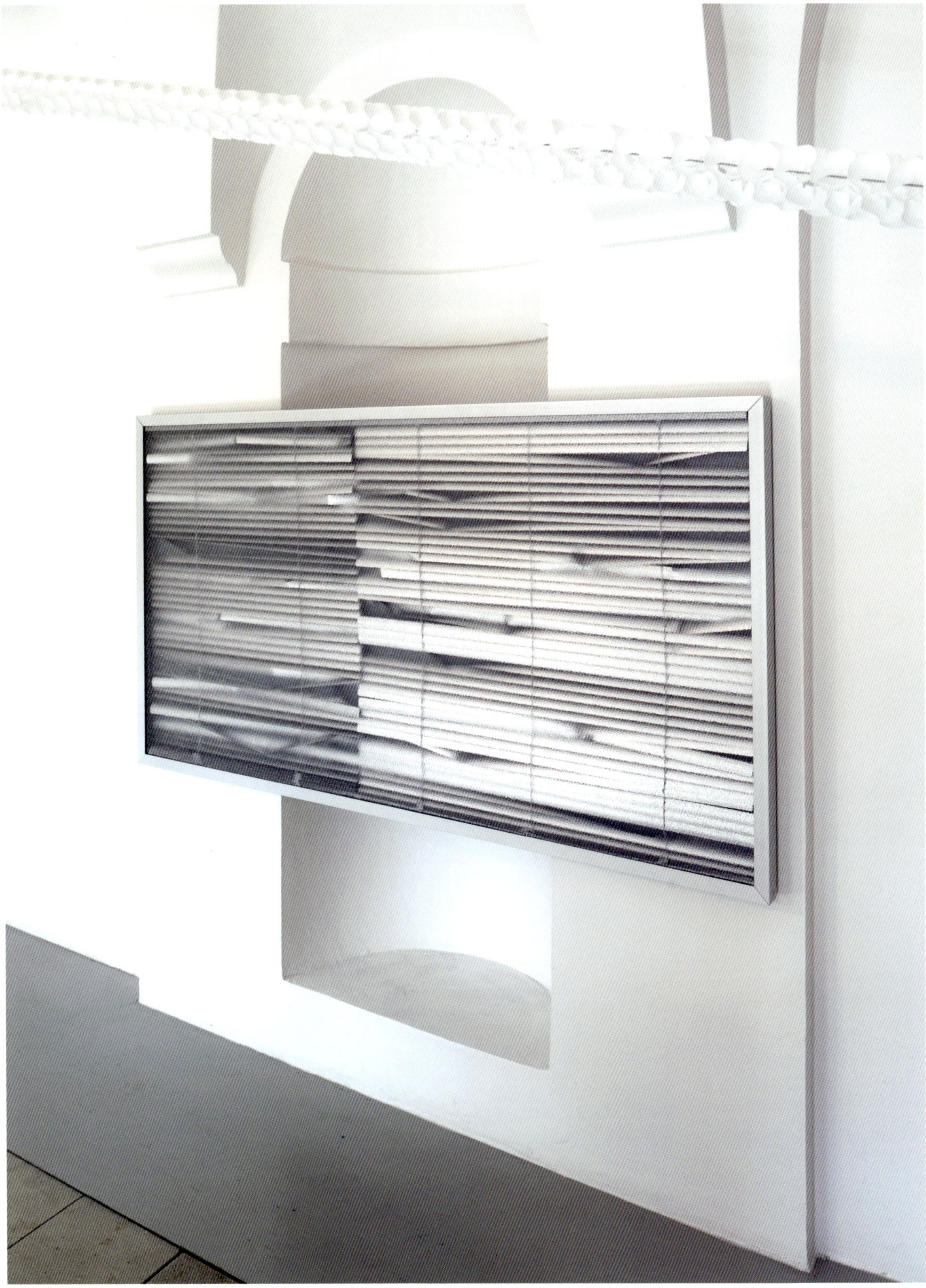

Austrian Cultural Forum Prague, 2010
p. 18: Untitled (Smokey Purple – green eyes), Ø 200 cm, make-up on wall, 2010
left page top: Untitled (Küppers II), 50 x 50 x 140 cm, chocolate, cardboard, 2006
left page bottom: Untitled, chlorine and acrylic on paper, 2010
this page: Untitled, 88 x 192 x 5 cm, aluminium, plexiglass, wood, jalousie, 2010

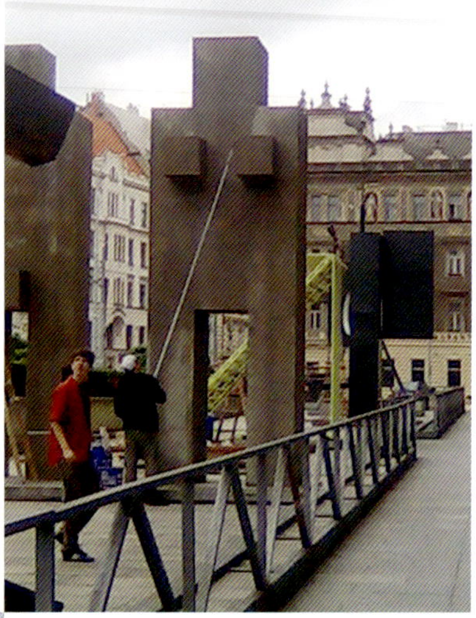

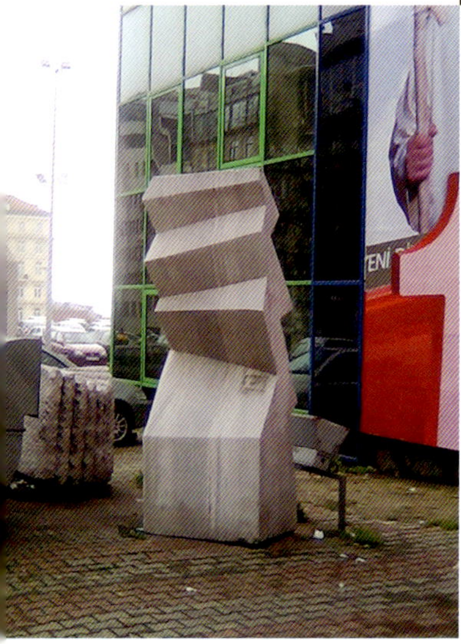

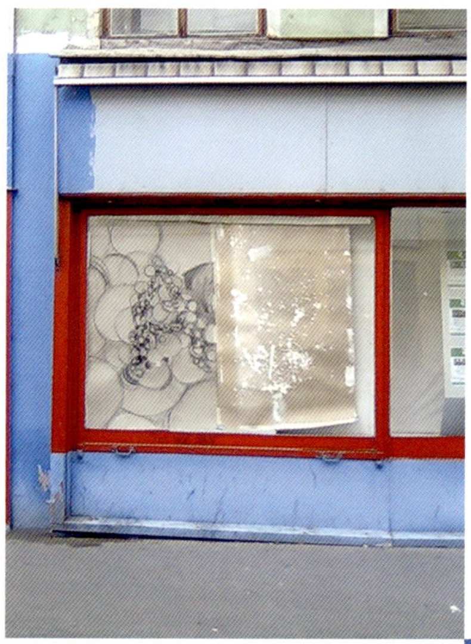

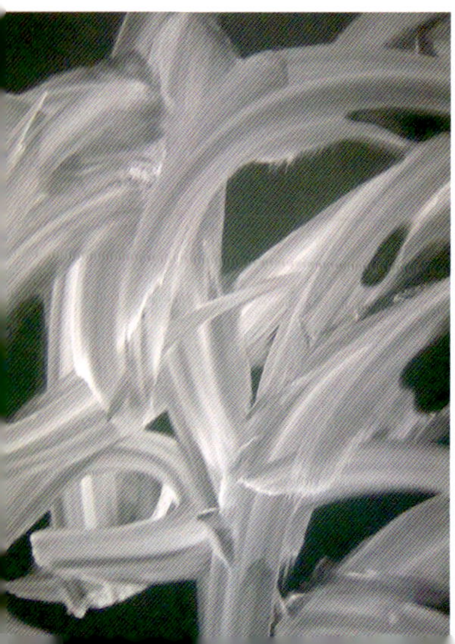

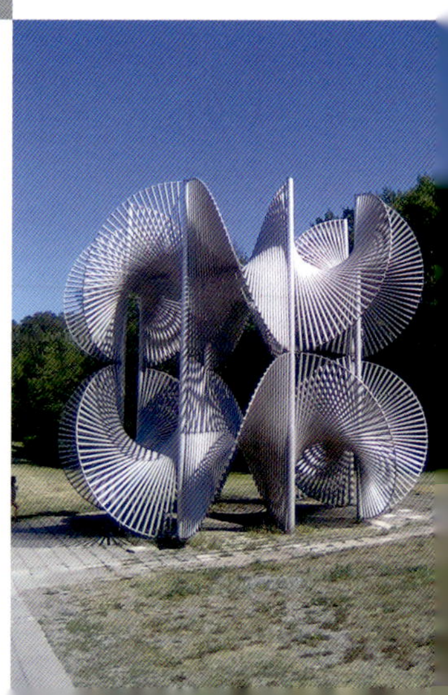

Kerstin Cmelka

Therapie

Seit Langem schon kommunizieren Manuel Gorkiewicz und ich viele unserer Themen über Bilder, die wir meist mit dem I-Phone aufnehmen und gleich einander zusenden. Auf Manuels Anraten hin landen sie in einem speziellen Ordner: „TPF" – die Abkürzung für „Therapy Folder".

Wir nennen sie Therapie-Bilder, weil sie den anderen aufheitern oder umsorgen sollen (am besten beides), indem sie nämlich auf die künstlerische Arbeit des anderen oder seine privaten Vorlieben (auch am besten beides) genauso wie auf miteinander Erlebtes anspielen. Die Therapie funktioniert gut, ich muss jedes Mal erstaunt laut auflachen oder berührt in mich hineinschmunzeln, bekomme ich ein neues Bild von ihm geschickt.

Öffne ich also besagten Ordner, was ich wirklich oft mache, dann sehe ich zum Beispiel einen Frauenhintern in Herzform ausgeschnitten, der für eine besondere Intimhygiene per extra in eine Toilette eingebautem Duschzylinder wirbt. Oder ich blicke in Schaufenster, einerseits in verlassene und vernachlässigte, die infolgedessen in Eigenregie eine Kunst-Patina erzeugen konnten, oder andererseits in solche, die fast überambitioniert von fremder Hand bestellt werden. Sie beheimaten zum Beispiel Gemälde zu Dekorationszwecken, die Motive der ausgestellten Kleidung aufnehmen, oder umgekehrt camouflieren die Kleider plötzlich ganz wie von selbst die Deko-Bilder – man weiß das oft nicht mehr so genau, was zuerst da war ... Extrem sind auch die zuletzt von Gorkiewicz zu Luftballons aufgeblasenen und sogleich fotografierten „Besamungshandschuhe" aus pinkem Plastik, die eigentlich als Schutz für Tierärzte, die In-vitro-Behandlungen vornehmen, dienen. Weiters finde ich im Ordner unfreiwillig zum Witz gewordene Bildbeispiele diverser unsinniger bis pseudo-sinniger privater und öffentlicher Baumaßnahmen – etwa einen auf eine Plastikplane gedruckten Sesamring, aus dessen Mitte sich vulgär ein Lüftungsschacht wölbt. Dann auch Hasen-, Hirschkuh-, Katzenfiguren – tierische Alter Egos aller Art, aktiv als Schrebergarten-Kunst, Living Sculptures oder traurige Kostümreste einer durchfeierten Nacht, die wohl auf dem Asphalt gelandet und den BesitzerInnen im zwischenmenschlichen Gefecht abhandengekommen sein müssen.

All das macht nicht nur enorm Spaß, sondern schafft zudem gehörige Inspiration. Wir kommunizieren natürlich auch über gewisse Insider-Codes in diesen angeblichen Abbildungen der Realität und sagen uns darüber Persönliches. Bei mir entsteht hin und wieder das Gefühl, einen intimen Anteil am Leben meines Bilderfreundes zu haben, so wie auch ich ihm durch unseren Foto-Tausch Einblick in meine Gefühle gewähre. Die Fotonachrichten bilden Bande, der andere kann sie hernach weiter binden, Knoten knüpfen, diese wieder auftrennen sowie dem anderen ein neues Band zuwerfen.

Diese Kommunikationsform ist natürlich nicht neu und schon gar nicht unsere Erfindung: zeitgenössische soziale Netzwerke und die dazugehörigen Meta-Kommentare der bildenden Kunst, das mittlerweile historisch gewordene Format Mail Art und so weiter – alles bereits da gewesen.

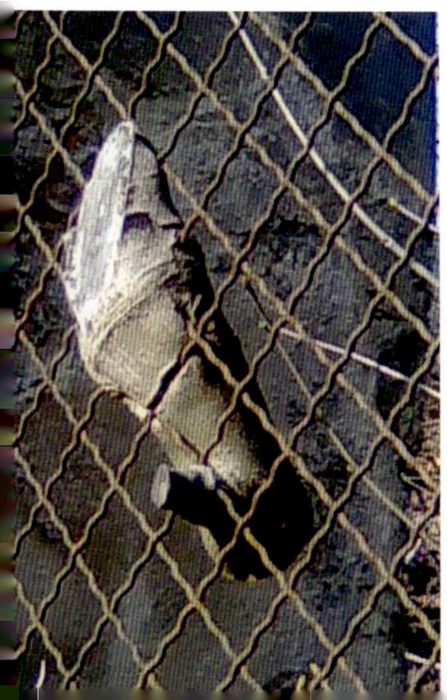

Auch das, was Manuel in dem hier vorliegenden Künstlerbuch macht, nämlich diese und ähnliche im öffentlichen Raum gesammelte *therapy files* seinen eigenen künstlerischen Arbeiten als Bezugssystem gegenüberzustellen, ist im Prinzip nichts Neuartiges, und ich finde eine solche Gestaltungsgeste oftmals auch zu pädagogisch, manchmal sogar altklug (siebengescheit). Warum ich das in diesem Fall gar nicht tue und außerdem die ganze Sache mit dem Therapie-Ordner erzähle, geschieht, weil hier sowohl für die im Buch reproduzierte Kunst als auch für die abgelichteten Szenen und Momente der Realität ein therapeutischer Mehrwert erzeugt wird.

Was aber ist das, ein therapeutischer Mehrwert? Und vor allem wie soll dieser in einem solchen Zusammenhang aussehen?

Während einer psychotherapeutischen Behandlung kann die/der PatientIn oft nicht erklären, was die wöchentlichen Sitzungen bewirken oder verändern, beziehungsweise ob sie so etwas überhaupt tun. Manchmal hält dieser Zustand auch noch an, wenn eine Behandlung schon längere Zeit vorbei ist, ohne dass jedoch gleichzeitig das Gefühl eintreten würde, die Therapie wäre deswegen missglückt. Ein Therapieerfolg ist meist nicht auf schnellem und direktem Weg messbar und schon gar nicht Unwissenden oder Nicht-Eingeweihten vermittelbar.

Stellt Gorkiewicz nun seine Werke dem Alltag, der sie umgibt, der sie auch speist und wieder verspeist, gegenüber, passiert einfach gesagt Folgendes: Seine Arbeiten werden – zumindest für fantasielose Anfänger der Kunstbetrachtung – seriöser, ernsthafter, und die uns umgebende Realität wird – zumindest für Kurzsichtige und Langeweiler – lustiger. Für alle anderen ist es aber auch toll, weil durch das Neben- und mehrfach belichtende Übereinander die Beziehungen der „Arbeiten“ und ihrer „Quellen“ und „Ziele“ immer wieder hin, her und wieder zurück blitzen und in dieser multistabilen Gymnastik ein neuer Denkansatz, so möchte ich sagen, fabriziert wird.

In seinen Produktionen verwendet Gorkiewicz nämlich meist einfache Materialien, die wir aus populären Bereichen kennen: Girlanden, Softeis und Schokolade vom Basteln als Kind und vom Basteln mit Kindern zum Beispiel. Indem er die eigenen Qualitäten und technischen Grenzen genauso wie die reale und mögliche Repräsentationsgeschichte seines jeweiligen Materials kennt und vor allem ernst nimmt, und weil er über technisches Know-how, Erfahrung und eine gewisse Haltung, die irgendwo zwischen Anti-Held und ritterlicher Verve verortet ist, verfügt, entsteht ein interessant abgeschirmter Raum aus folgender Ambivalenz: Er arbeitet streng material-inhärent und mutet seinem Material dabei immens viel zu, fügt den fragilen Papieren, Stoffen, Folien, Flüssigkeiten Manipulationen, Grenzverschiebungen und -erweiterungen, Skalierungen und Verschiebungen zu, sodass bei den Betrachtenden das heute eher für ungewöhnlich erachtete Gefühl der Frohheit produziert wird. Die Besucher_innen seiner Arbeiten sind froh, weil sie die Materialien und auch ihre Bedeutung wiedererkennen (zum Beispiel „Wow, aus DER Girlande, die ich noch vom Kindergeburtstag her kenne, baute der eine so massive Skulptur!? Das ist doch sicher ein anderes Material, das nur so aussieht wie ... oder??“). Gleichzeitig sind sie (noch viel) froh(er), weil sie sehen, was man mit den Dingen, die jedem zur Verfügung stehen (und damit auch aus sich selbst), alles machen kann!

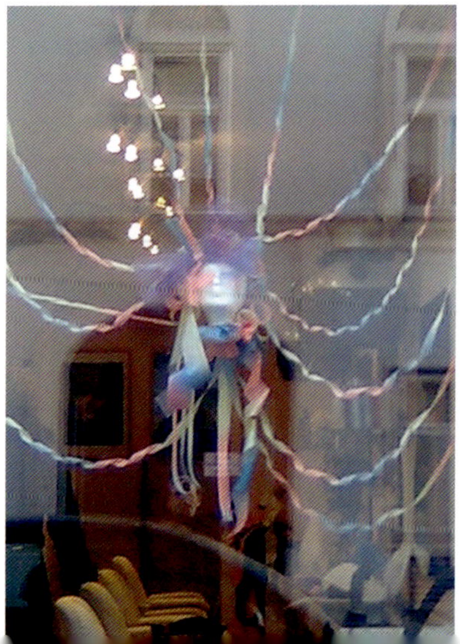

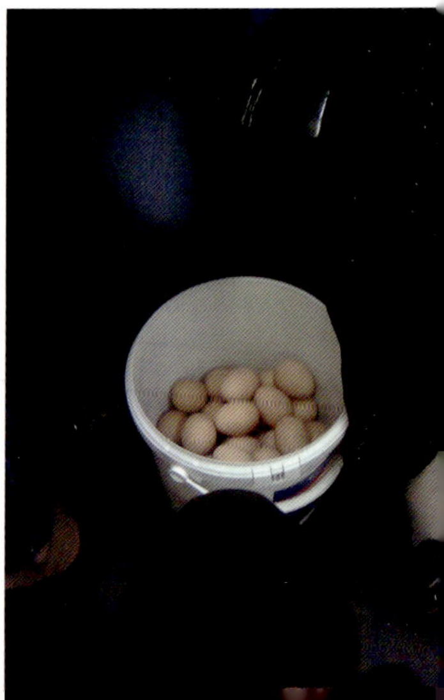

Gorkiewicz expandiert seine ausgewählten Materien, Konstruktionen und Bedeutungen oft überdimensional, indem er ganze Straßenzüge vergirlandet oder pompös barocke Luster wie aus papierenen Scherenschnitten baut – und all diese Dinge funktionieren auch noch ganz normal! Der Luster ist eine formale Skulptur, ein Objekt und ein Gebrauchsgegenstand, den man praktisch wie jede alltägliche Lampe an- und ausknipsen kann, mit dem sich ein kleines Zimmer wie ein riesiger Tanzsaal anfühlt, der ein weiter und weiter zu spinnender Kommentar auf Pop Art ist, die Idee des englischen Gartens noch einmal von einer anderen Seite aus kitzelt und der Hightech, frühe Moderne und Camp zusammen beheimaten kann. Diese Gedanken- und Produktionsgänge als Betrachter_in mitzugehen, macht froh und ist gleichzeitig therapeutisch – selbst ohne die im Buch dazu gedruckten Therapiebilder.

Was diese ausgewählten Fotos von Situationen aus Manuel Gorkiewicz' Welt-Streifzügen aber zusätzlich machen, ist, dass wir nach der Gorkiewicz-Lektüre solche Szenarien, an denen wir tagtäglich vorbeischlendern, plötzlich schneller, fokussierter und selektiver wahrnehmen, dass wir sie lustvoller begreifen und in der Folge auch das Erkannte, Erlebte immer wieder neu nachvollziehen und herbeiholen können. Wenn wir noch dazu Künstler_innen sind, verstehen wir umso mehr, dass wir selbst eine ähnliche Geste, ein ähnliches Gefühl, eine ähnliche Produktion zu aktivieren imstande sind. Durch die Gorkiewicz-Brille die Welt zu sehen, führt zu einer speziell erweiterten Sichtweise von Manuels eigenen künstlerischen Arbeiten. Nicht um diese dann irgendwie nachzumachen, kopieren zu wollen (oder zu können), sondern vielmehr um ihr reales Bezugssystem, die uns umgebende ästhetische Oberfläche, aufwerten zu können. Natürlich nicht in dem Sinn, dass wir dann mit dem, was um uns ist (sowohl in der Kunst als auch in der Realität), plötzlich zufrieden wären, sondern dass wir es – in echt – produktiv machen können, dass eine solche schwungvolle Geste der Produktion zumindest erzeugt werden kann – vorausgesetzt allerdings man besitzt wie Gorkiewicz die Verve, sie auch im Alleingang auszuführen. Therapie bedeutet, dass man am Ende selber zurechtkommt und wieder etwas kann, das vorher verschüttet war.

Es ist so wie in der Chaosmagie, wo es drei Arten gibt, einen magischen Moment herbeizuführen: Neben der sogenannten Dämpfungs- und der diametral dazu stehenden Erregungsgnosis gibt es eine dritte Option, die „indifferente Leere", in der jener magische Moment nämlich im Vorübergehen erzeugt wird, so nebensächlich, dass man ihn gar nicht merkt oder gleich wieder vergisst, ja man muss ihn sogar verdrängen können, sonst kann er gar nicht wirksam werden, geschweige denn erneut entstehen. Und ja, ich glaube, dieses schwierige, Umwege, aber Lust bringende Unterfangen ist es, was uns Gorkiewicz in diesem Künstlerbuch offen darlegt und damit als wechselwirkendes Produktionsverfahren generös anbietet: Durch die erfinderische genauso wie trickreiche Verquickung und damit einhergehende Aufhebung von gebauter und ungebauter Realität, von alltäglicher Welt und Alltagsinszenierung zeigt er einen therapeutischen Mehrwert und die Möglichkeit(en) einer Therapie – auch, aber vor allem in der Kunst.

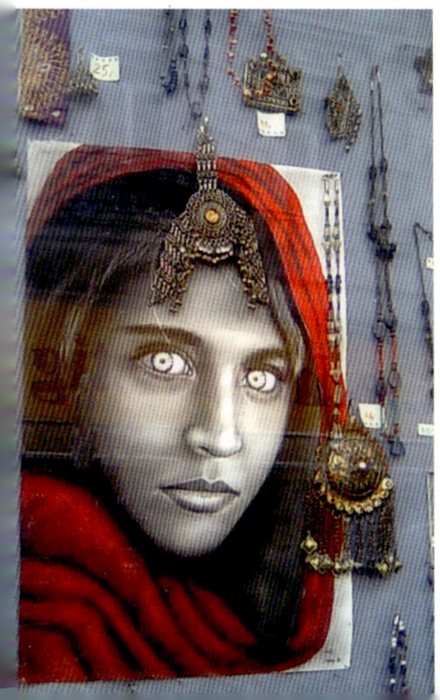

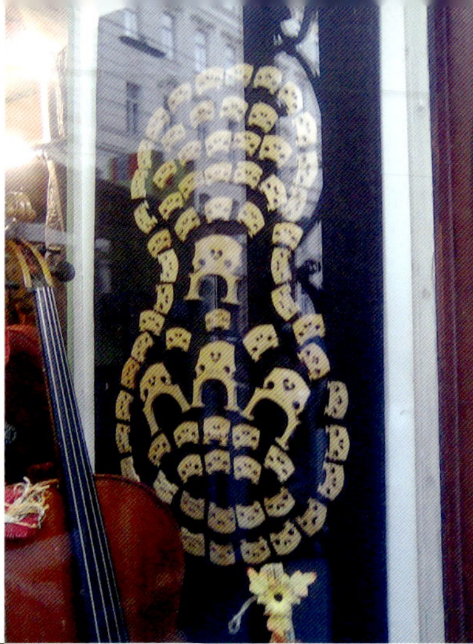
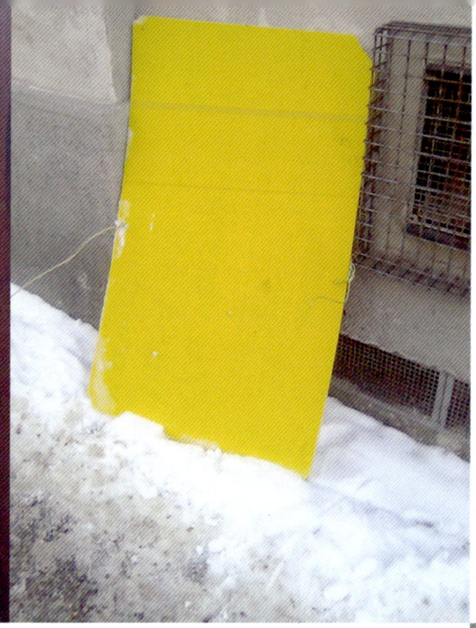
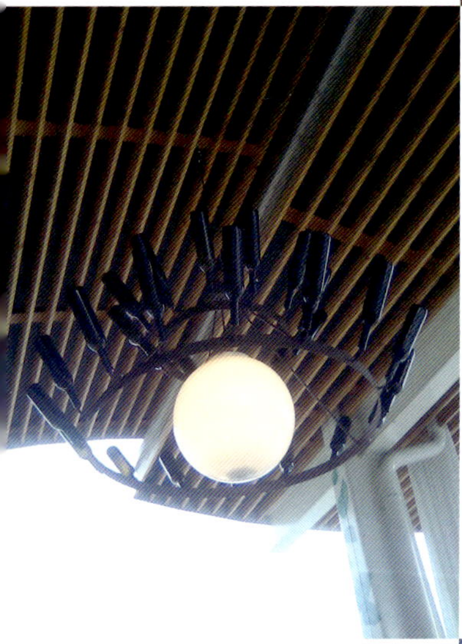
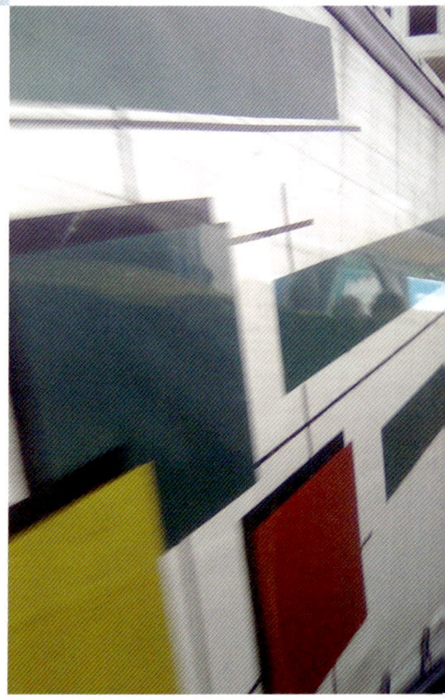
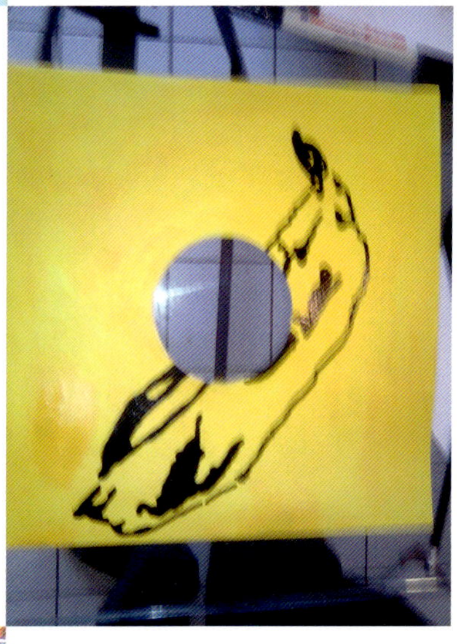
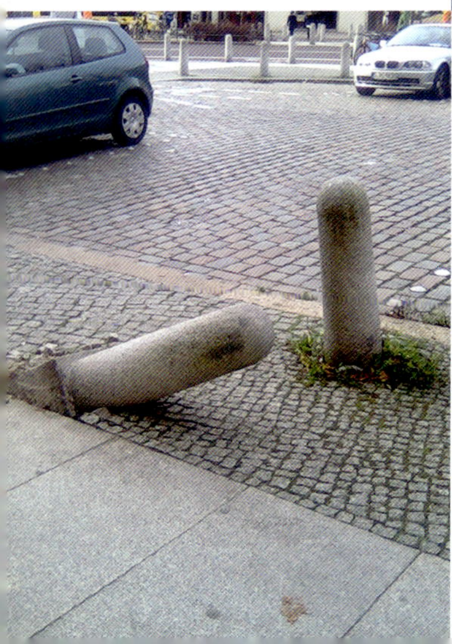
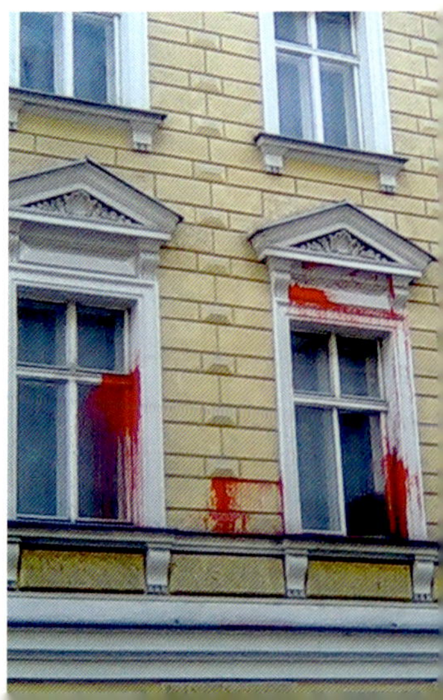

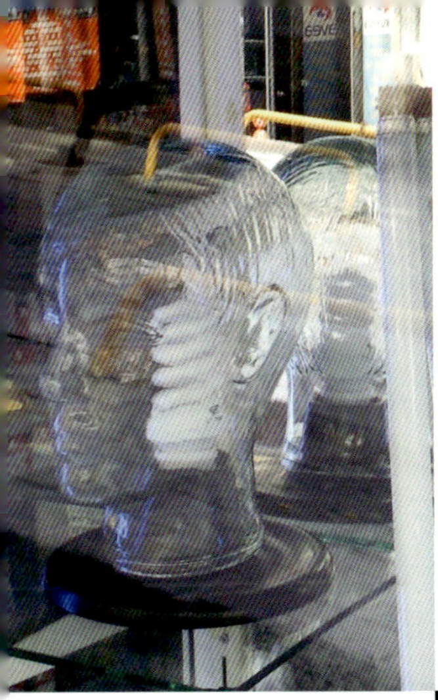

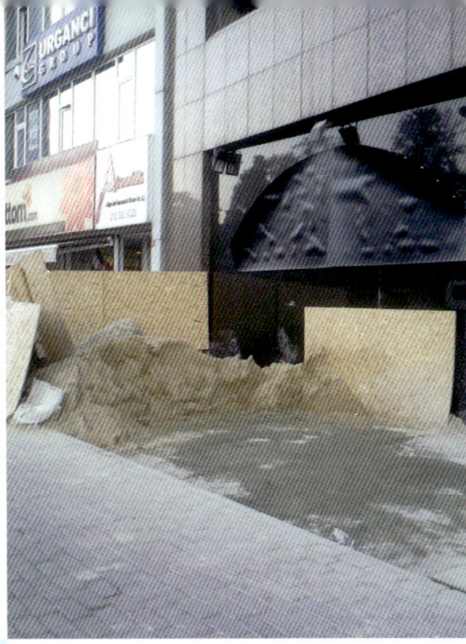
URGANCI

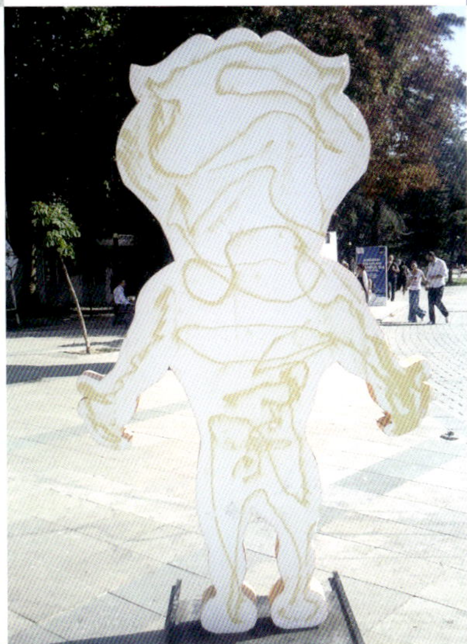

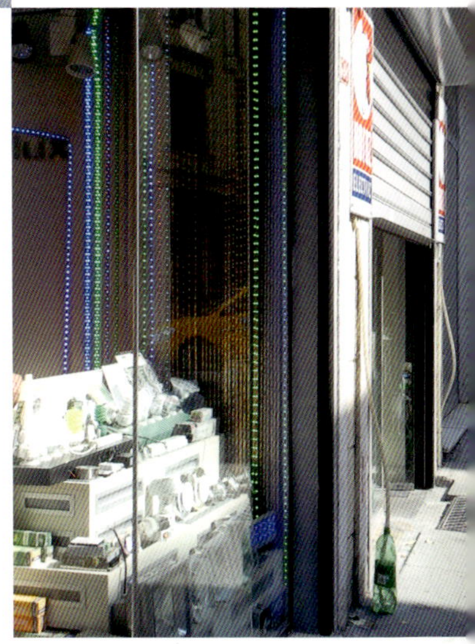

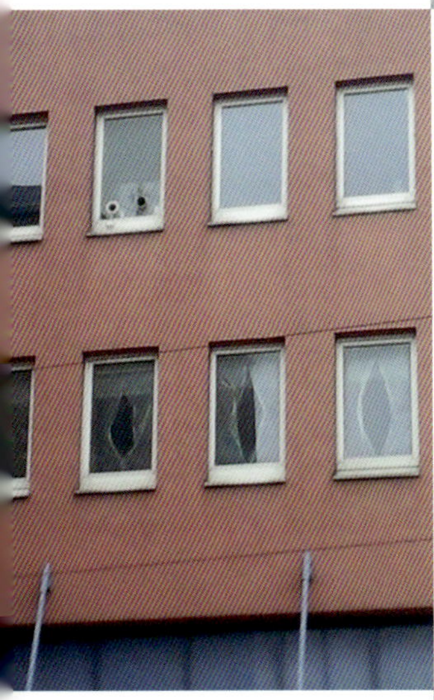

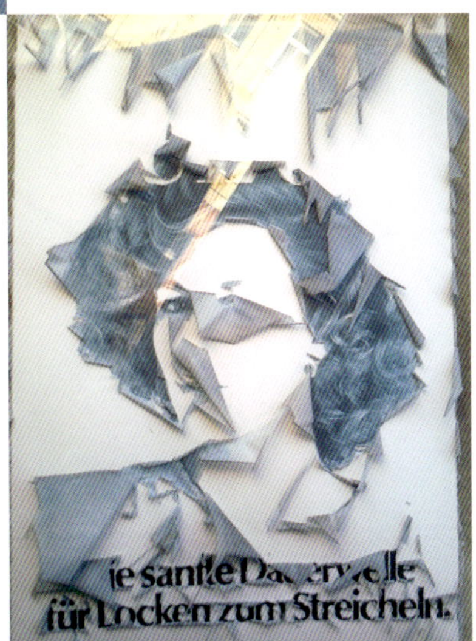
für Locken zum Streicheln.

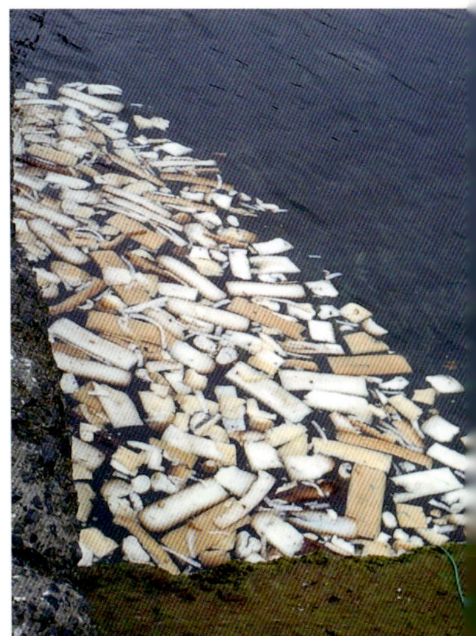

Therapy

Manuel Gorkiewicz and I have long communicated many of our issues through pictures, photos that we usually take with our iPhones and immediately send to each other. At Manuel's suggestion, they are filed in a special folder marked "TPF" – short for "Therapy Folder."

We call them therapy pictures because they are meant to cheer up or comfort (preferably both) one another, usually alluding to the other's artistic work or private preferences (preferably both), as well as to shared experiences. The therapy works well; every time Manuel sends me a new photo I have to laugh out loud in surprise or smile to myself in appreciation.

When I open that folder, which I do quite often, I see, for example, a woman's behind cut out in the shape of a heart to advertise a unique method of intimate personal hygiene by means of a showerhead that can be specially installed in toilets. Or I peer into shop windows that have been abandoned and neglected to produce a patina of art entirely on their own or almost over-ambitiously arranged by another hand. They are inhabited, for example, by decorative paintings that pick up on motifs in the clothing on display or vice versa, the decorative paintings suddenly camouflage the clothing as if by magic. It is often hard to tell exactly which came first... The "insemination gloves" that Manuel recently inflated into balloons and photographed are also amazing: Made of pink plastic, they are actually intended to serve as protection for veterinarians undertaking in-vitro treatment in female cattle. The folder also contains pictorial examples of various involuntarily ridiculous private and public construction projects that range from nonsensical to pseudo-clever – like a sesame ring printed on a plastic tarp, from the center of which a ventilation shaft bulges vulgarly. Then there are the figurines of rabbits, does, cats – animal alter-egos of every kind that serve out their existence as garden art, living sculptures, or the sad remnants of a costume that has landed on the pavement after a wild night out, lost by its owner in the course of an interpersonal battle.

Not only is this all a great deal of fun, it also provides considerable inspiration. In these supposed depictions of reality we also communicate through certain insider codes, conveying personal things as well. Now and again I feel as though I am sharing intimately in my picture-pal's life, and at the same time allowing him insight into my feelings through our exchange of photos. The photo messages form bonds that the other can tie into, knot up, unravel again, or add a new strand to.

This form of communication isn't new, of course, and certainly isn't our invention: Contemporary social networks and the associated meta-commentary in the visual arts, the by now historical concept of "mail art" – it has all been done before. What Manuel does in the artist's book presented here, by juxtaposing these and similar *therapy-files* collected in public spaces with his

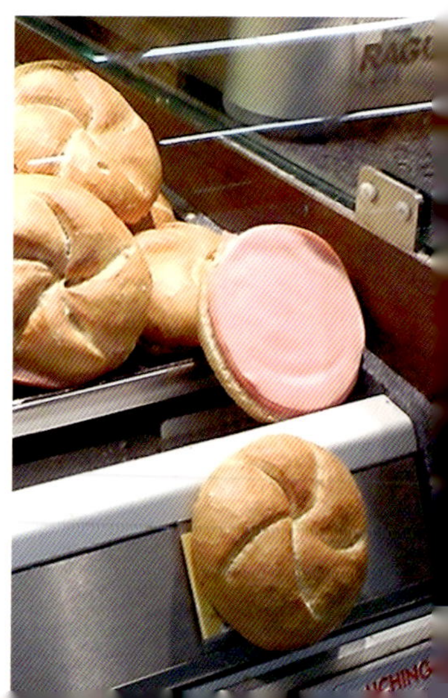

own artistic work as a reference system, is essentially not a new idea either, and at any rate I find that such creative gestures often come across as too schoolmasterly, sometimes even overweening (smart-alecky). In the case of Gorkiewicz's work however, I don't feel that way at all, and the reason for this, the reason I am telling this story about the therapy folder in the first place, is because it gives an added therapeutic value both to the art reproduced in this book as well as to the scenes and moments of reality captured in the photographs.

But what is that added therapeutic value? And above all, what is that supposed to look like in this context?

In the course of psychotherapeutic treatment, the patient often can't explain what effects or changes weekly meetings bring about, respectively whether they bring about anything at all. This condition sometimes lingers on long after the treatment has ended, yet without provoking the feeling that the therapy was unsuccessful as a result. The success of treatment is usually not quantifiable in a quick and direct way and certainly can't be communicated to the ignorant or uninitiated.

So when Gorkiewicz places his work side by side with the everyday scenes that surround it, that feed into it and then feed on it, the following occurs: His work – at least for unimaginative art-viewing amateurs – becomes more serious, more earnest, while the reality that surrounds us – at least for the short-sighted and bores – becomes funnier. But it is also great for everyone else because precisely this juxtaposition and superimposition allows the relationships between the "work" and its "sources" and "intents" to flash back and forth, forth and back, fabricating, I would like to say, a new impulse in this multistable gymnastic exercise.

Gorkiewicz usually uses simple, commonly familiar materials in his productions, like garlands, soft-serve ice cream, or chocolate reminiscent of childhood and handicraft work. Gorkiewicz knows, and takes seriously, the qualities and technical limitations of his respective materials as well as their real and possible representational history. He also has technical know-how, experience, and a certain attitude situated somewhere between anti-hero and chivalrous verve. Taken as a whole, this creates an interestingly isolated space consisting of the following ambiguity: He works strictly with the qualities inherent in his materials, making significant demands of the fragile papers, fabrics, films, and fluids he uses. They are subjected to manipulations, shifting and expanding boundaries, changes in scale, and displacements, eliciting a sense of joy in the viewer that today might be considered somewhat unusual. Viewers of his work take pleasure in recognizing the materials and their significance (along the lines of: "Wow, he built a huge sculpture from THAT garland!? I still remember it from kids' birthday parties... It must be another material that just looks like it...no??"). At the same time, they are (even more) pleased because they see what is possible with things that are available to everyone (including themselves)!

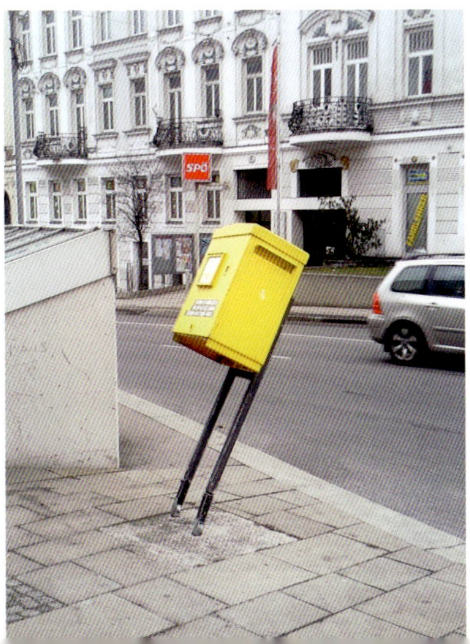

Gorkiewicz often scales up his selected materials, structures, and meanings, draping entire streets in garlands or creating pompous Baroque chandeliers as though from paper cut-outs – and what's more, they all still work perfectly normal! The chandelier is a formal sculpture, an object, and functional item that can essentially be flicked on and off like any other ordinary lamp. It makes a small space feel like an enormous ballroom, serves as a commentary on Pop art that can be spun out ever further, plays with the idea of the English garden from a different angle, and is capable of simultaneously embodying high-tech, early modernism, and camp. As a viewer, following these mental and production processes is a pleasure and at the same time therapeutic – even without the "therapy photos" that are printed in this book.

Yet these selected situational snapshots from Manuel Gorkiewicz's forays into the world have another effect as well: Read a little Gorkiewicz and suddenly those scenes we pass by every day come more quickly and sharply into focus, we perceive them more selectively and pleasurably, and as a result we can continually recall and reconstruct our experiences anew. If, on top of that, we are artists as well, we understand all the more that we are capable of tapping into a similar gesture, a similar feeling, a similar production. Looking at the world through Gorkiewicz-glasses gives us a specially enhanced view of Manuel's own artistic work. Not that we would then want (or be able) to imitate or copy it; rather, it makes us value more highly the real-world reference system behind the work, the aesthetic surface of our environment. Not, of course, in the sense that we might suddenly be satisfied with what we find around us (both in art and real life), but in the sense that we can make it genuinely productive, or at least that such a sweeping gesture of production is possible – provided, of course, that like Gorkiewicz we have the verve to pull it off on our own. Therapy means ultimately learning to get along by ourselves, able once more to do things that previously had been blocked.

In chaos magic, there are three ways to bring about a magical moment: In addition to so-called inhibitory gnosis and its diametrically opposite, excitatory gnosis, there is the third option of "in-different vacuity," in which that magical moment is produced in a passing so incidental that one does not notice or immediately forgets it. In fact, being able to suppress it is crucial or it cannot be effective, let alone occur again. And yes, I believe it is this difficult, indirect yet pleasurable undertaking that Gorkiewicz demonstrates to us in this artist book, generously proffering it as an interactive means of production. Through inventive and clever merging – and thereby voiding – of realities both constructed and not, of the everyday world and everyday theatricality, he points out an added therapeutic value and the therapeutic possibilities – also, but especially, in art.

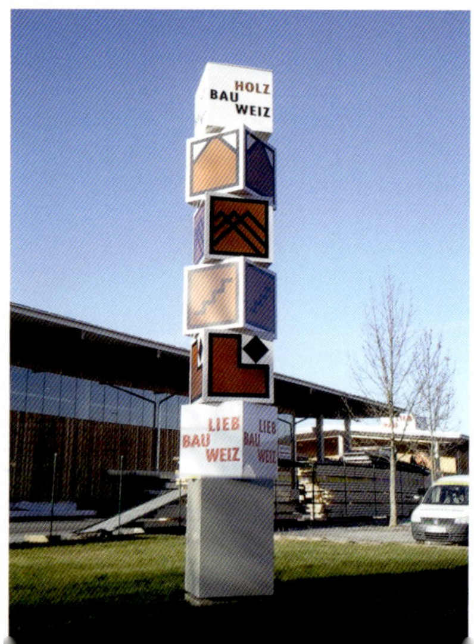

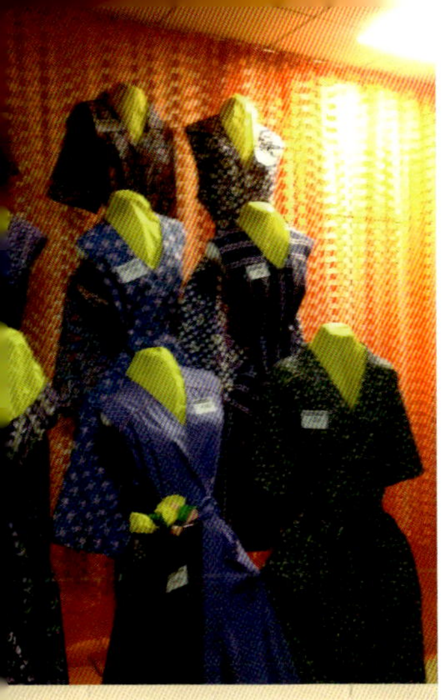

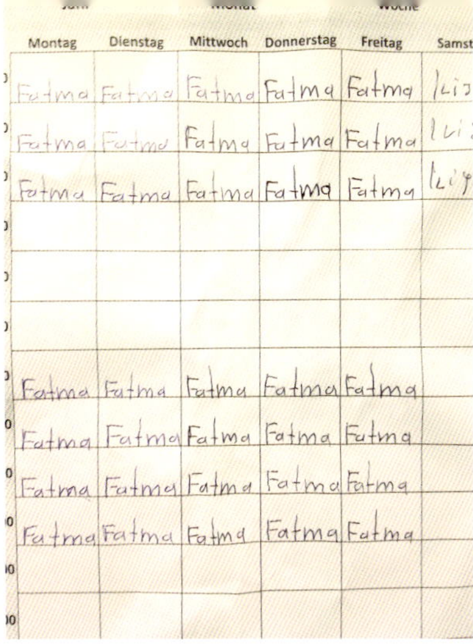
Montag Dienstag Mittwoch Donnerstag Freitag Samst
Fatma Fatma Fatma Fatma Fatma
Fatma Fatma Fatma Fatma Fatma
Fatma Fatma Fatma Fatma Fatma
Fatma Fatma Fatma Fatma Fatma
Fatma Fatma Fatma Fatma Fatma
Fatma Fatma Fatma Fatma Fatma
Fatma Fatma Fatma Fatma Fatma

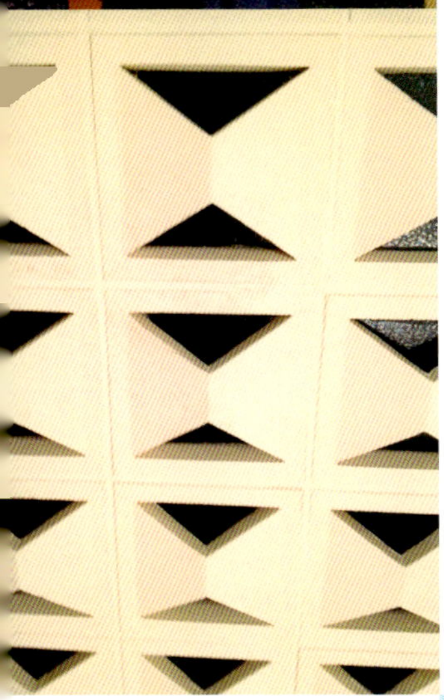

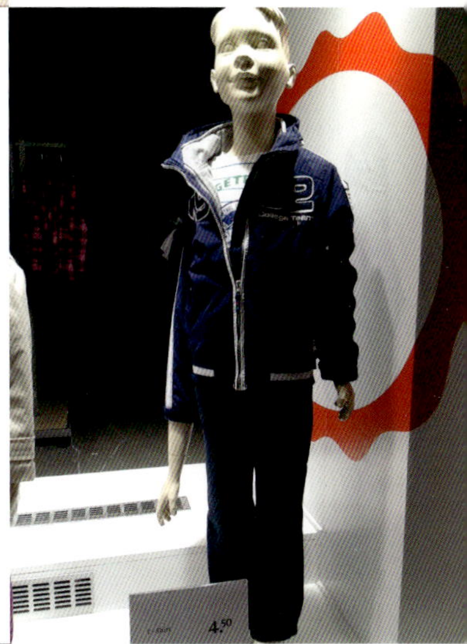
4,50

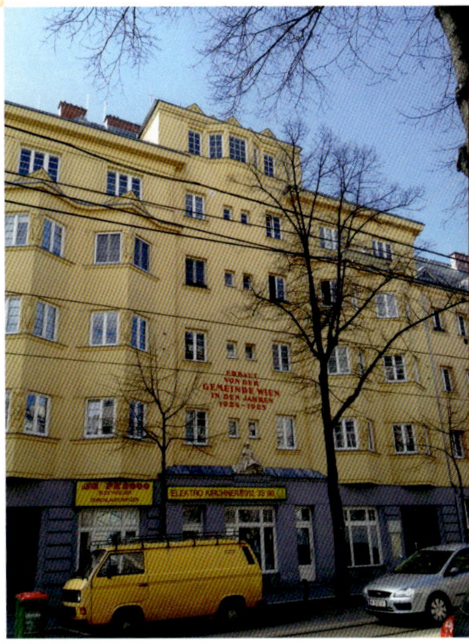

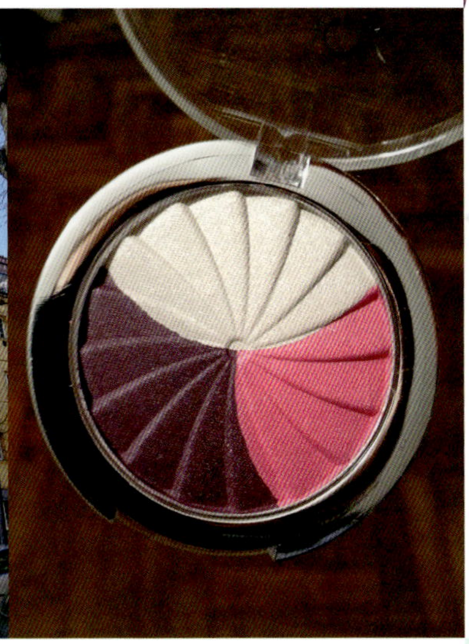

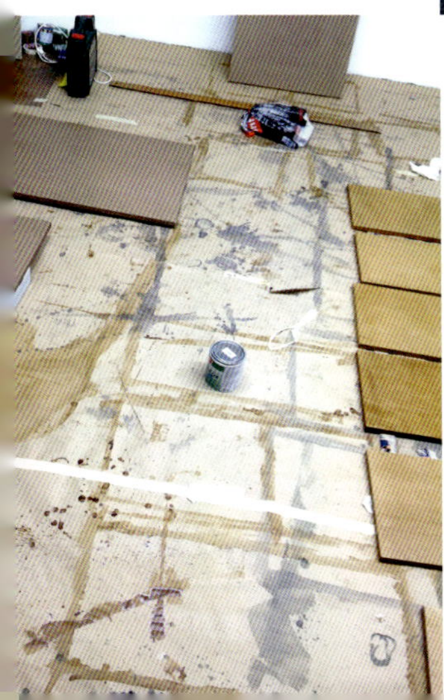

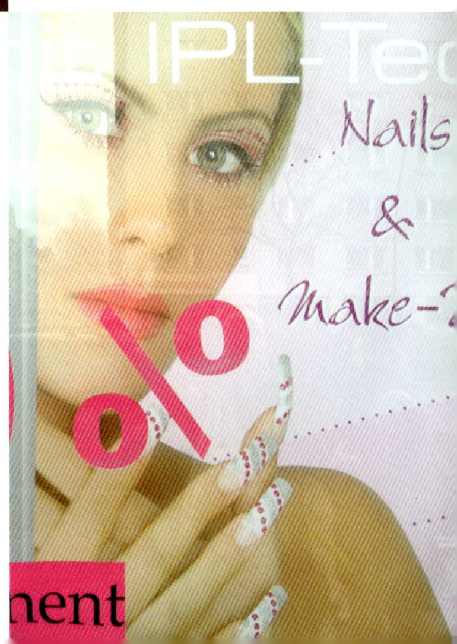
IPL-Tec
Nails
&
Make-
%
nent

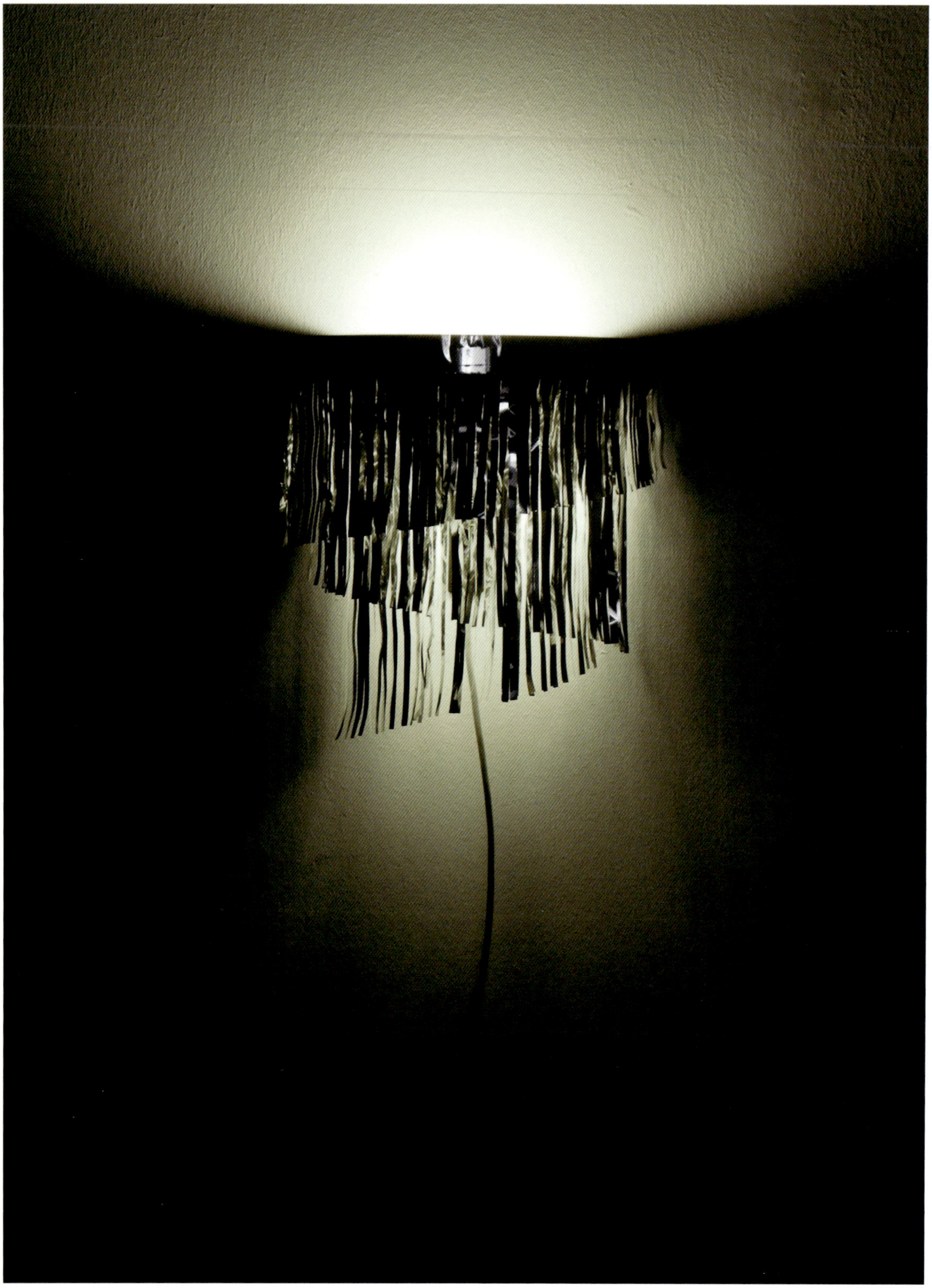

"Stolen from my subconscious", Kunstwerke Berlin, 2011
Untitled, 30 x 30 x 15 cm, iron, plastic foil, light bulb, cable, 2011

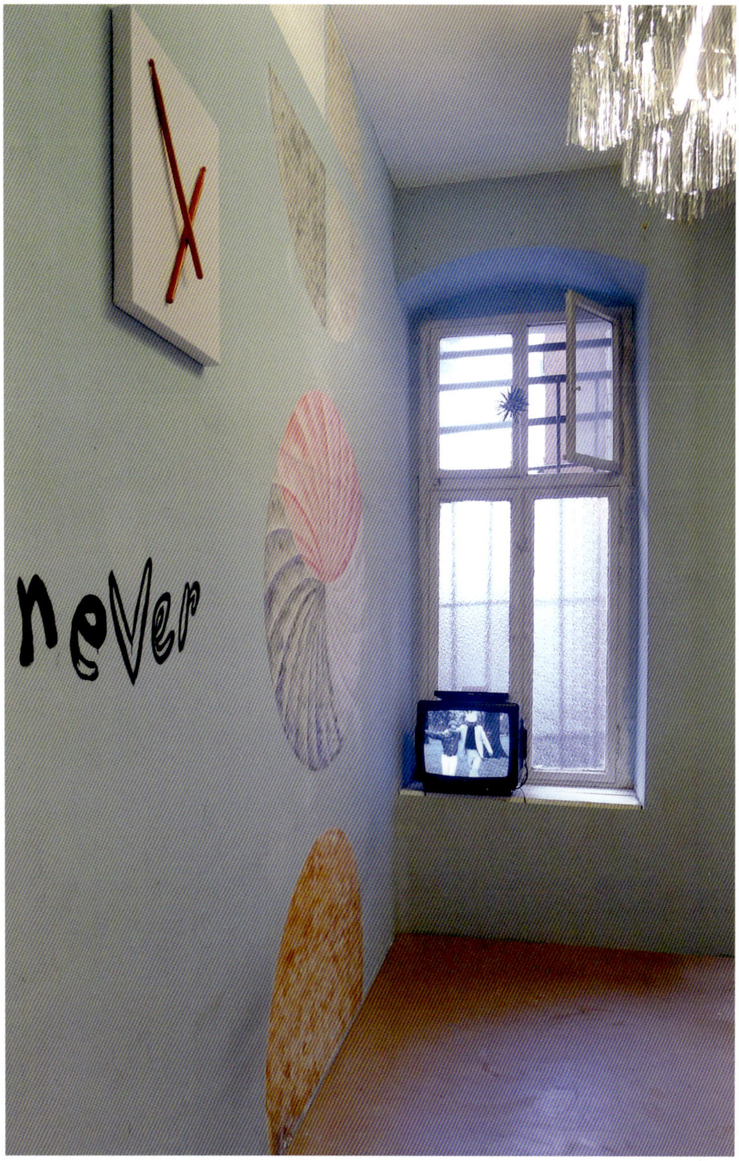

"this time dressed", Der Grieche, Berlin, 2012 with Marten Frerichs and Kerstin Cmelka

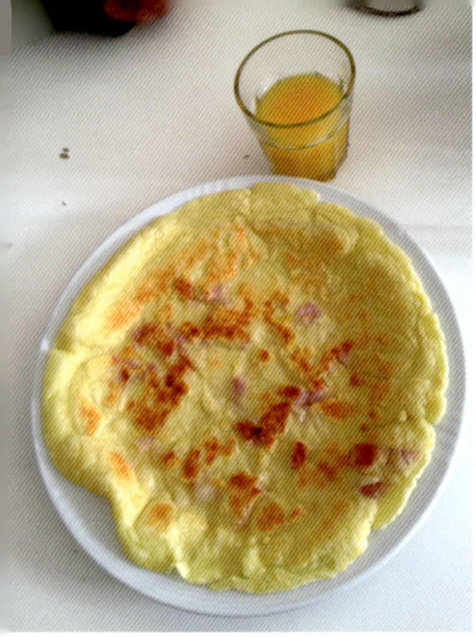

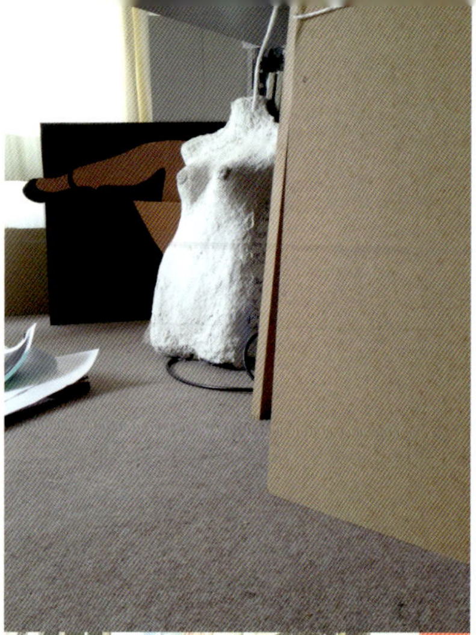

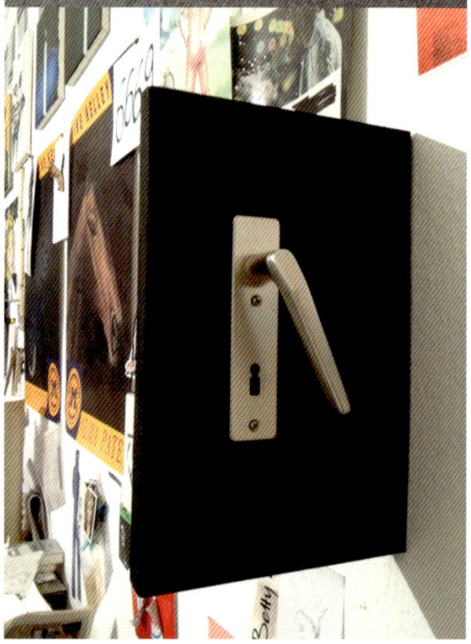

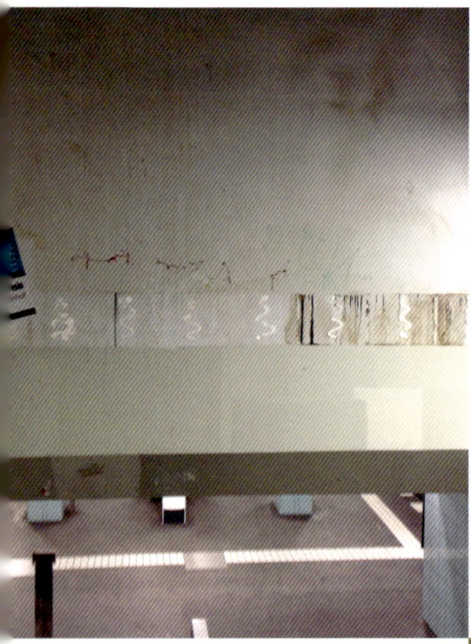

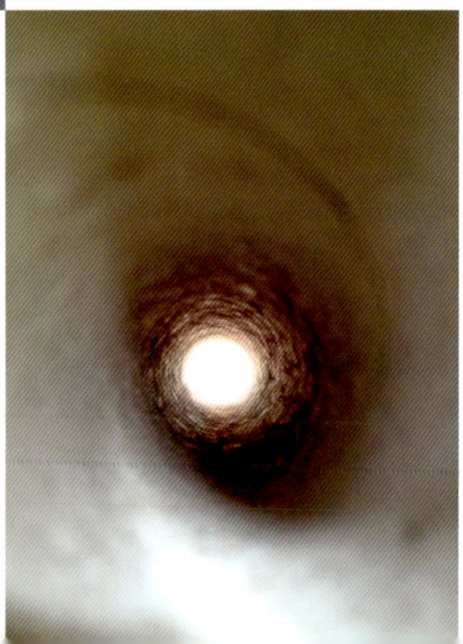

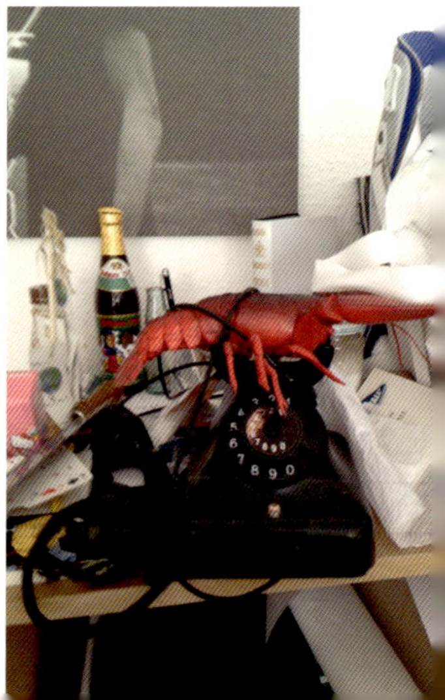

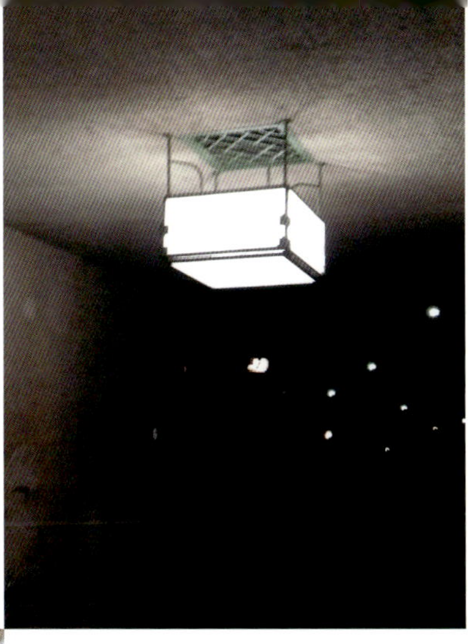

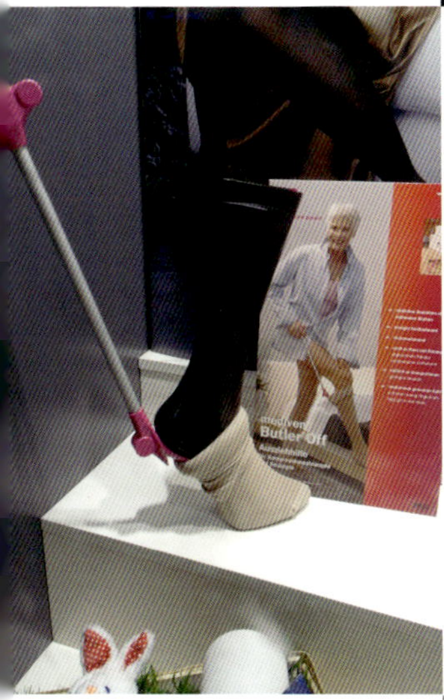
Butler Off

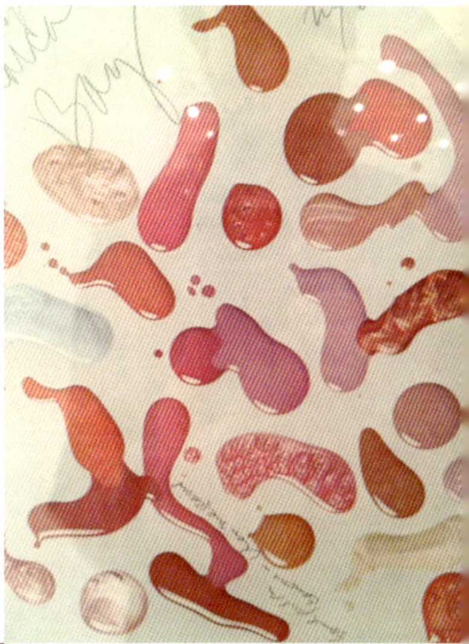

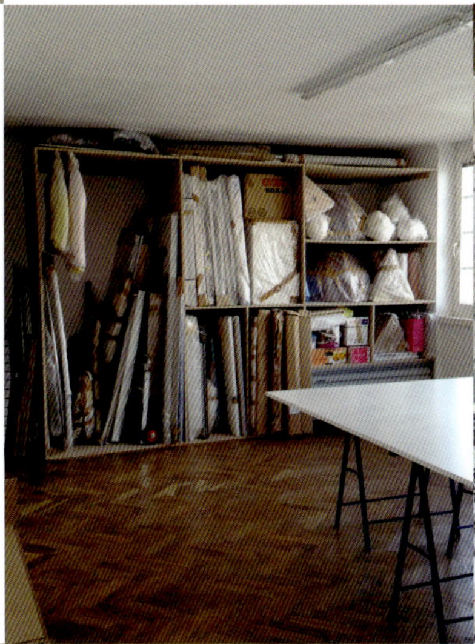

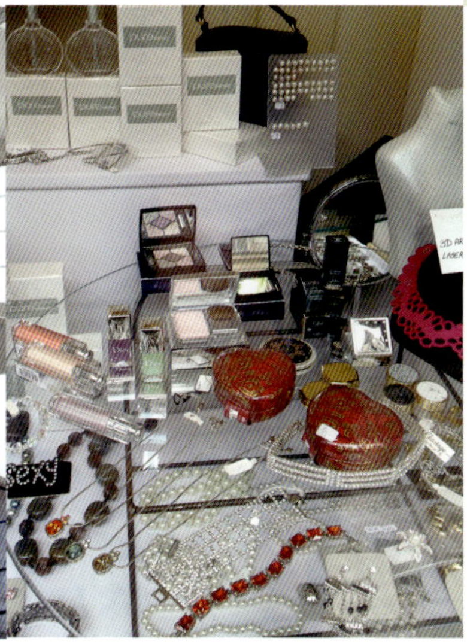
sexy

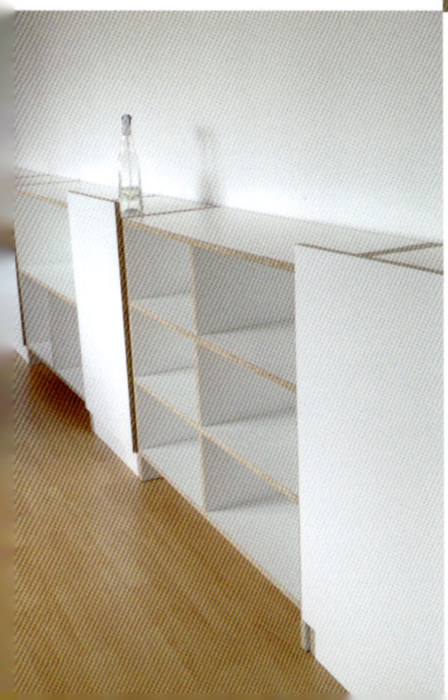

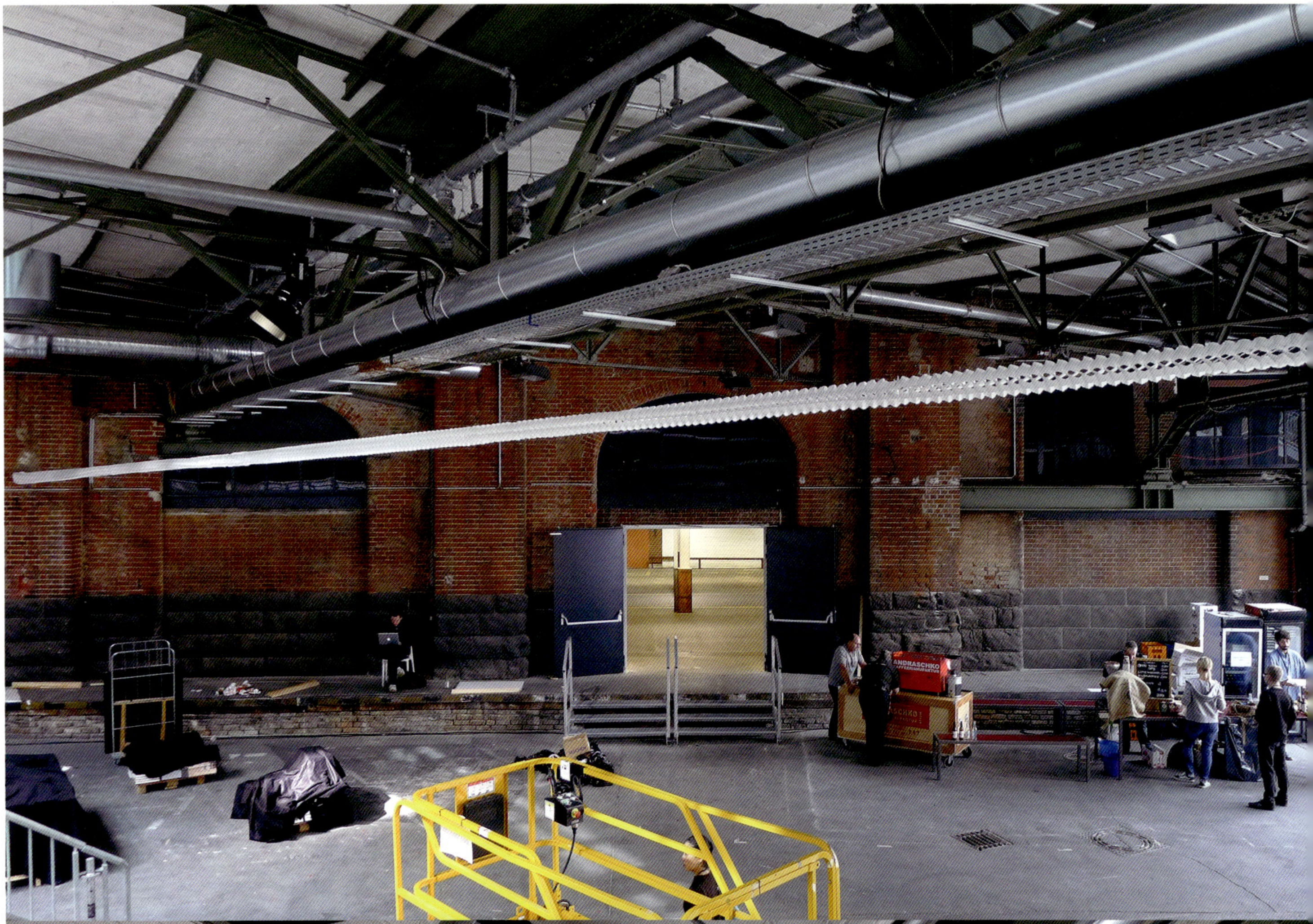

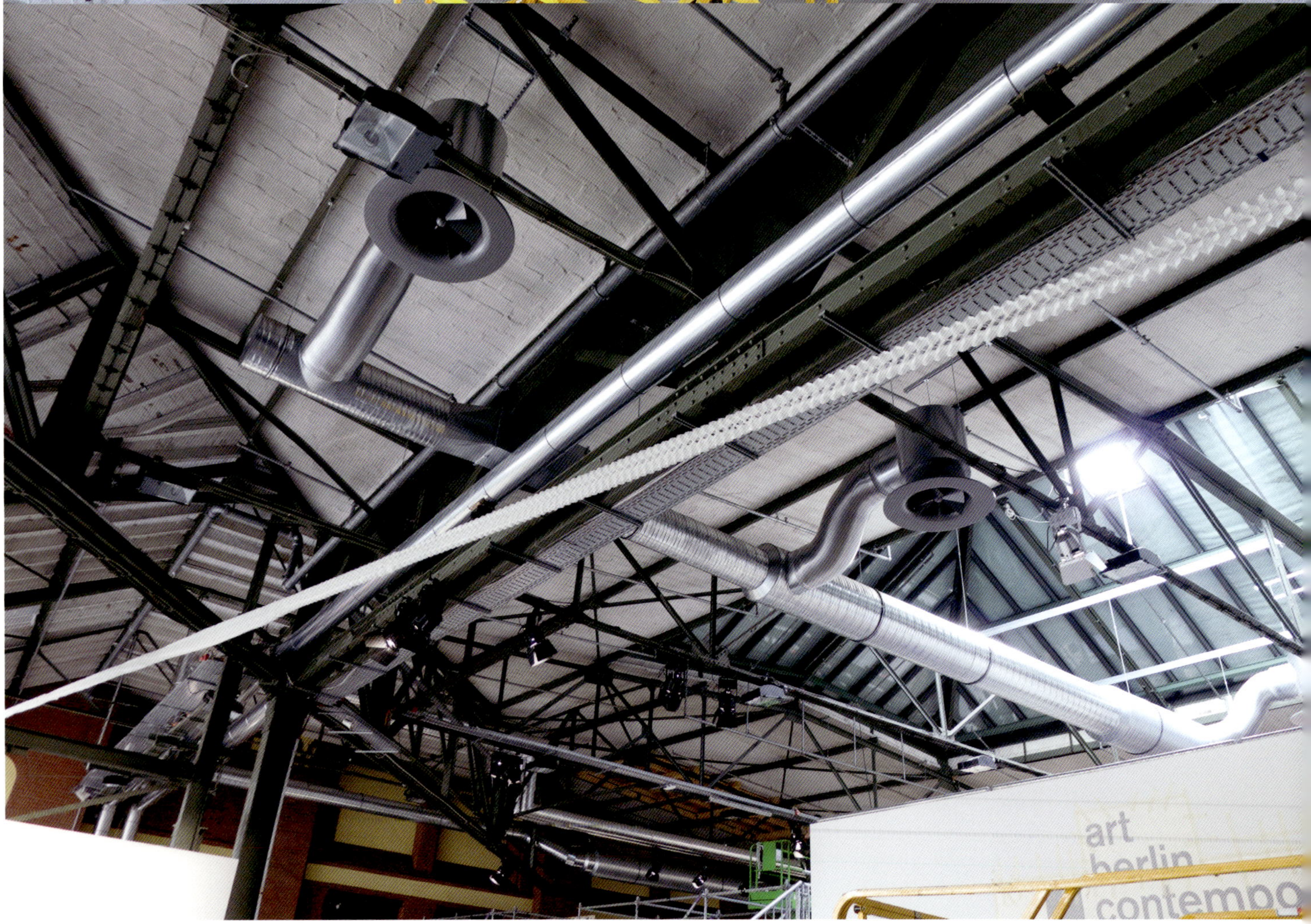
art
berlin
contempo

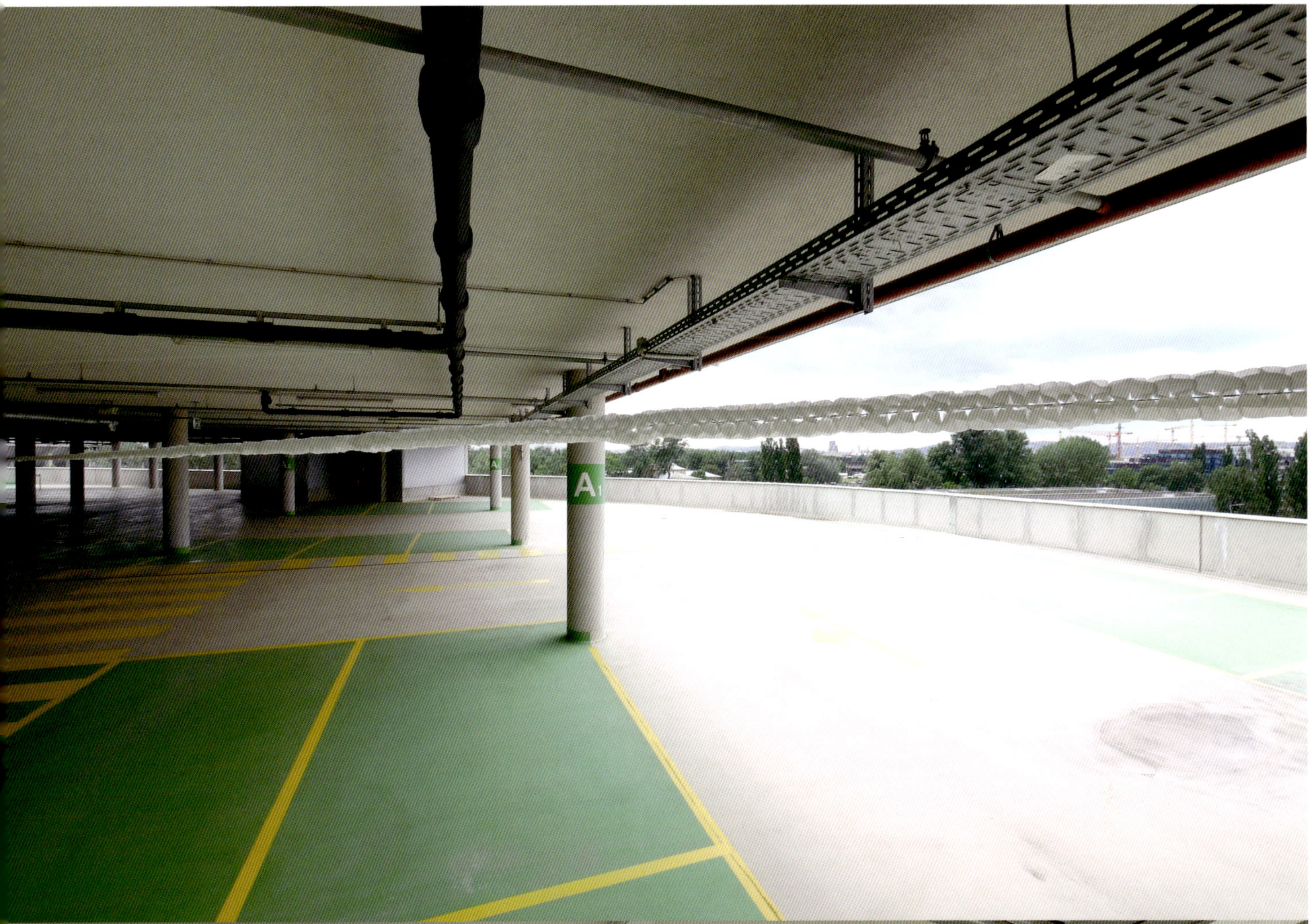

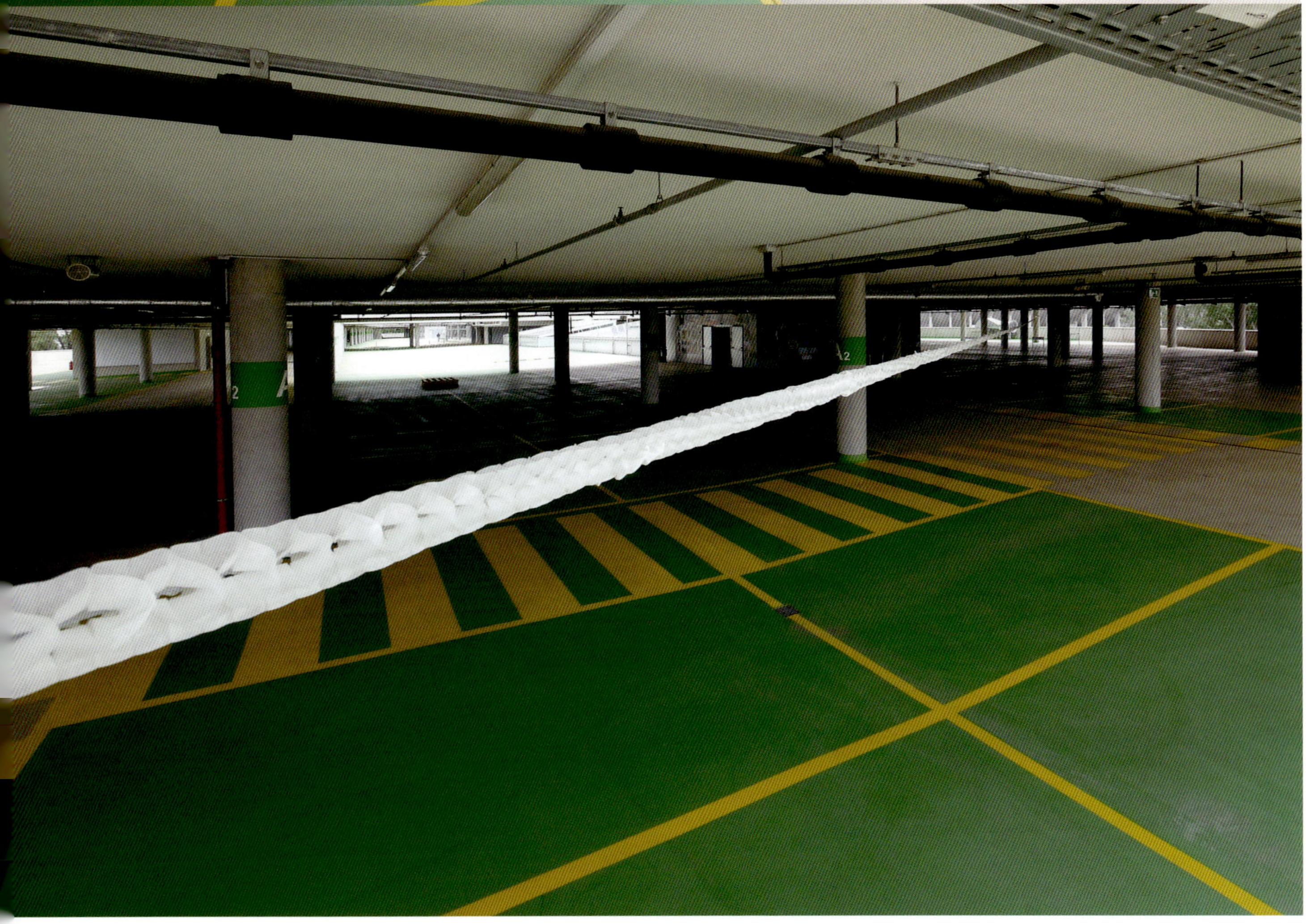

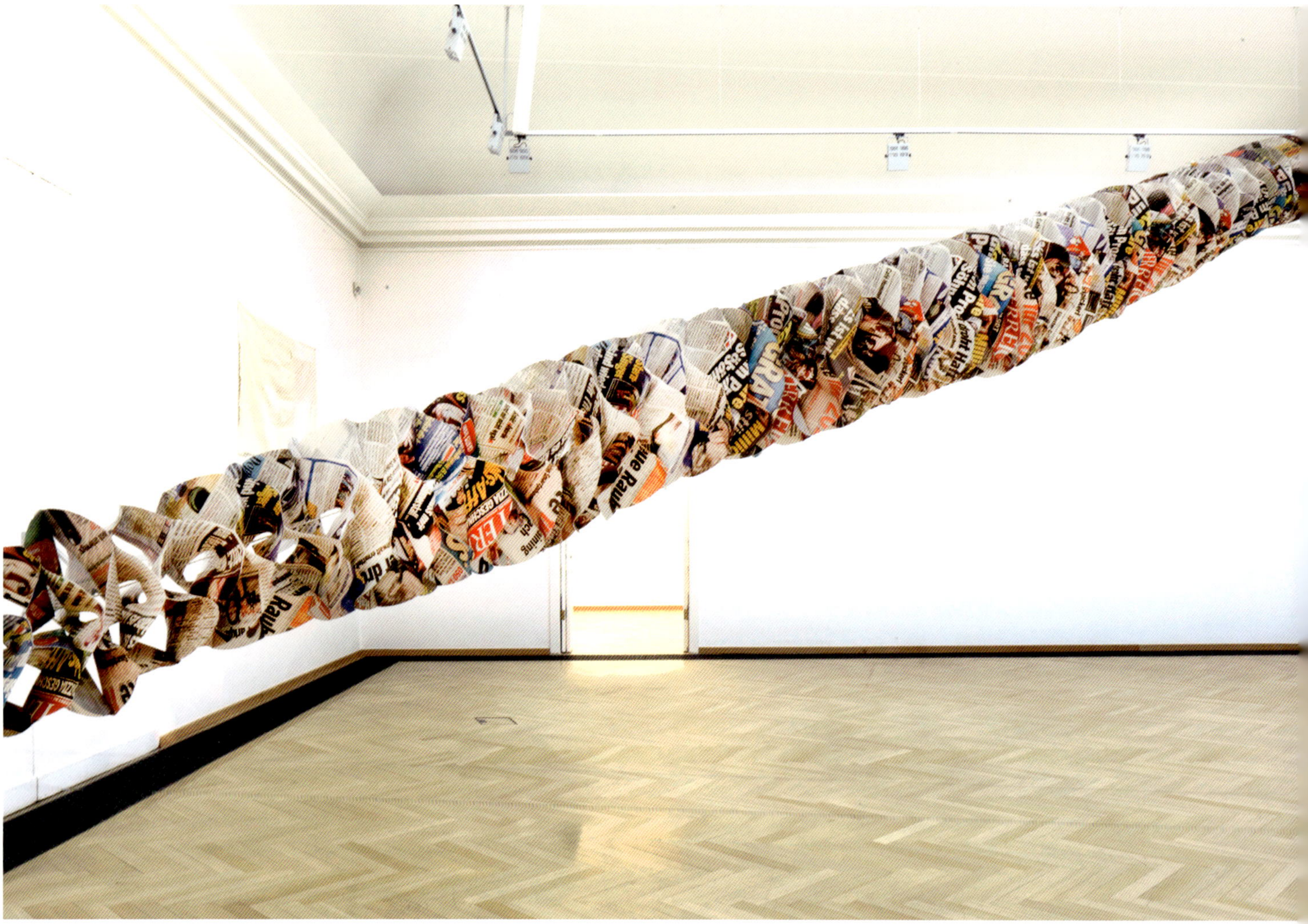

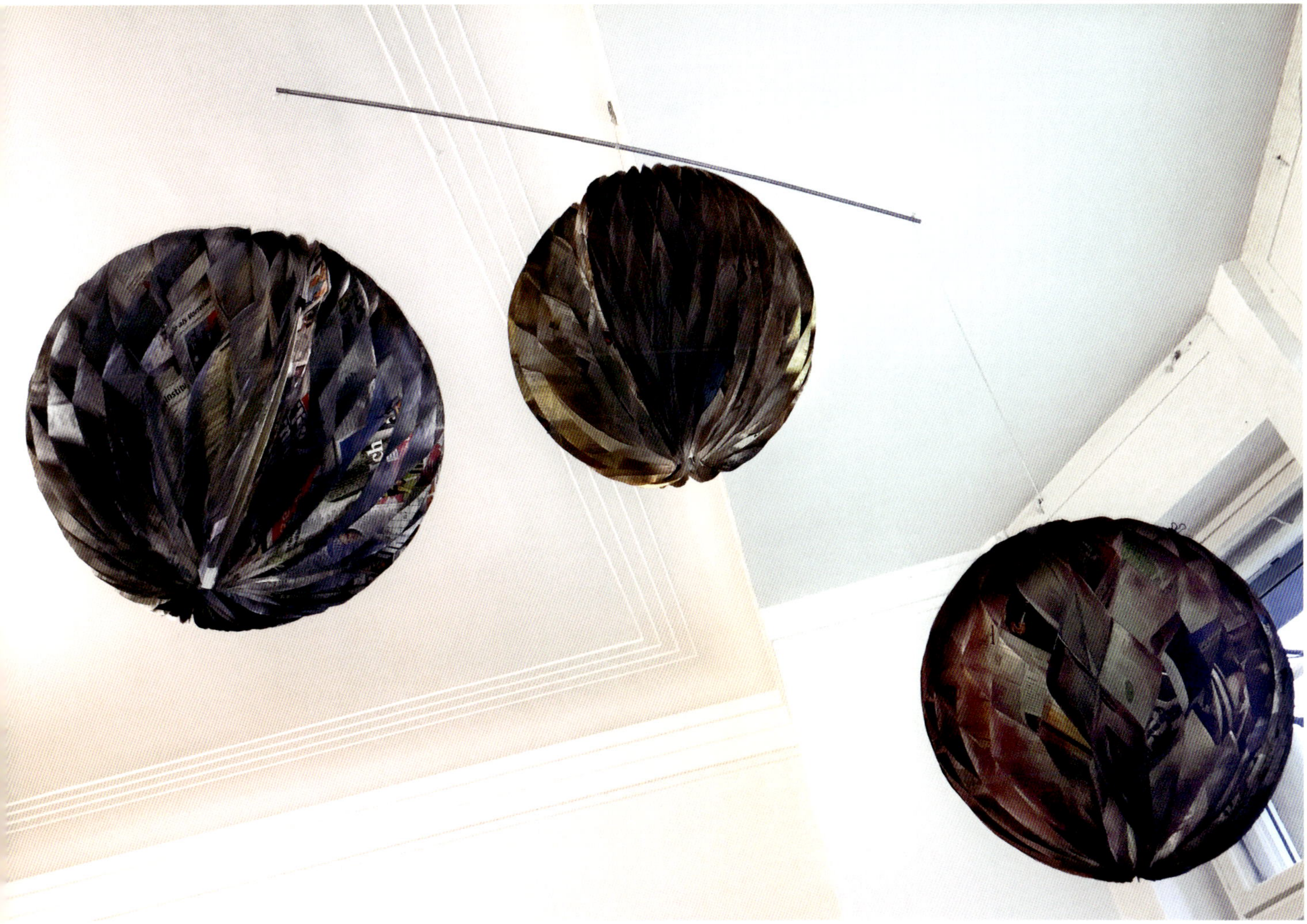

"Don't Eat the Yellow Snow", Wiensowski & Harbord, Berlin, 2011
Untitled, ca. 160 x 60 x 180 cm, newspaper, acrylic, aluminium, nylon, 2011
p. 30: abc – art berlin contemporary 2012, Untitled, ca. 30 m, paper, steel, 2012
p. 31: Parkfair Vienna 2011, Untitled,10 x 10 x 6000 cm, paper, steel, 2011
left page: "Die illustrierte Ausstellung", Künstlerhaus Klagenfurt 2012
Untitled, ca. 20 x 20 x 300 cm, steel, newspaper, 2012

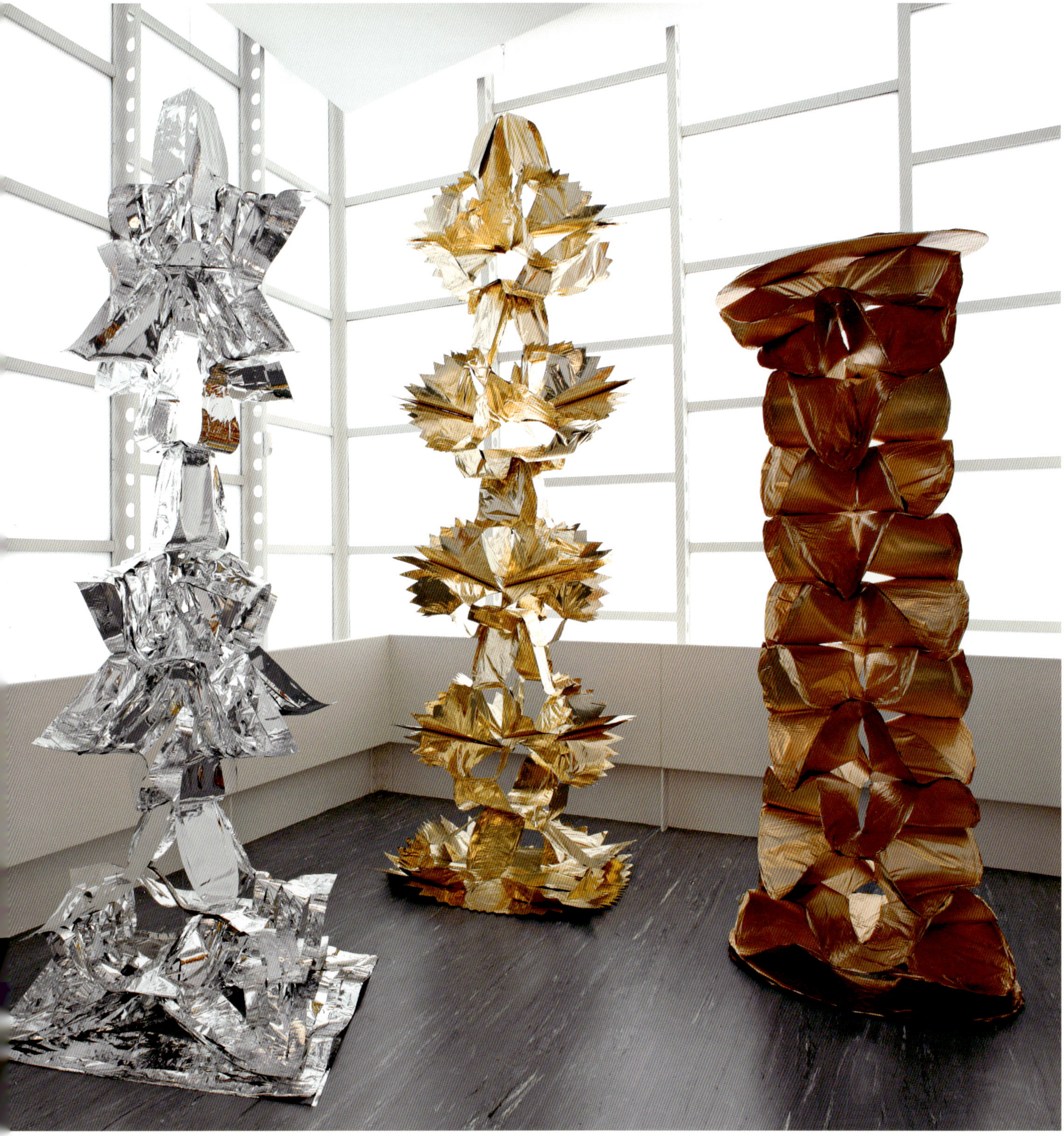

"Die Sammlung", 21er Haus, Vienna, 2012
Untitled, 120 x 120 x 400 cm, 120 x 120 x 500 cm, 80 x 80 x 300 cm,
plastic foil, cardboard, steel cable, 2006

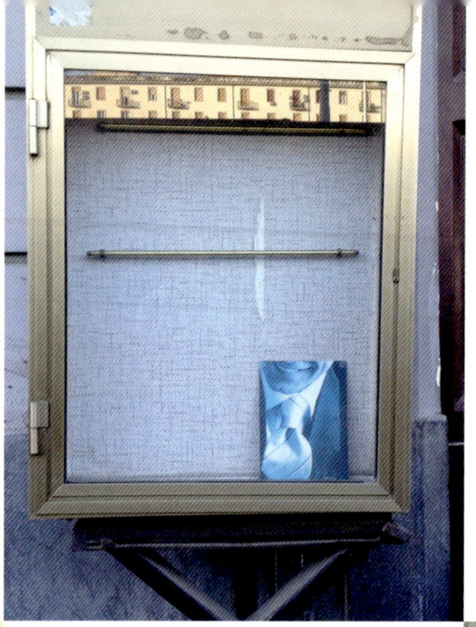

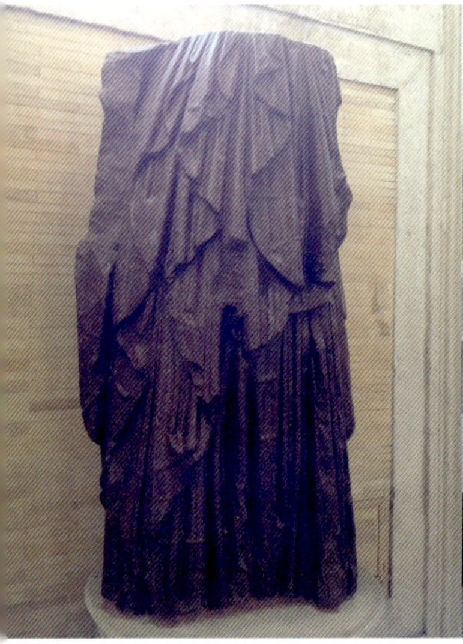

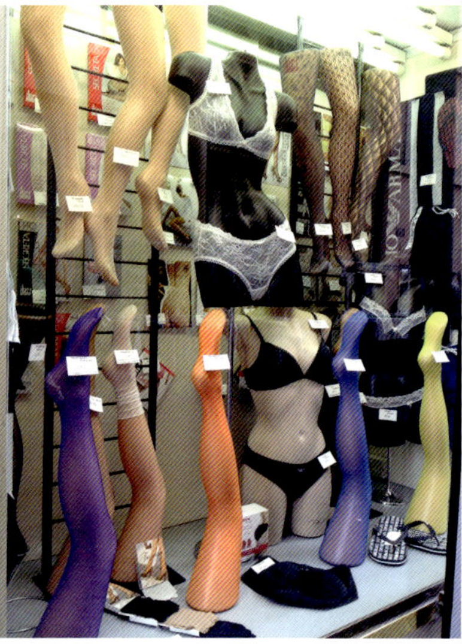

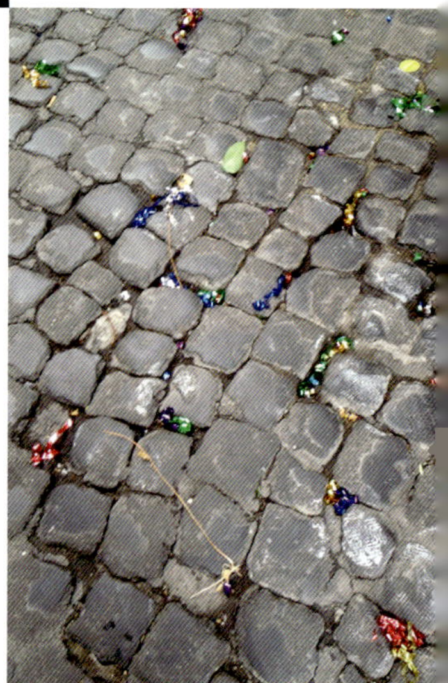

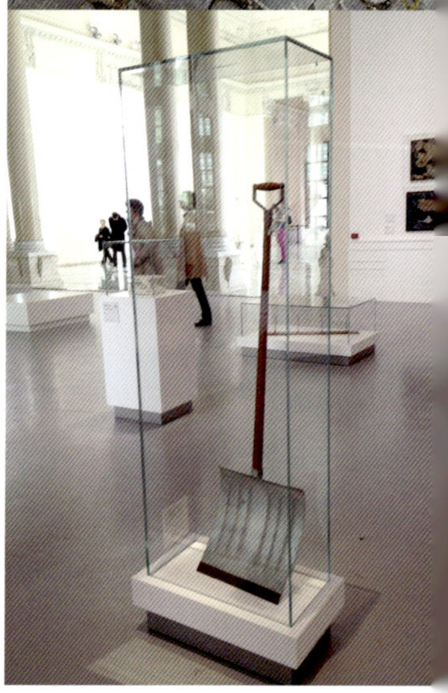

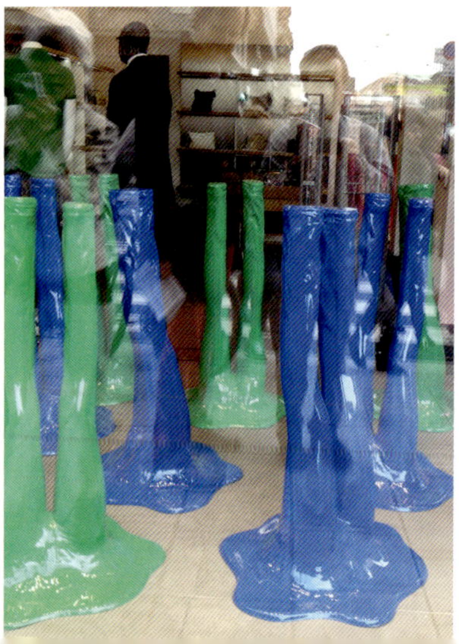

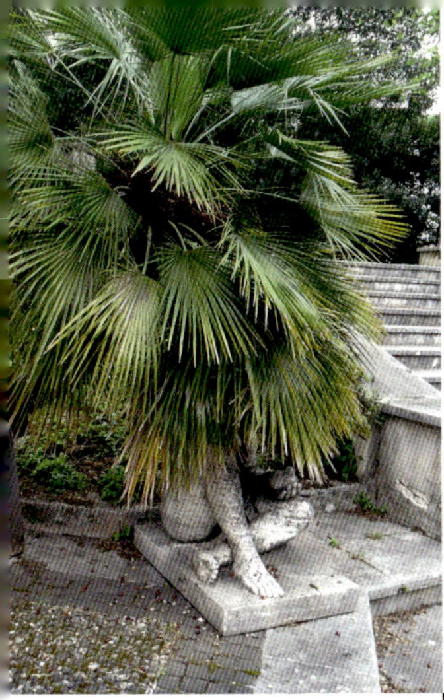

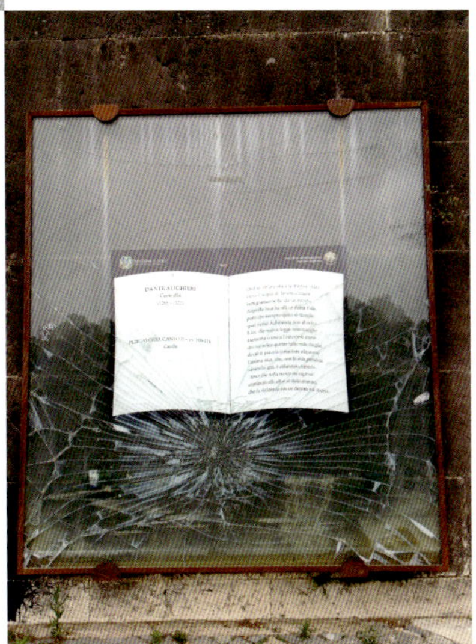

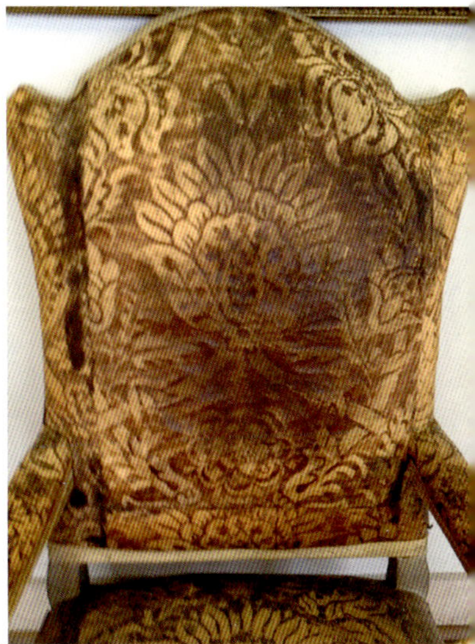

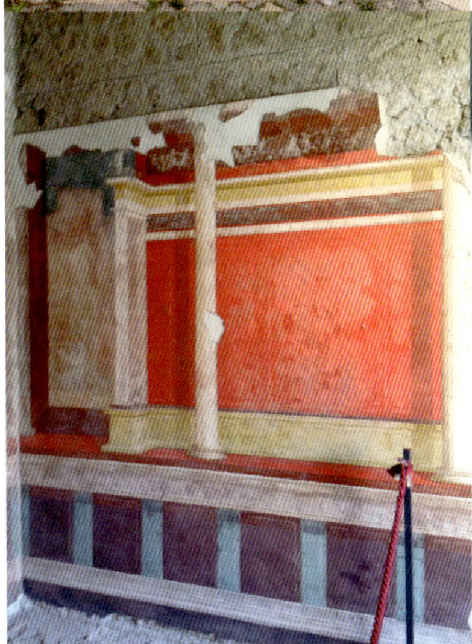

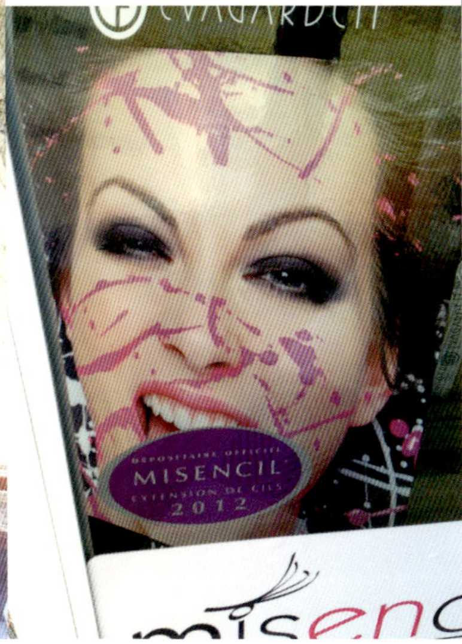
DÉPOSITAIRE OFFICIEL
MISENCIL
EXTENSION DE CILS
2012

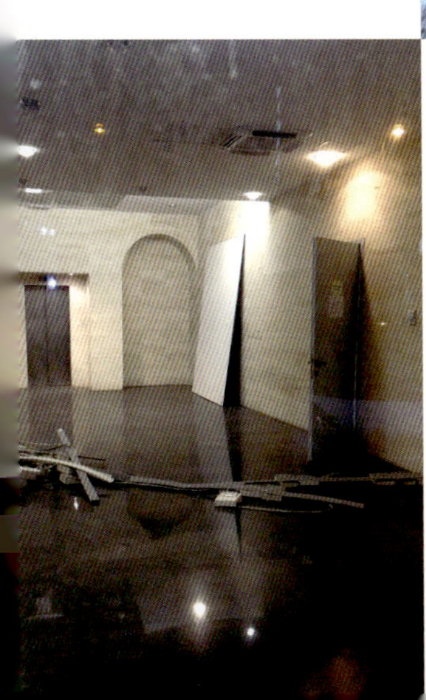

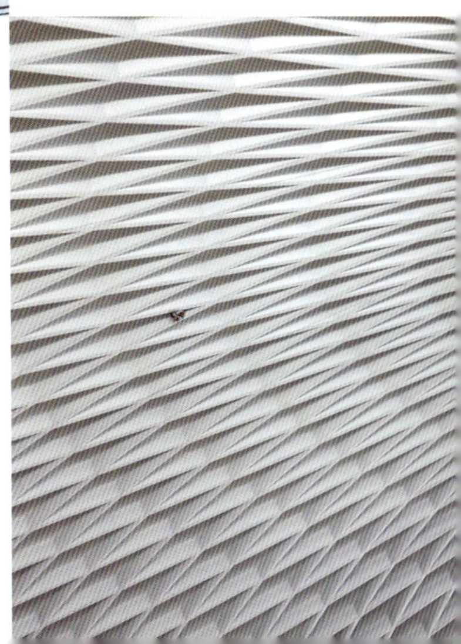

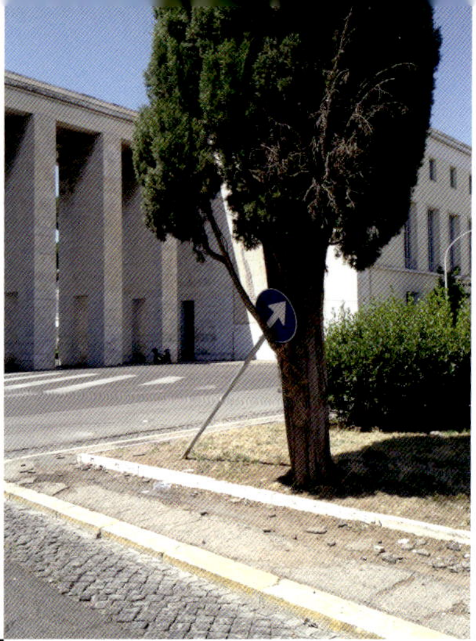
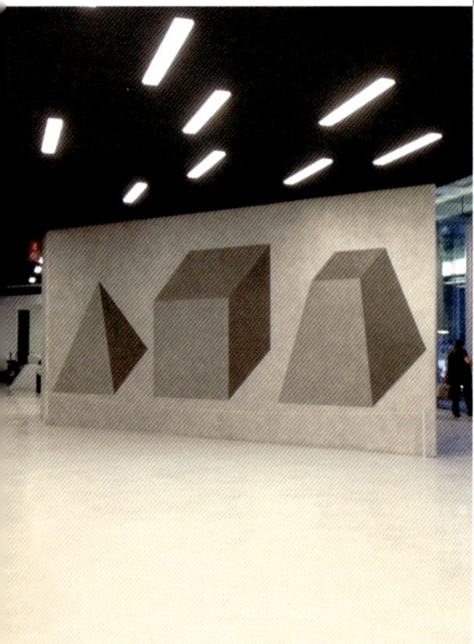
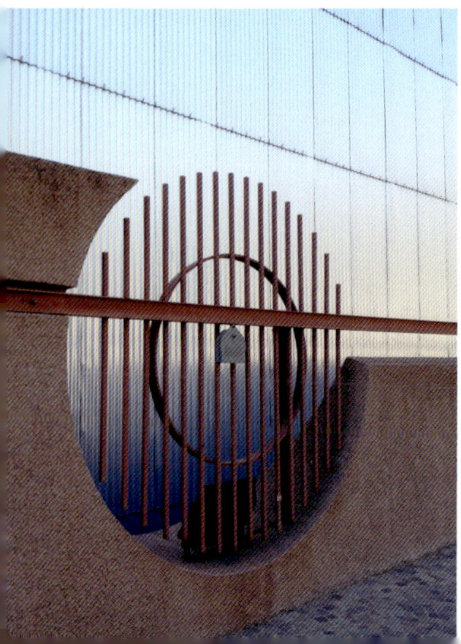

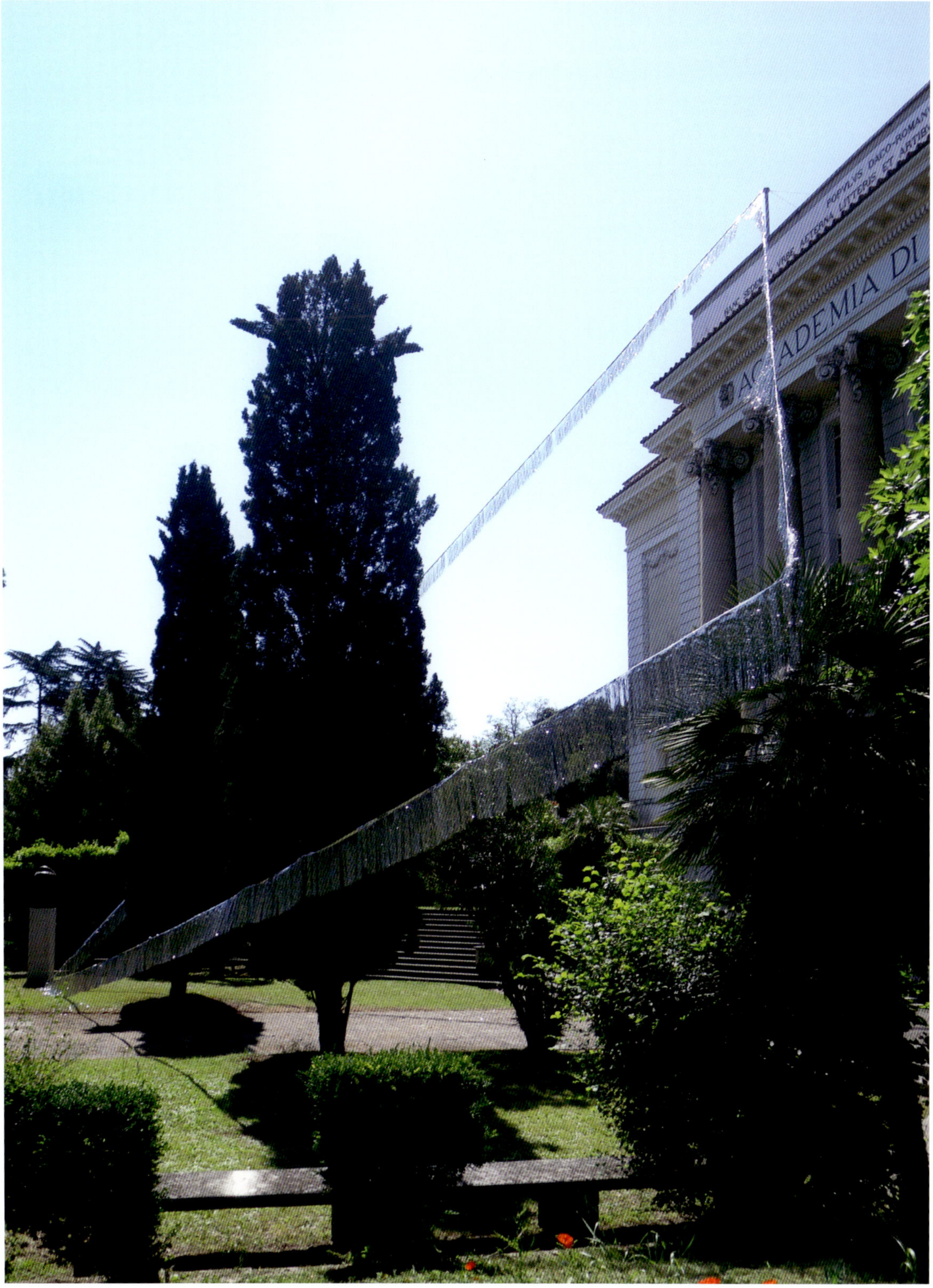

"Spazi Aperti X", Accademia di Romania Rome, 2012
Untitled, ca. 2500 x 2500 x 1000 cm, steel, plastic foil, 2012

Make-Up Works

Manuel Gorkiewicz in conversation with Martin Guttmann

Martin: When did you start doing make-up works?

Manuel: In 2010.

Martin: Five years ago?

Manuel: Yes, the first piece I did was in Prague. I showed some older works there along with a new work consisting of make-up.

Martin: So this is Wandmalerei, fresco?

Manuel: Yes, kind of.

Martin: Let's talk about this aspect of the fresco. How do you relate to the fresco tradition? I guess you could think about Pompey, you know, or the Renaissance "al fresco"?

Manuel: Yes, that's where it starts.

Martin: What is fresco for you?

Manuel: First I saw these boxes that contained eye shadow, skin powder, etc. in a shop and it reminded me of the fresco color palette. I was interested in the limitation of colors within these palettes, without knowing much about make-up in particular.
I guess at that point I'd heard more about the use of color in Renaissance murals than how these cosmetic products are used.

Martin: So what happens if you transfer it to a mural?
Painting, as we know, begins with the movable "quadro" – a "square" made of canvas or wood that you can move from one space to another; that's the art of the bourgeois era. The mural is still painting of the aristocratic era, because the aristocrats had a stable house that was passed on from one generation to the next. So if you make a mural, it stays there. The "quadro" is for the bourgeoisie who move – they don't stay in the same place. People came back to it, like Sol Lewitt, and others in a different way, but I think if you ask an art historian what fresco means, it would be art before the bourgeois era.

Manuel: Well, make-up is a very temporary item. In its appropriate use on the skin it stays for one day or even less. And periods in today's contemporary art are also very short-term. You build up a show and two or three months later everything is removed.

Martin: To force the issue of temporality by quoting the "quadros" which were not temporal.

Manuel: Yes.

Martin: Ok, so let's stay a little bit longer with the make-up.
When Daniela Salvioni and Cornelia Lauf saw your make-up works they both thought the real issue behind them was queerness. I said to myself, "Of course! That's how people would see your work in New York!" What do you think about that?

Manuel: I always knew that there is this connotation within this body of work. People always try to project content on a work of art. When you know that it's made out of make-up it evokes many associations. Especially when the artist is male. But my intentions are coming from the readymade. To use a product which a lot of people use every day and think about how I could use it within my parameters. It's about color that is not produced for making art, but if you use it as so it already delivers a lot of meaning. So it's more about unsettling pre-built opinions in general.

Martin: But you often use cheap glittery stuff, it's not just the make-up.
In the outdoors you have that cheap stuff that glitters, that's "chintzy."
Again, you can also continue the theme and say, there is always a kind of maybe, not bad taste, but a kind of shallow populist taste.
Do you want to demote high art or show the beauty of low art, or neither?

Manuel: On one hand it brings a very low element into high art, but also it brings high art issues to people who have nothing to do with contemporary art, especially in the public space. I guess I try to go both ways.

Martin: Like Claes Oldenburg – is this a good comparison?
Because he would take classics of everyday design and make them big; part of it is about showing how beautiful the things of everyday life are.

Manuel: Yes, that's Oldenburg.

Martin: That's his version of Pop. As opposed to, let's say Warhol, maybe it's also to demote high art as well. Because in the end it's not like you say "Wow, the Brillo is so beautiful, or the soup cans," but it's also about the story of someone who talks about what he knows about life. Warhol said that when he was little they had Campbell soup every day, so that's his "nature," that's his "landscape" his "portrait."

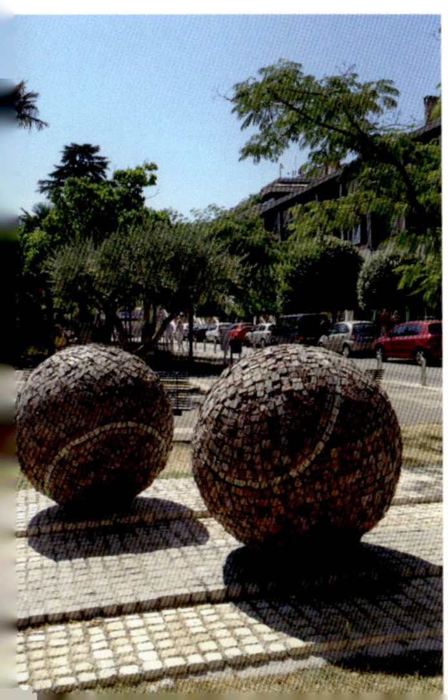

Manuel: I would say there've been a lot of changes in the relation between art and everyday life since the 1960s the impact of event culture on art institutions, for example.

Martin: I want to push this a little bit further, because I think it's a major element in your work. Rauschenberg was going around the block and picking up whatever elements in reality, taking them to the studio and pasting them because it was about this holiness of everyday life, the unmediated relationship to the commercial environment. So it was really like Allen Ginsberg looking at everyday reality like a mystic, as opposed to a deep pessimist like Warhol, who says that he was doomed to low objects because that's who he is. So there is more a mystical Pop and a more pessimistic Pop. Mike Kelly for example is a very pessimistic Pop artist.

Manuel: I guess what I try to show is that that these opposites are not so far away from each other – that there is a limbo in between.

Martin: Ok I see. Let's take another comparison – between your work and Franz West's and Heimo [Zobernig]'s for example.
So Franz used African fabrics, right? But these African materials look really beautiful on his chairs. There is not a trace of irony in the end. In the case of Heimo, whenever he uses cheap materials, like toilet paper rolls, cardboard, or stuff like that, at the end it is so appropriate and formally persuasive that you don't have any trace of the lowliness of the material. But in your case there is a trace. You can look at the chintz and can see that it's actually beautiful but you never forget that it is chintzy – and the same with make-up. It can look like a Piero della Francesca, like these pastel colors, but you will never forget for one second the lowliness of the material. In my opinion it is one of the distinctions of your work. I think with Franz West it's particularly obvious. You know, he has those cheap African materials, but on his couches they just look gorgeous. But in your case it never translates completely. There is always the cheapness of the effect, that stays there, and it does not disturb the beautiful aspect, it sits next to it but it lets you never forget that it comes from another social zone.

Manuel: I understand your point. Maybe that's why I've often been asked to do works outdoors, where they can be perceived by people who wouldn't enter the museum.
Because, like you said, the material keeps its identity, so it is familiar to almost everybody. For me it works best, when the piece leaves you with certain suspense.

Martin: But it goes a little bit further, I think. Let me explain. Kant makes a distinction between pleasure and gratification – especially, aesthetic pleasure and gratification. And he says aesthetic pleasure has nothing to do with what you are used to whereas gratification does. For example, gratification is if you like the color magenta and then you see a magenta painting and say "Ah, I love this painting, it's magenta." That's gratification, because it's a preexisting condition. Beauty, he says, has nothing to do with what you like or don't like beforehand.
It has to give you a sense of pleasure, but the pleasure comes from the fact that you cannot change anything, that everything fits together. To make a long story short, for the person who looks at the chintz and likes the sparkle, it's gratification.
So it's a bit of a debasement of the aesthetic experience. Which I think has something

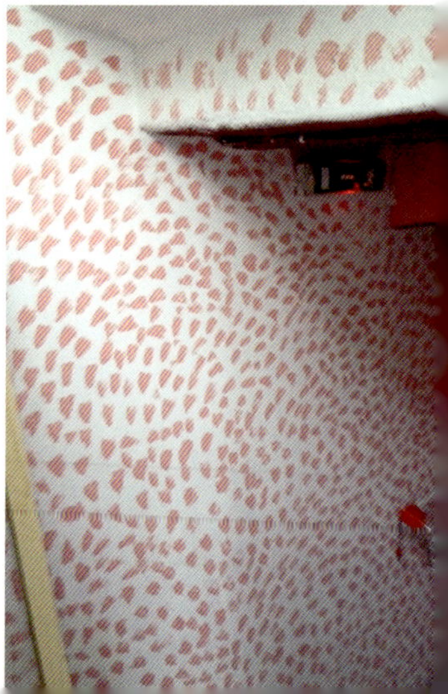

profoundly to do with Pop art, the debasement of an aesthetic experience. You see it's not just like the fact that when you like it you expose yourself to a lowly background or something like that. It goes further than that because it is like gratification confused, artfully confused with aesthetic pleasure. That's why I say there is something interesting here, because it really gets to the source of the aesthetic experience somehow. In the case of Warhol, it's the identity of the product that creates the debasement; according to Kant, though, these type of considerations really have to be put aside during an aesthetic judgment. But when something is sparkly or chintzy – as with some of your artworks – the "cheapness" enters into the aesthetic experience itself. It's not about the social identity of the product; it's within your sense of vision – a purely visual type of Pop – taking Pop sensibility and putting it in the vision itself.

Manuel: The key issues are located in the visual experience and your preexisting expectations related to the material, and not about "pure beauty."

Martin: You know, at the end the work is quite beautiful, but it never lets you forget the confusion between beauty and gratification; in a certain sense it puts into question the very distinction. Maybe that's what transvestites feel, you know? That this gratification-bound and "shallow" part of aesthetics, actually has a profound transcendental aspect.

Manuel: (laughs) It's "Divine."

Martin: Yes, I was really thinking about John Waters, but with John Waters, it is never beautiful. It really stays ugly. And it really shows you a parallel aesthetic system, where beauty doesn't really enter, because chintzy-ness and sparkly-ness completely overtake the sense of beauty. And it's done quite self-consciously. The kitschy-ness of late Elvis, to take another case, and his kind of aesthetics will never become beautiful – it will always remains a parallel, class-bound system that has more to do with the lower sentiment of gratification than with genuine "Kantian" beauty – always about the colors that you like, the visual effects that are kind of sparkly to the eye, but in your case there is a kind of resolution – the make-up work transcends, but never forgets its lowly aesthetic origins.
I think that's pretty interesting.

Manuel: People often do not recognize the materials I use at first sight – things they have seen many times before. They ask me how I made them, what does the shape mean, is it related to whatever comes to their mind. Like the chintzy stuff, these are just very cheap garlands from the decoration supply, and you can see them quite often, because they are made to decorate space. I mean garlands have a very long tradition since Ancient Greece or longer. If you walk through Vienna you see them on historicist facades, or you can find them in Dutch still life or the murals in Pompey, they often include painted or cast garlands. The chintzy I use is just a contemporary version of that. What I do is change their everyday use, as little as necessary, to turn it into something else. To stretch them straight, give them a geometric shape, extend them into monumental, etc. But mainly people tell me about their perceptional experience, when they speak about my work, rarely about the basic objects it is made of.

Martin: Ok, I'll make another comparison. The minimalist slogan was:

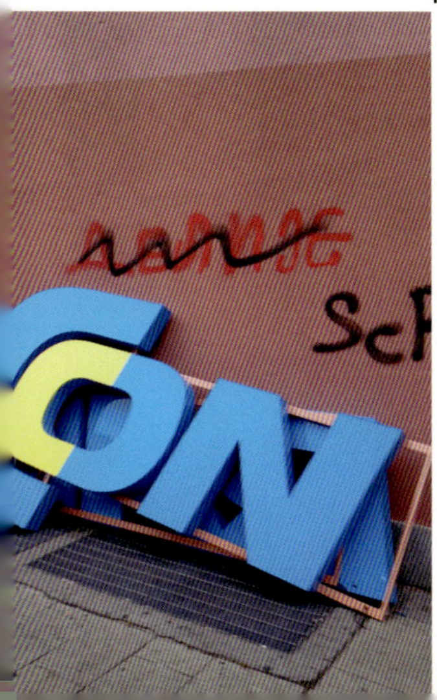

"Go to a hardware store, and just buy the stuff as it is." It so happens that hardware store-bought materials often have very classic proportions; because of that the minimalists imported very classical qualities into their work – why many minimalist works look so classical – which they didn't expect at all, this was an unintended consequence. I don't think any of them, in the beginning, thought their work would have this timeless elegance. So that's another parallel, because they would use everything as it was and some of the qualities would rub off on the work. In your case it doesn't get this timeless elegance, but there's this thing that's still…

Manuel: For the minimalists it was this idea of anti-choice, which is far less obvious in my work but it's always there.

Martin: Yes, but they are different. You can almost build an argument that it's a critique of minimalism. The minimalist said that if you take it as it is, then you get rid of the issue of choice, of the issue of a social character and all that, and it's like your work proves that it's not true. You can take it as it is, and it will contribute to the work, but you'll never have this clean sense that you're just looking on structures and intentions. Let's go to Mike Kelley. He was a real pessimist. And it has this kind of real Pop pessimism. When he was taking heavy metal flags and doing them out of real silk, and stuff like that, he would've said that some artists want to transcend their work upwards, and I want my work to fall down like a lead zeppelin, and in your work there is this kind of Pop pessimism, it never totally transcends but it is never ugly, never.

Manuel: Maybe it has to do with the circumstances; that these works were developed mainly in times of global financial crisis. It is a fact that during crisis the consumption of make-up escalates, to cover the lines of worry, to put it simply. I always liked to play with this meaningful idea to make up an art space or decorate the institution, surely tongue-in-cheek. But after a while I got matching feedback about different works of mine from various people. They often talked about this melancholic undertone, which exists parallel to their eye-pleasing effects and beauty. Maybe that's why it is neither optimistic nor pessimistic, but relates to a certain embedded economic sentiment.

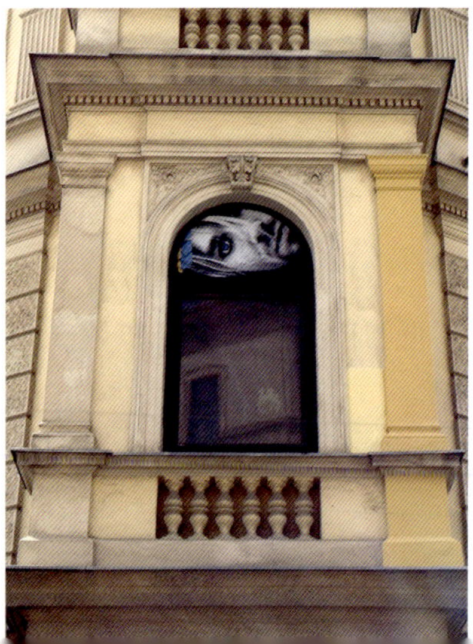

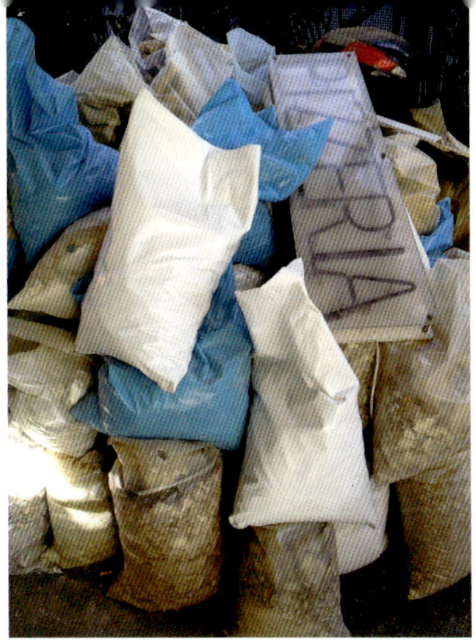

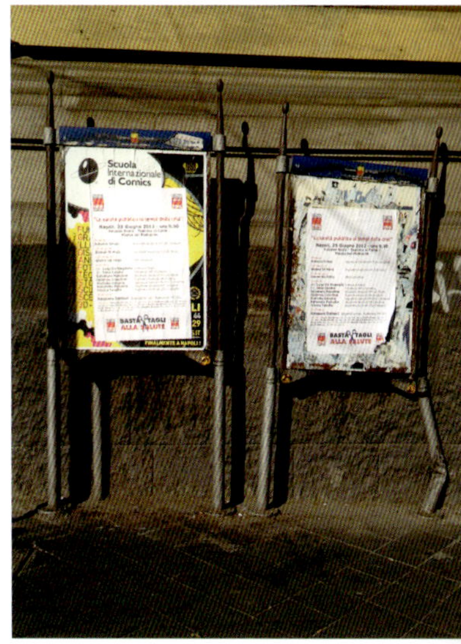
Scuola
Internazionale
di Comics

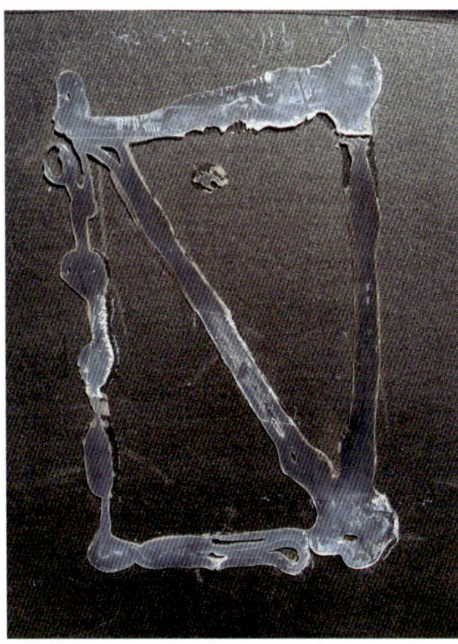

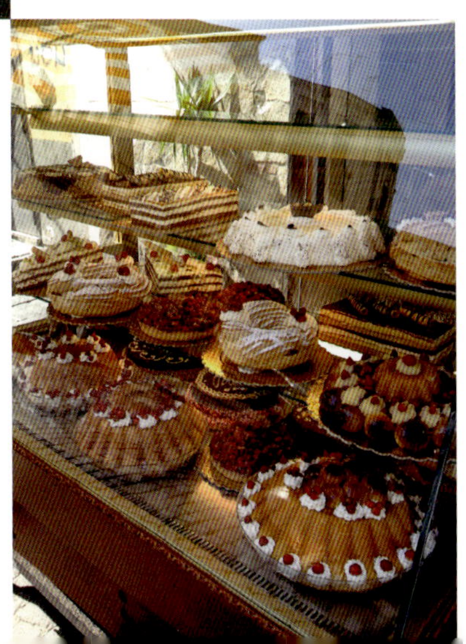

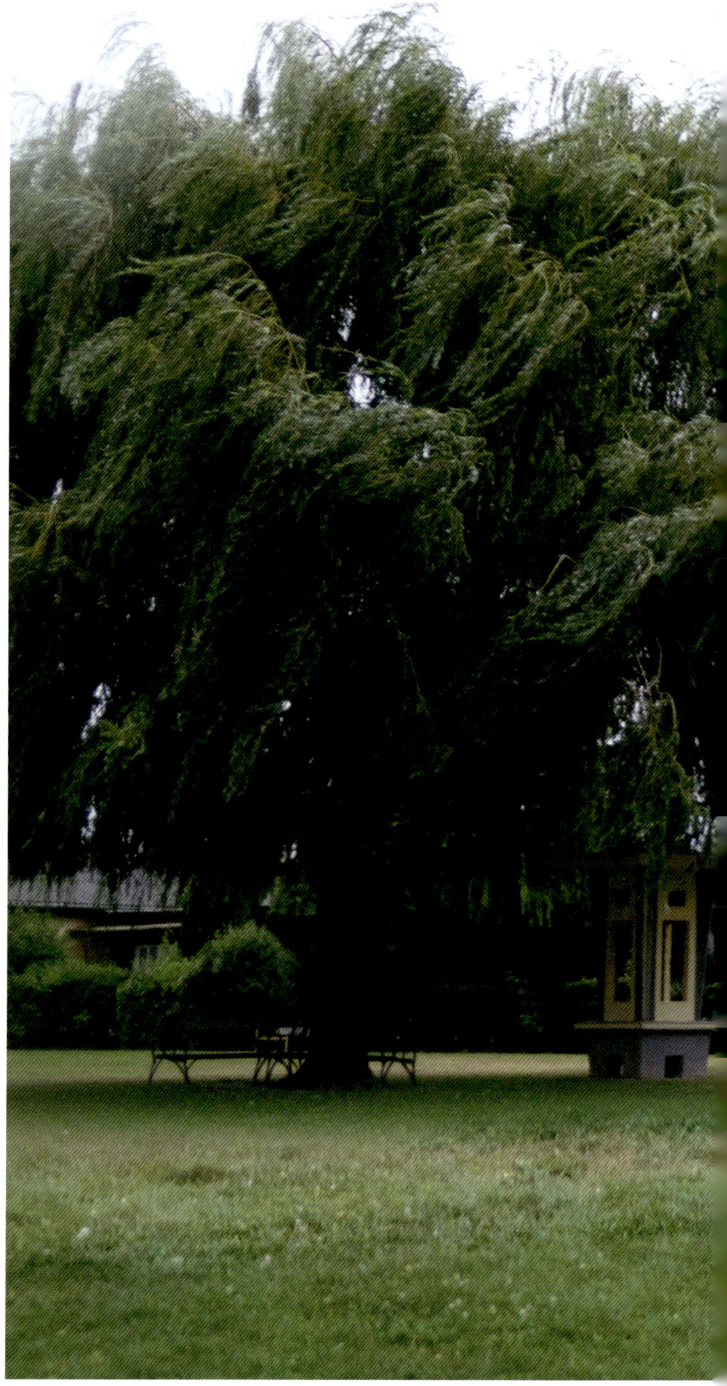

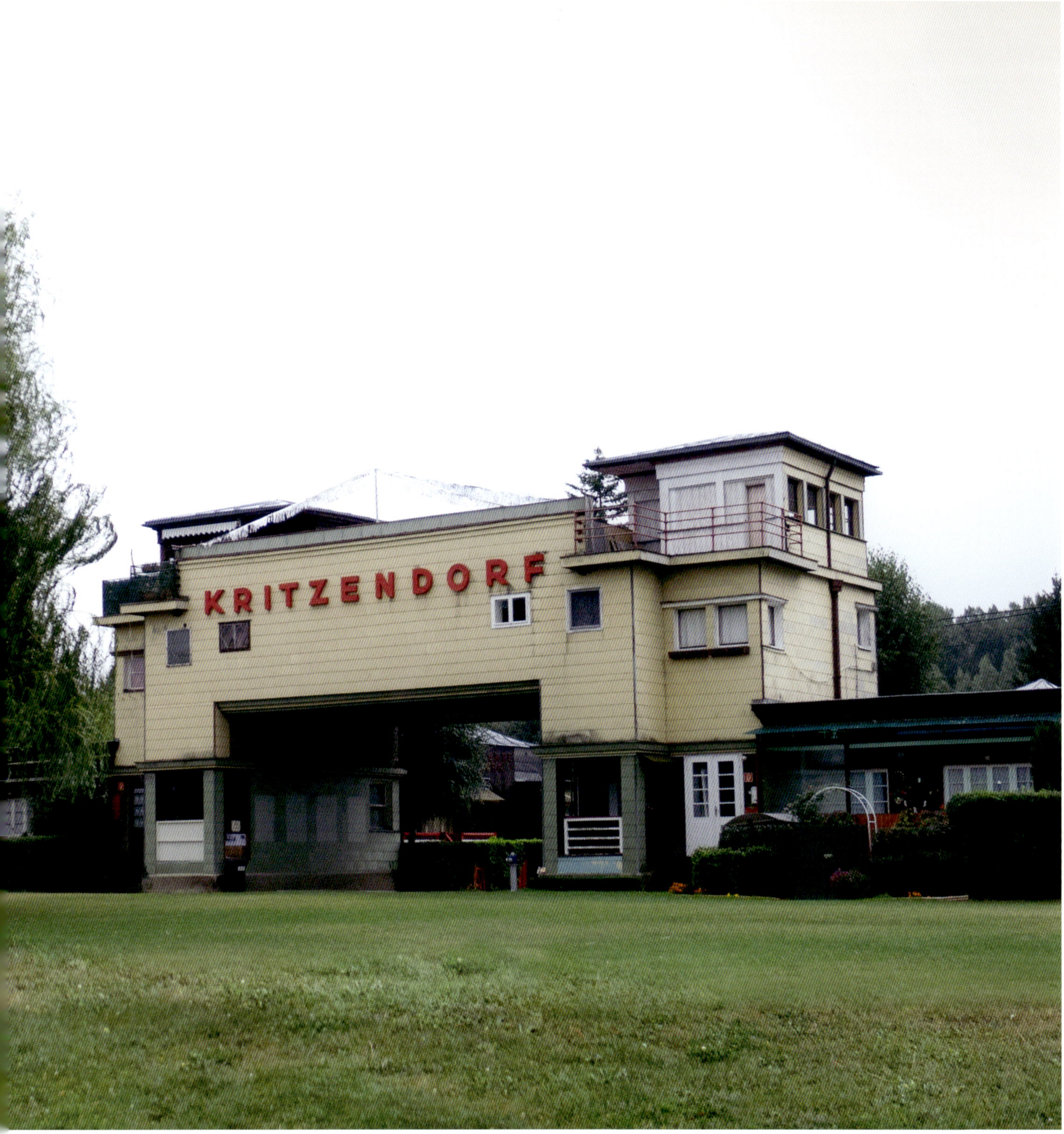

"Sculpturegarden", Strombad Kritzendorf, 2012
Untitled, 300 x 1000 x 850 cm, plastic foil, steel, 2012

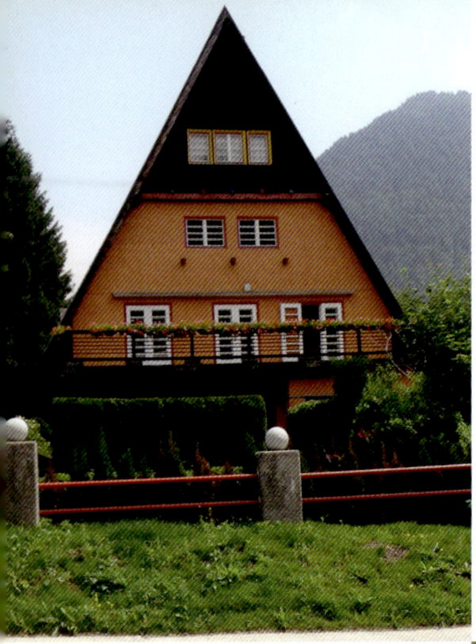

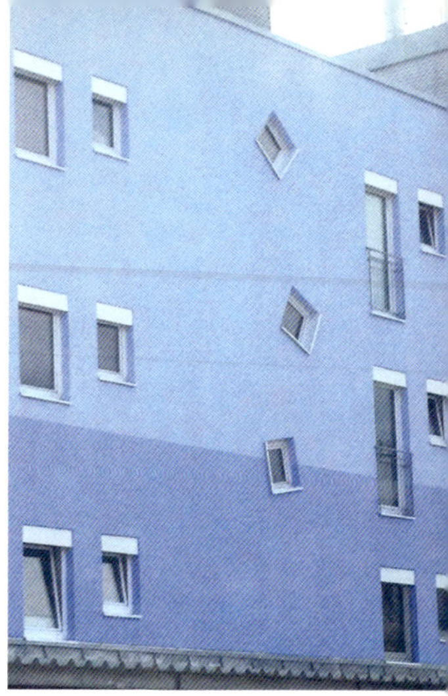

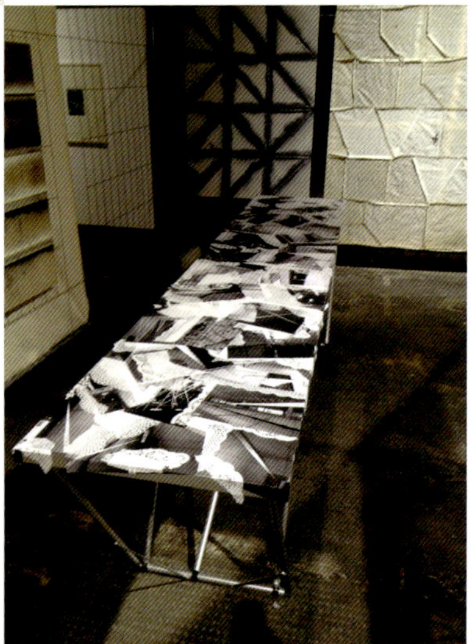

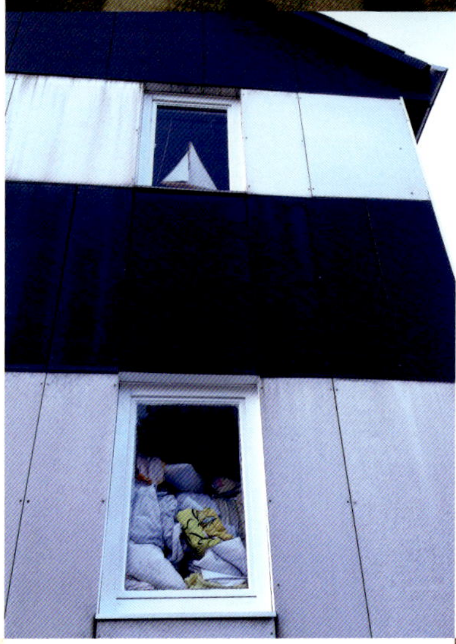

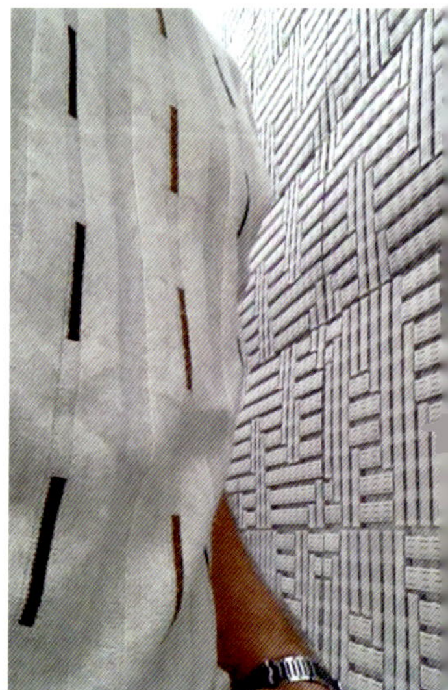

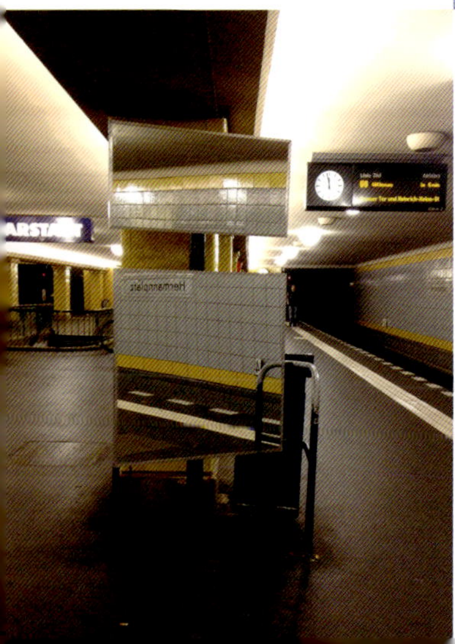

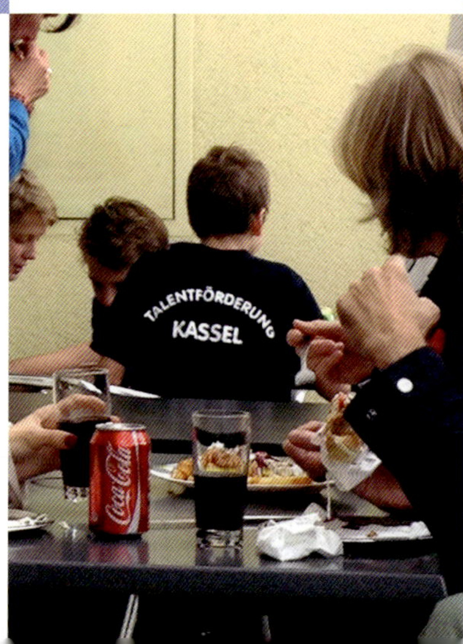
TALENTFÖRDERUNG
KASSEL
Coca-Cola

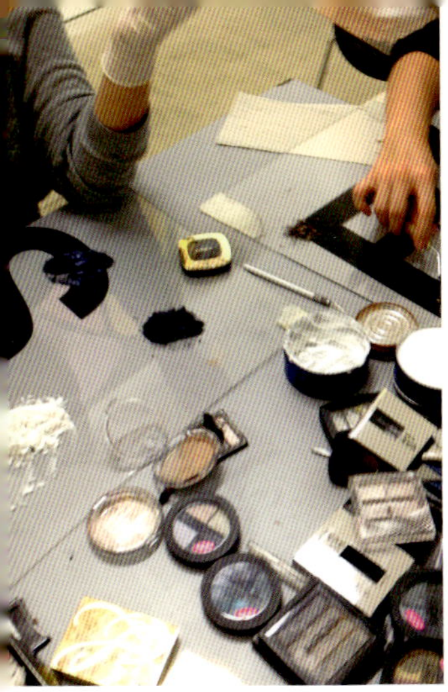

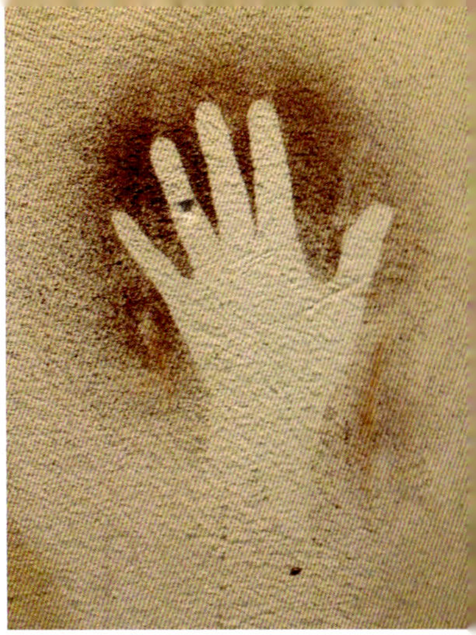

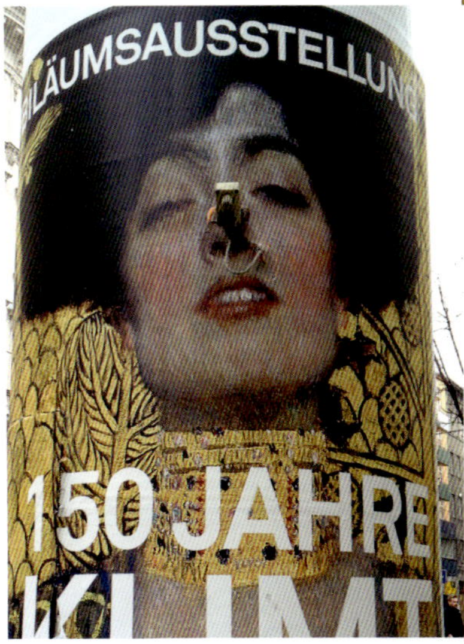
150 JAHRE

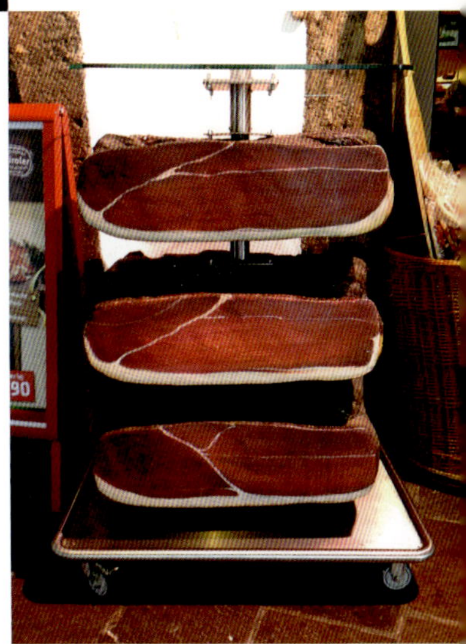

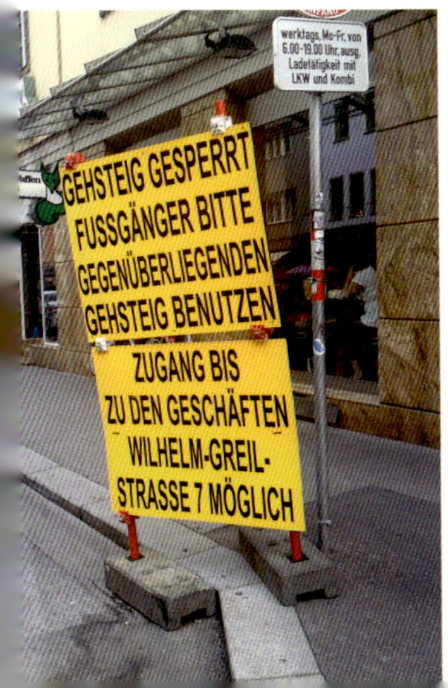
werktags, Mo-Fr, von 6.00-19.00 Uhr, ausg. Ladetätigkeit mit LKW und Kombi
GEHSTEIG GESPERRT
FUSSGÄNGER BITTE
GEGENÜBERLIEGENDEN
GEHSTEIG BENUTZEN
ZUGANG BIS
ZU DEN GESCHÄFTEN
WILHELM-GREIL-
STRASSE 7 MÖGLICH

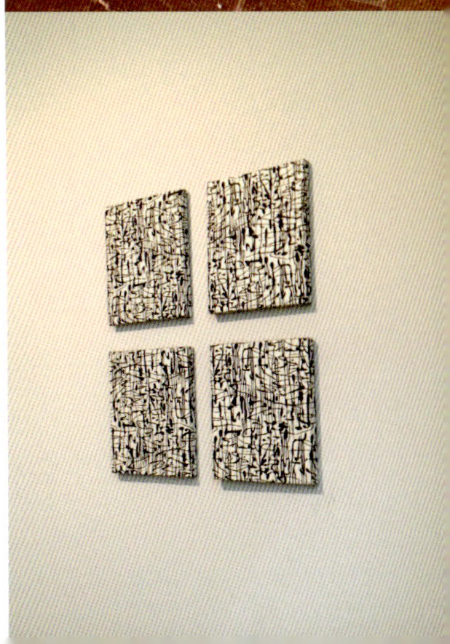

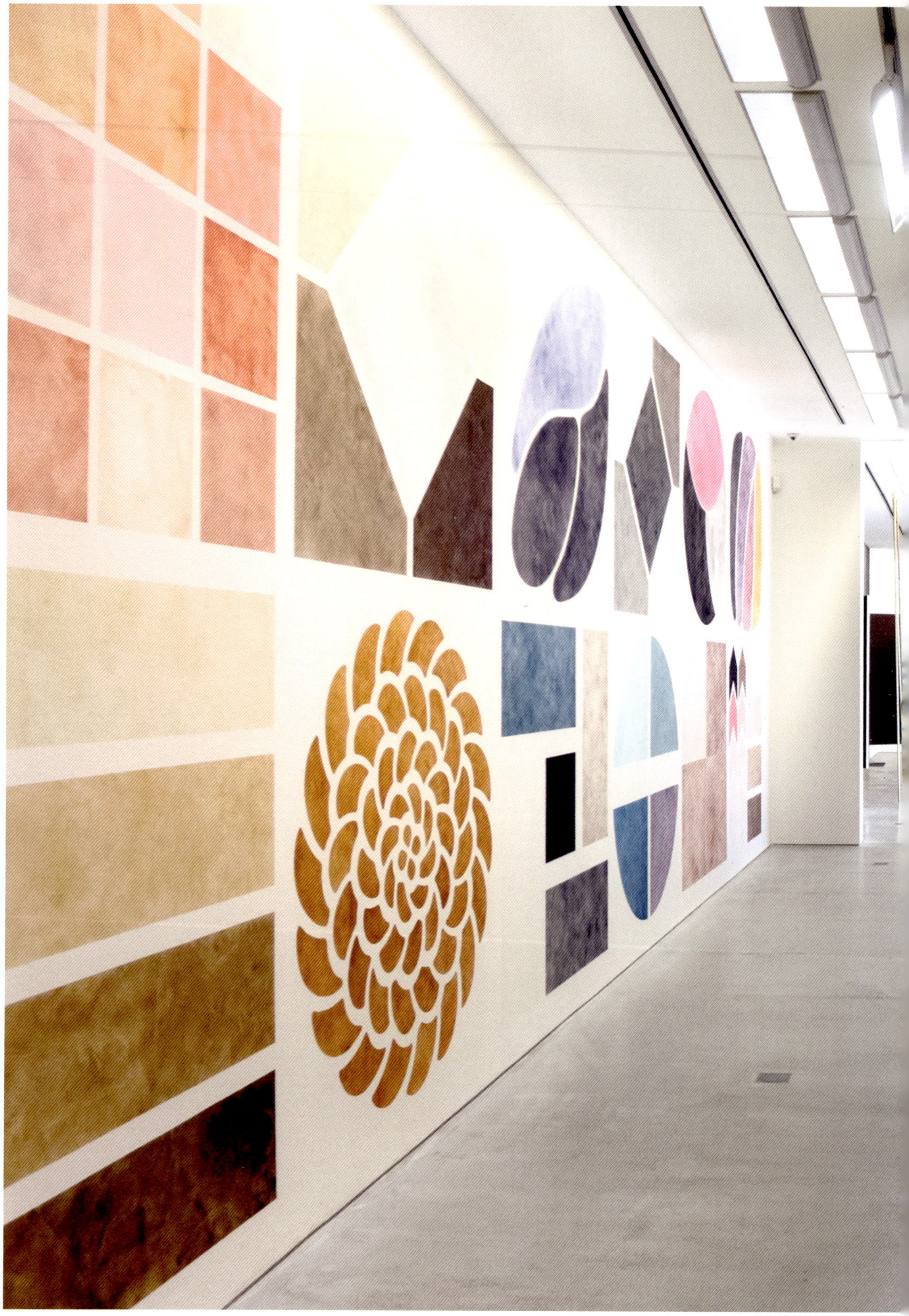

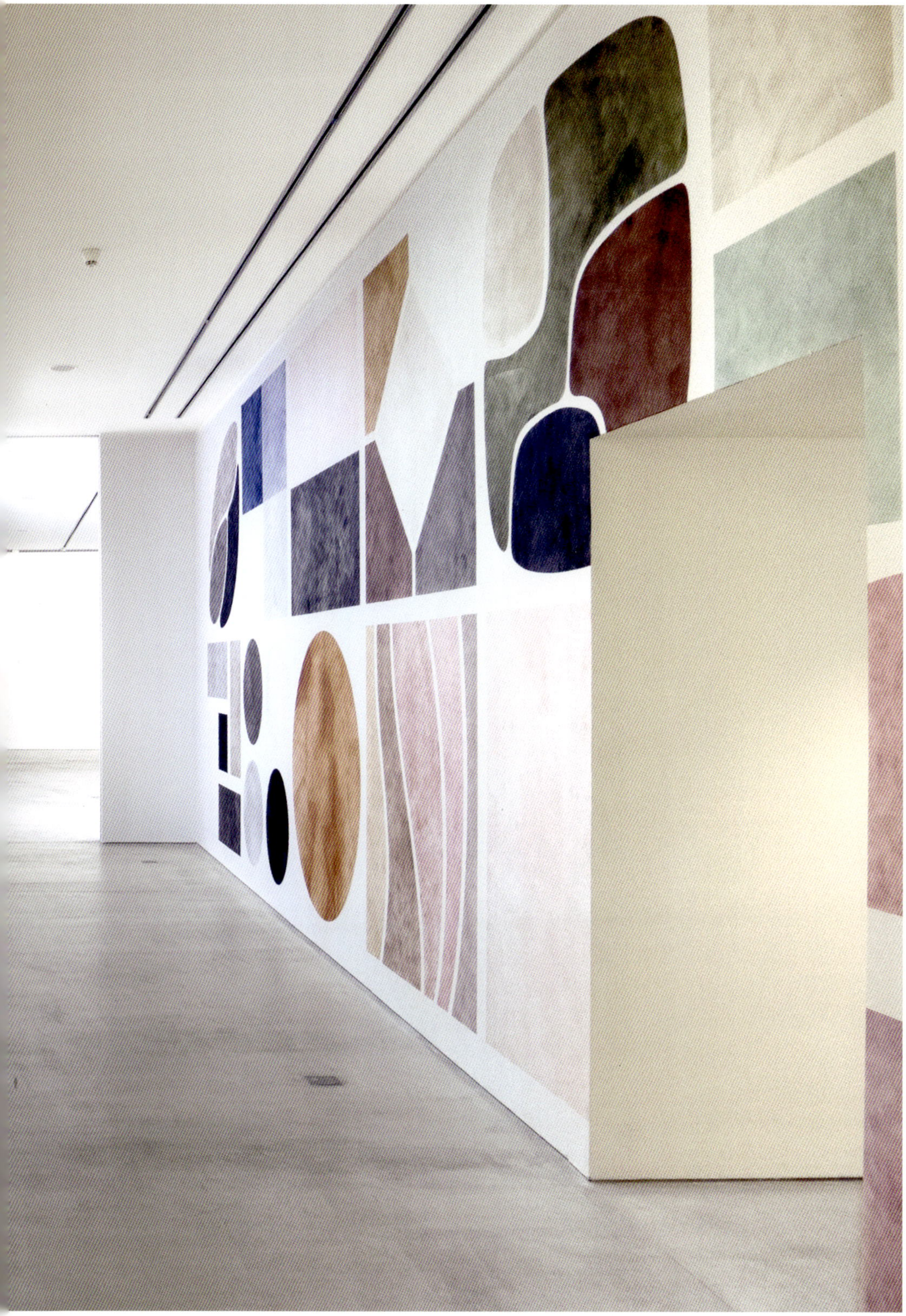

"Increasingly Colorful – Current Painting from Austria"
Galerie im Taxispalais, Innsbruck, 2012
Untitled, each side 310 x 950 cm, make-up and skin cream on wall, 2012

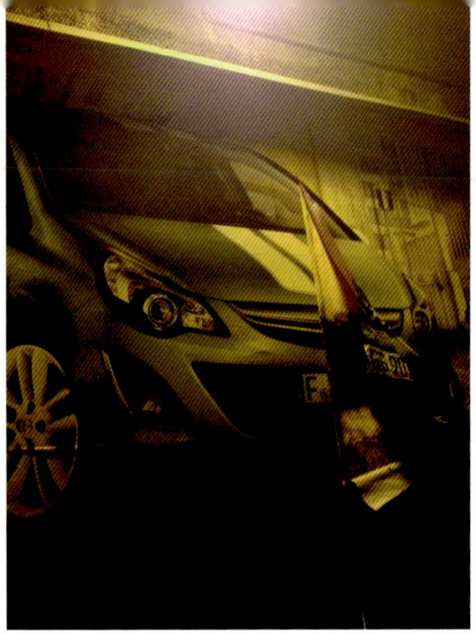

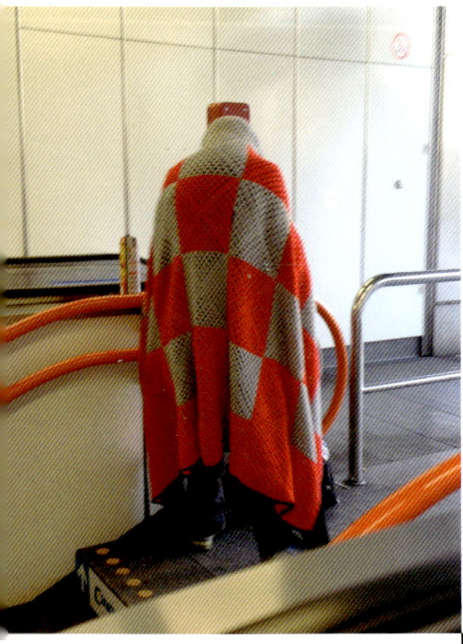

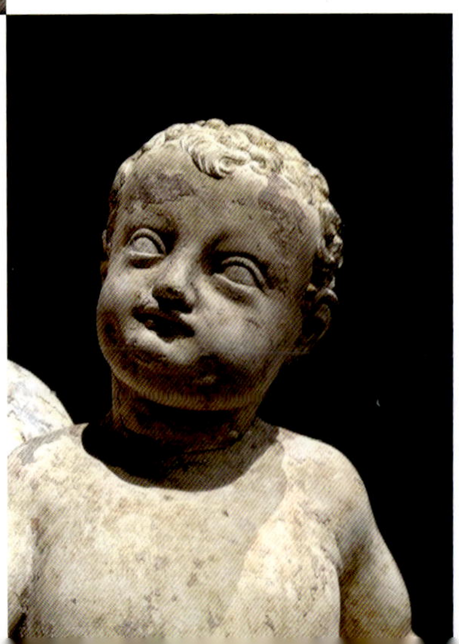

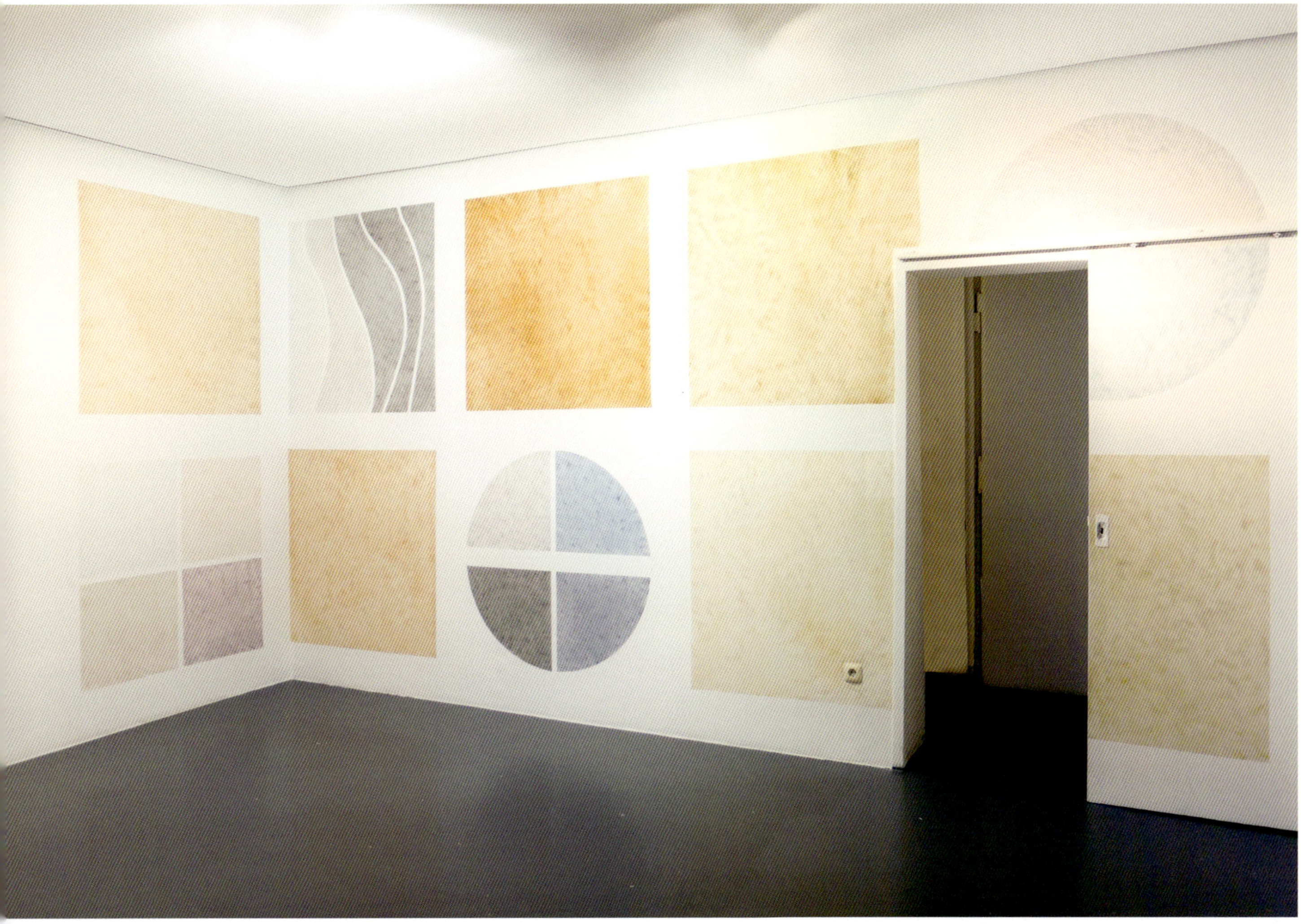

Galerie Perpétuel Frankfurt am Main
Untitled, 240 x 630 cm, make-up and skin cream on wall, 2012

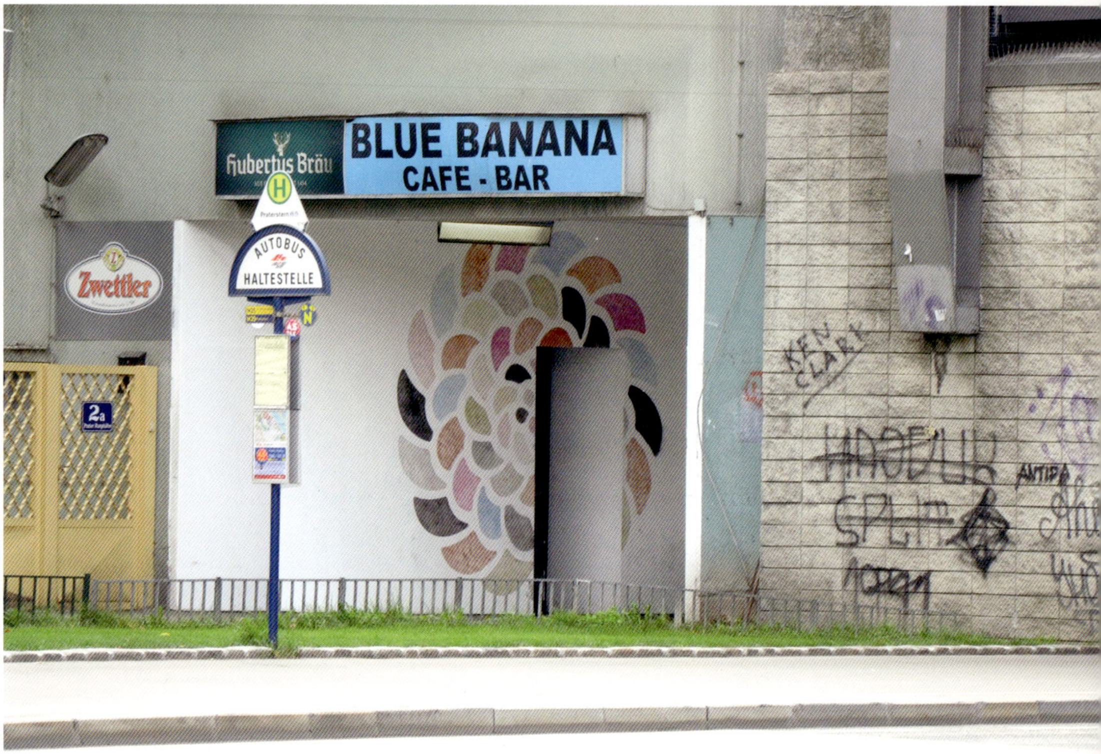
Hubertus Bräu
BLUE BANANA
CAFE - BAR
Zwettler
AUTOBUS
HALTESTELLE

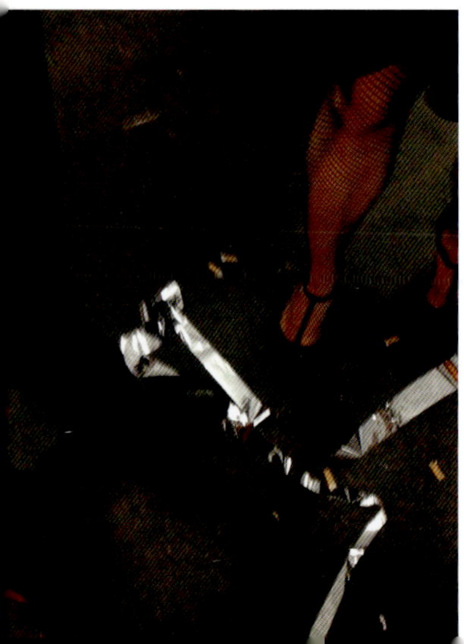

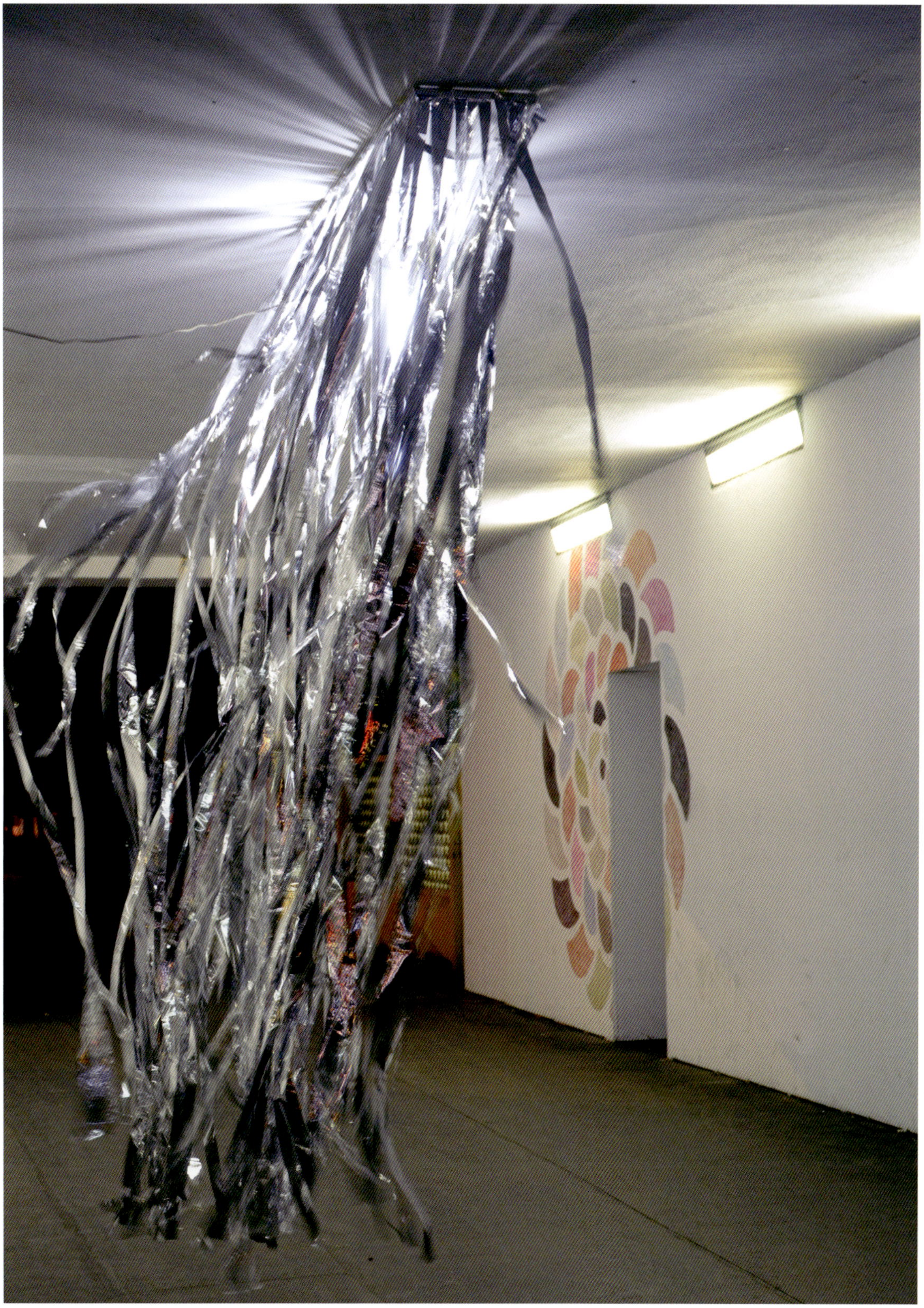

Pro Choice, Vienna, 2012
feat. Daniela Salvioni “Richard Hell, Arthur Rimbaud and their Hair”
Untitled, 300 x 300 cm, make-up and skin cream on wall, 2012
Untitled, plastic foil, neon tube, cable, ca. 300 x 130 x 30 cm, 2012

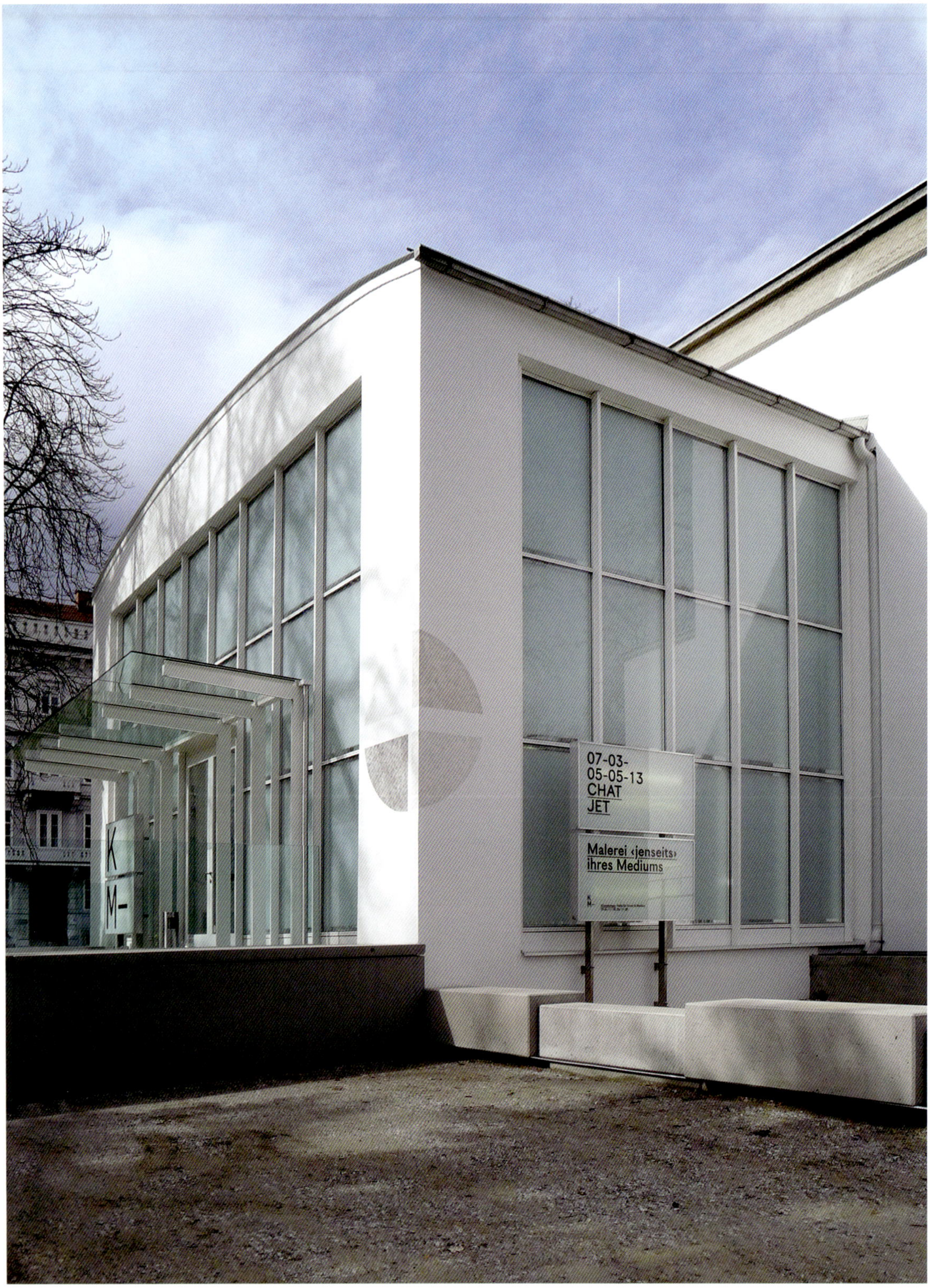

"Chat Jet, Painting ‹Beyond› The Medium"
Künstlerhaus, Halle für Kunst & Medien, Graz, 2013
Untitled (Q21 Platinium), 160 x 160 cm, make-up and sunmilk, 2013
right page top: Untitled (Pink Cupcake), 160 x 160 cm, make-up and sunmilk on wall, 2013
Untitled (Meteorites), 160 x 160 cm, make-up and sunmilk on wall, 2013
right page bottom: Untitled (Luminous Blue), 160 x 160 cm, make-up and sunmilk on wall, 2013
Untitled (Les Hombres), 160 x 160 cm, make-up and sunmilk on wall, 2013

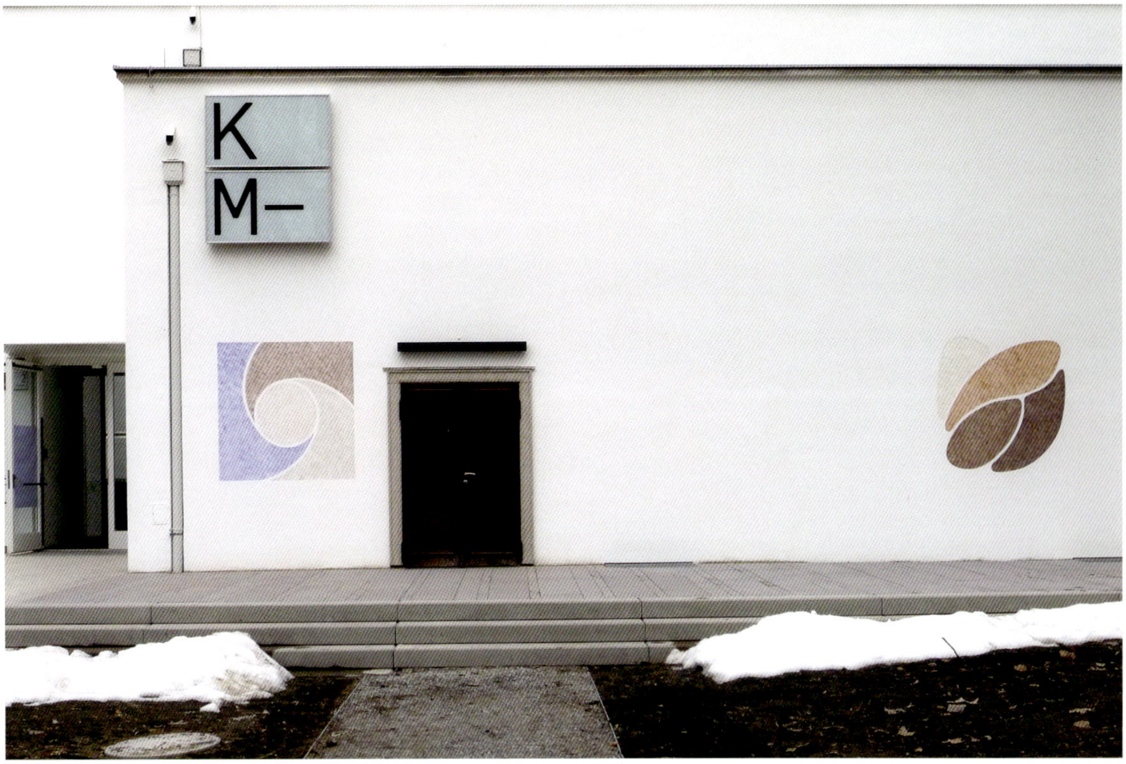
K
M–

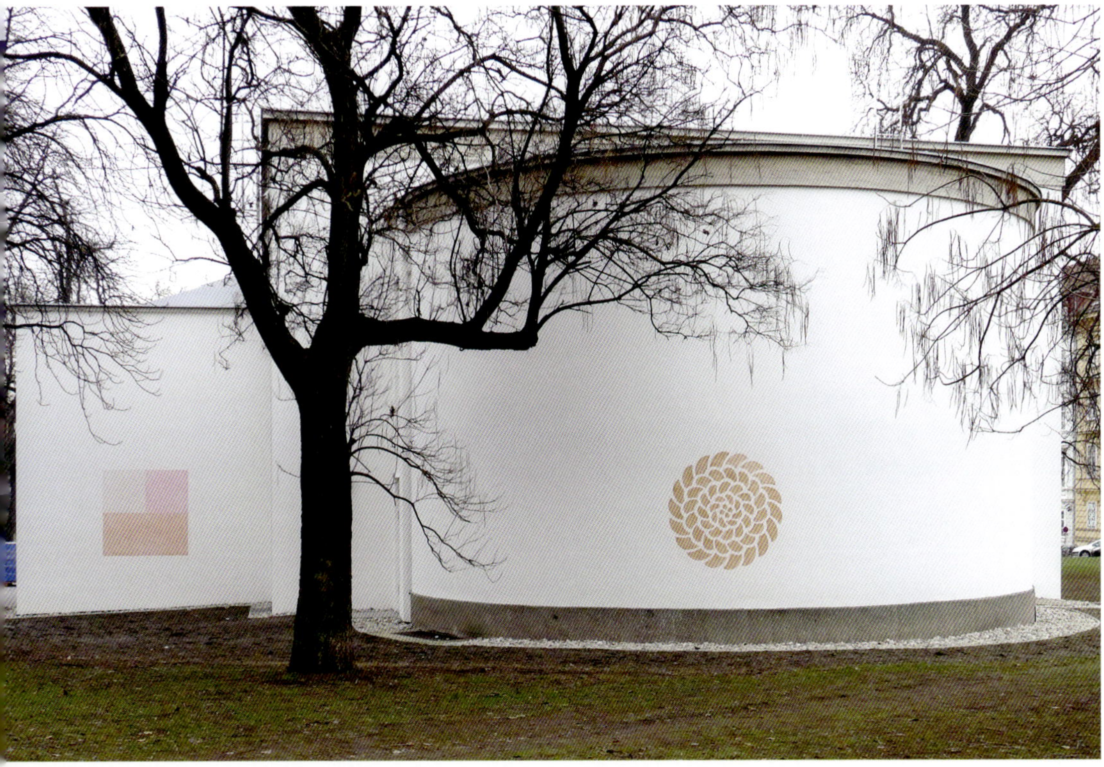

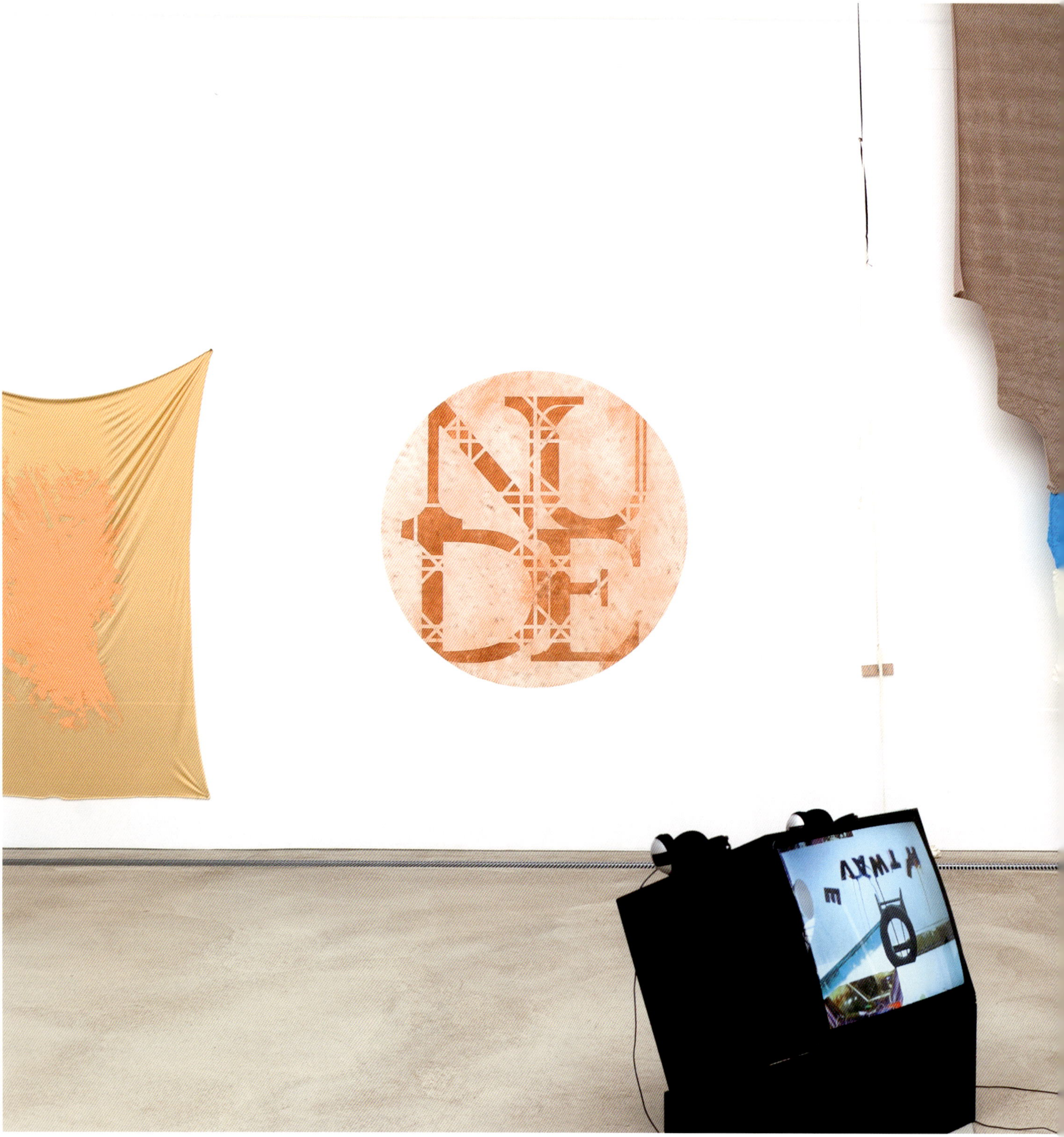

"Chat Jet, Painting ‹Beyond› The Medium"
Künstlerhaus, Halle für Kunst & Medien, Graz, 2013
Untitled (Nude), 150 x 150 cm, make-up and skin cream on wall, 2013
right: Untitled (Peach Boy), 150 x 150 cm, make-up and skin cream on wall, 2013

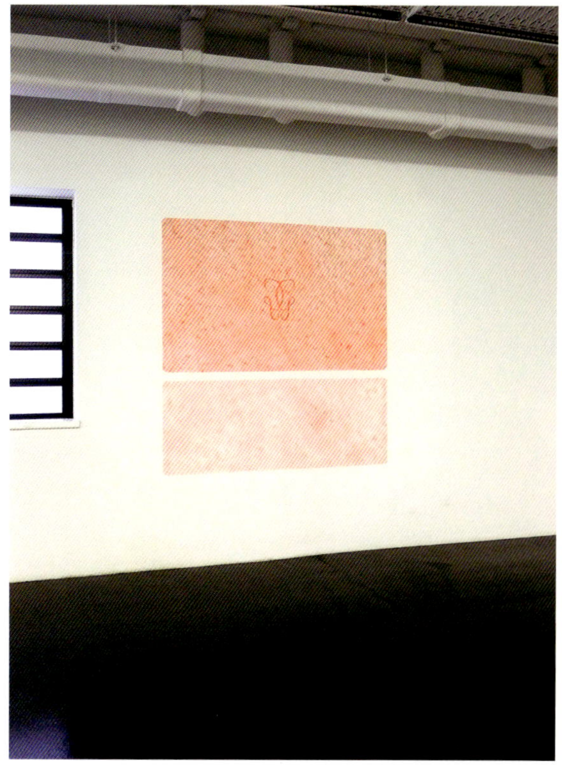

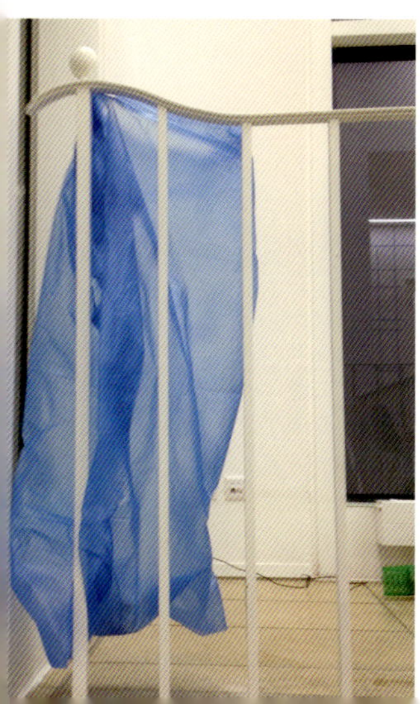

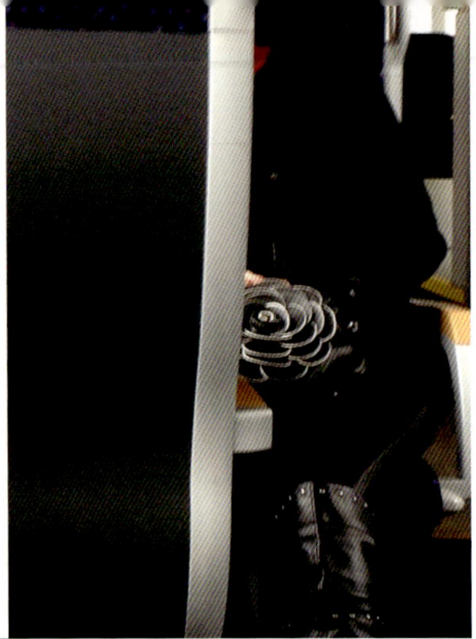

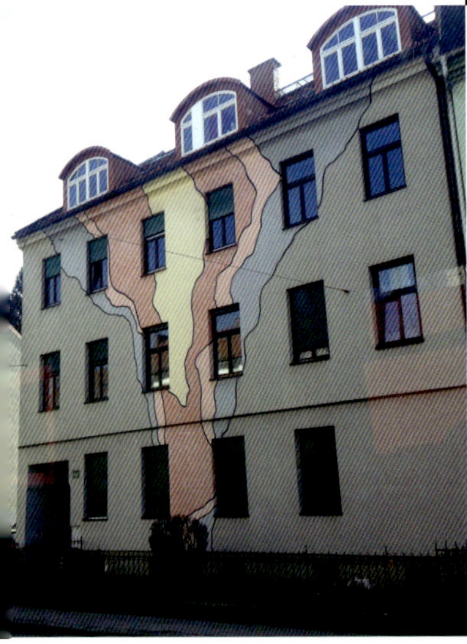

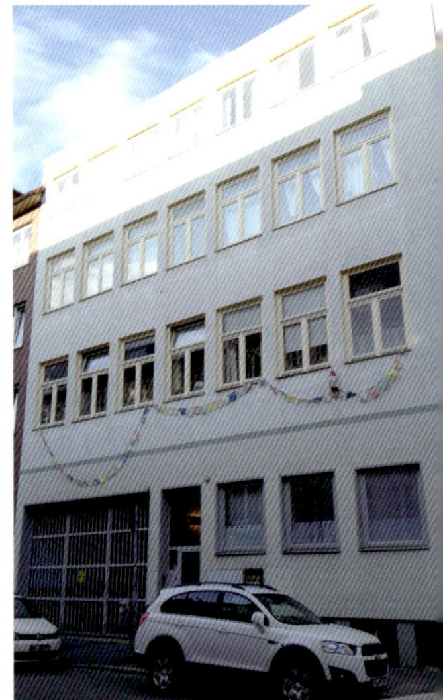

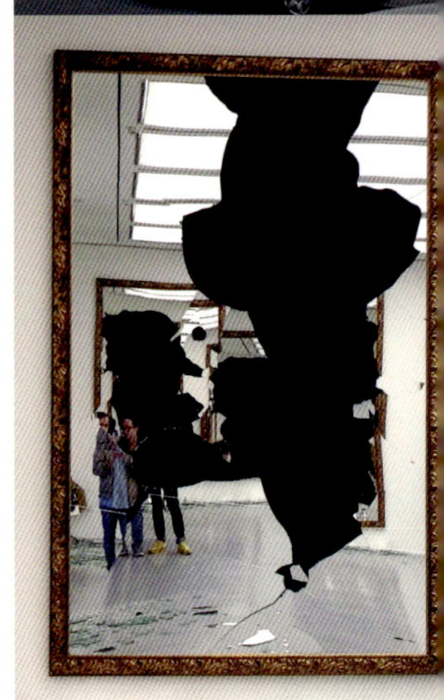

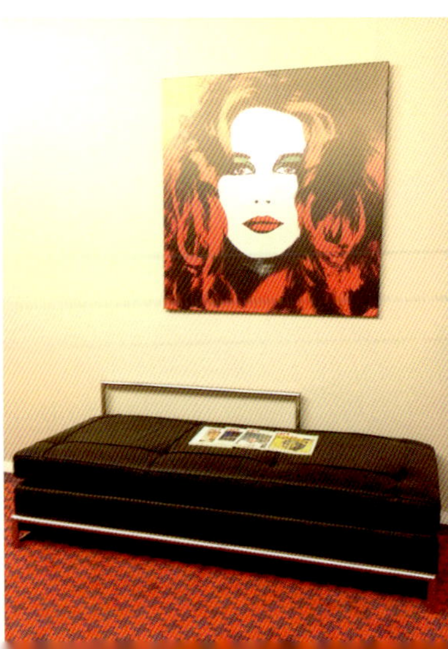

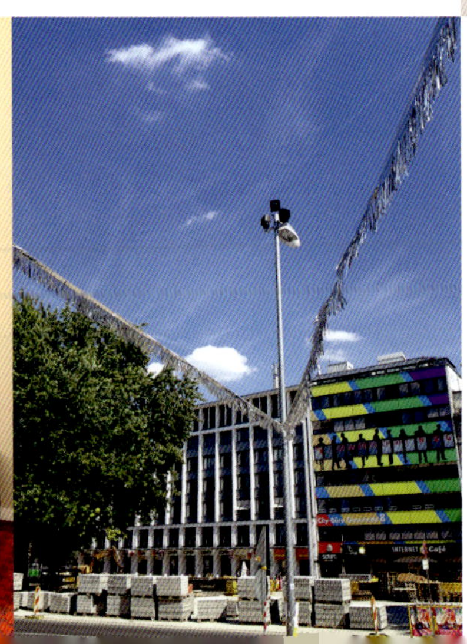

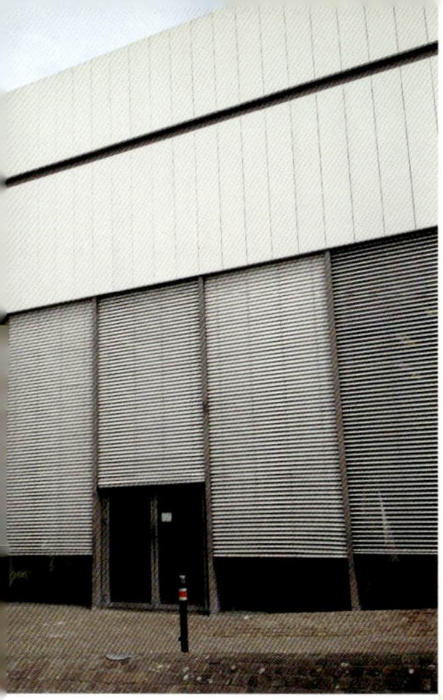
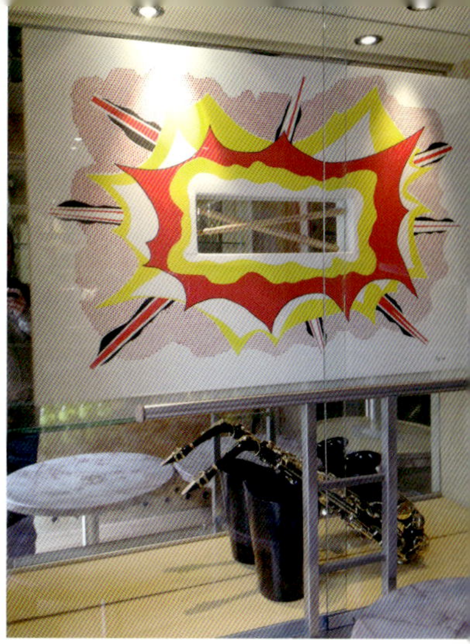
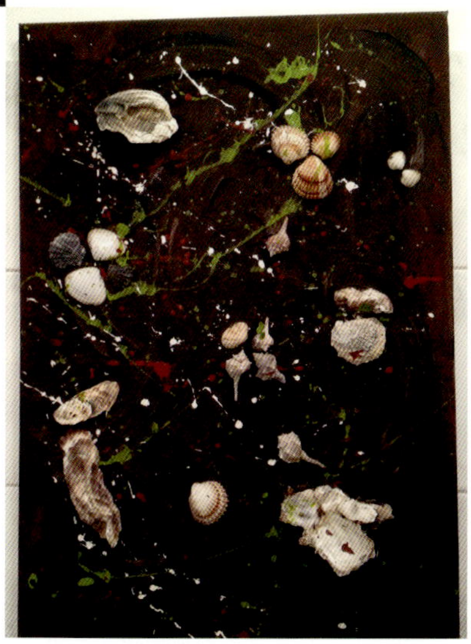
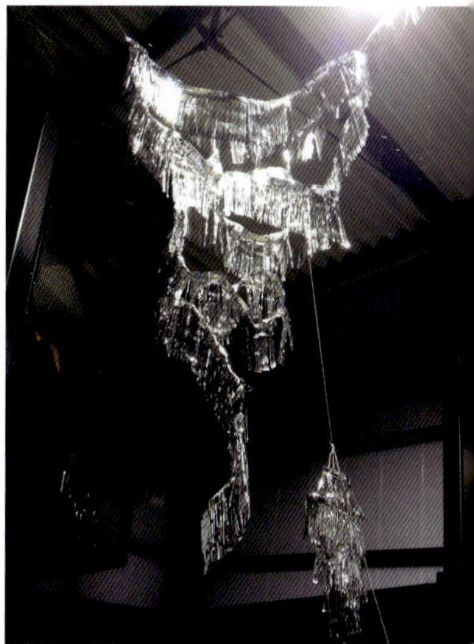
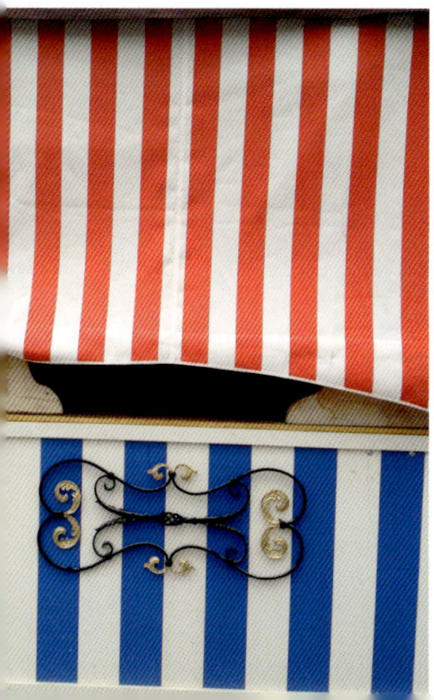
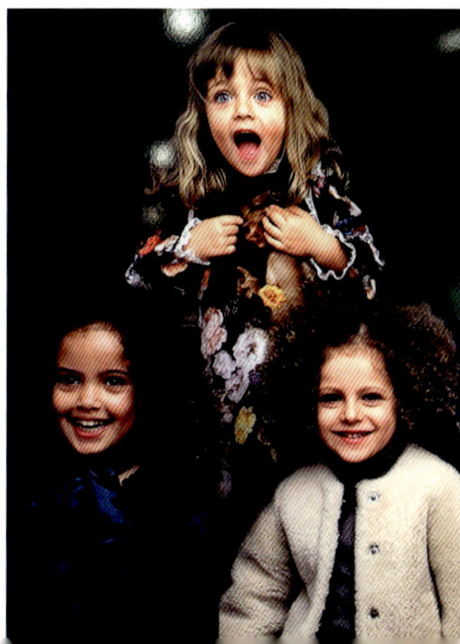

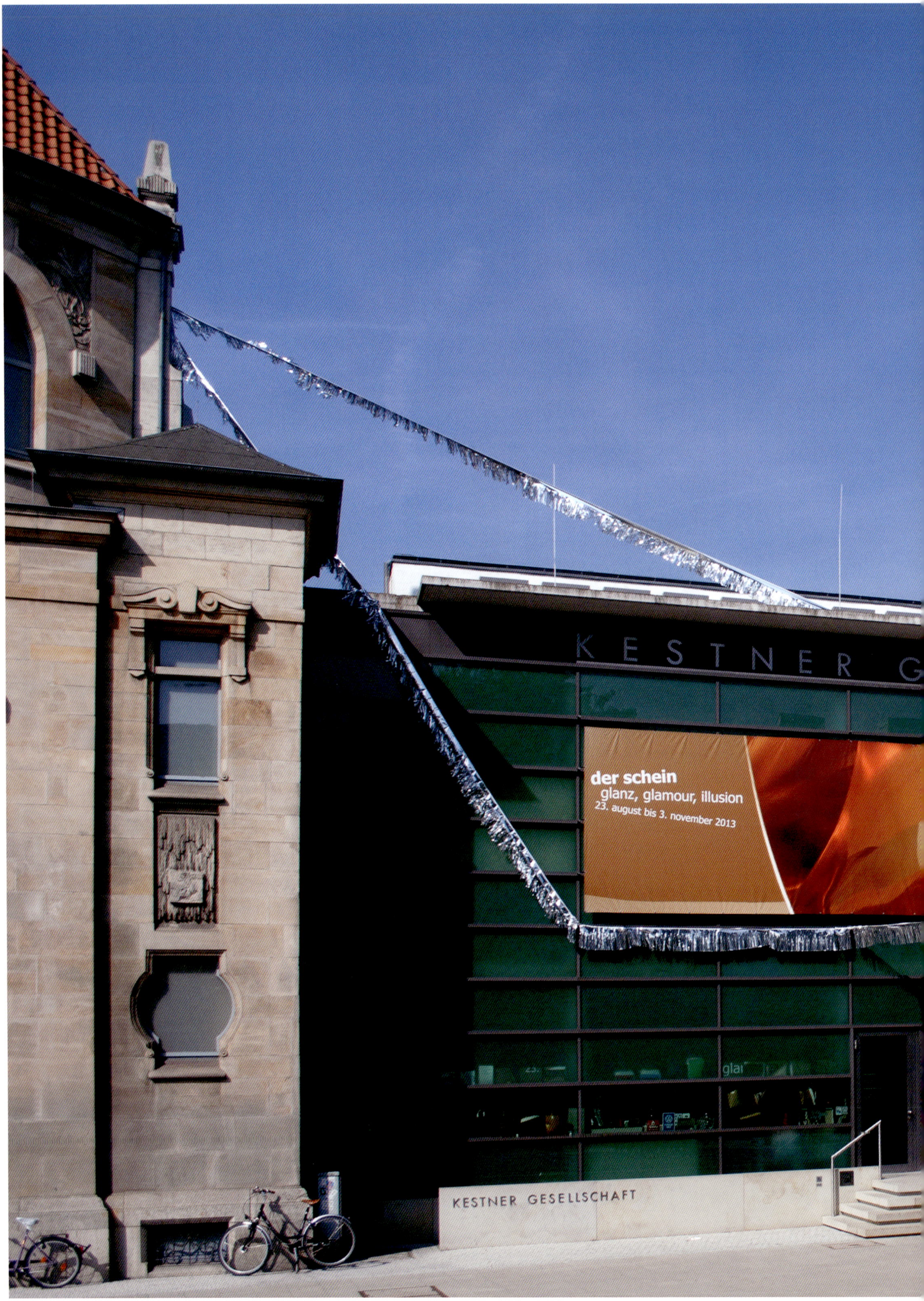
KESTNER G
der schein
glanz, glamour, illusion
23. august bis 3. november 2013
KESTNER GESELLSCHAFT

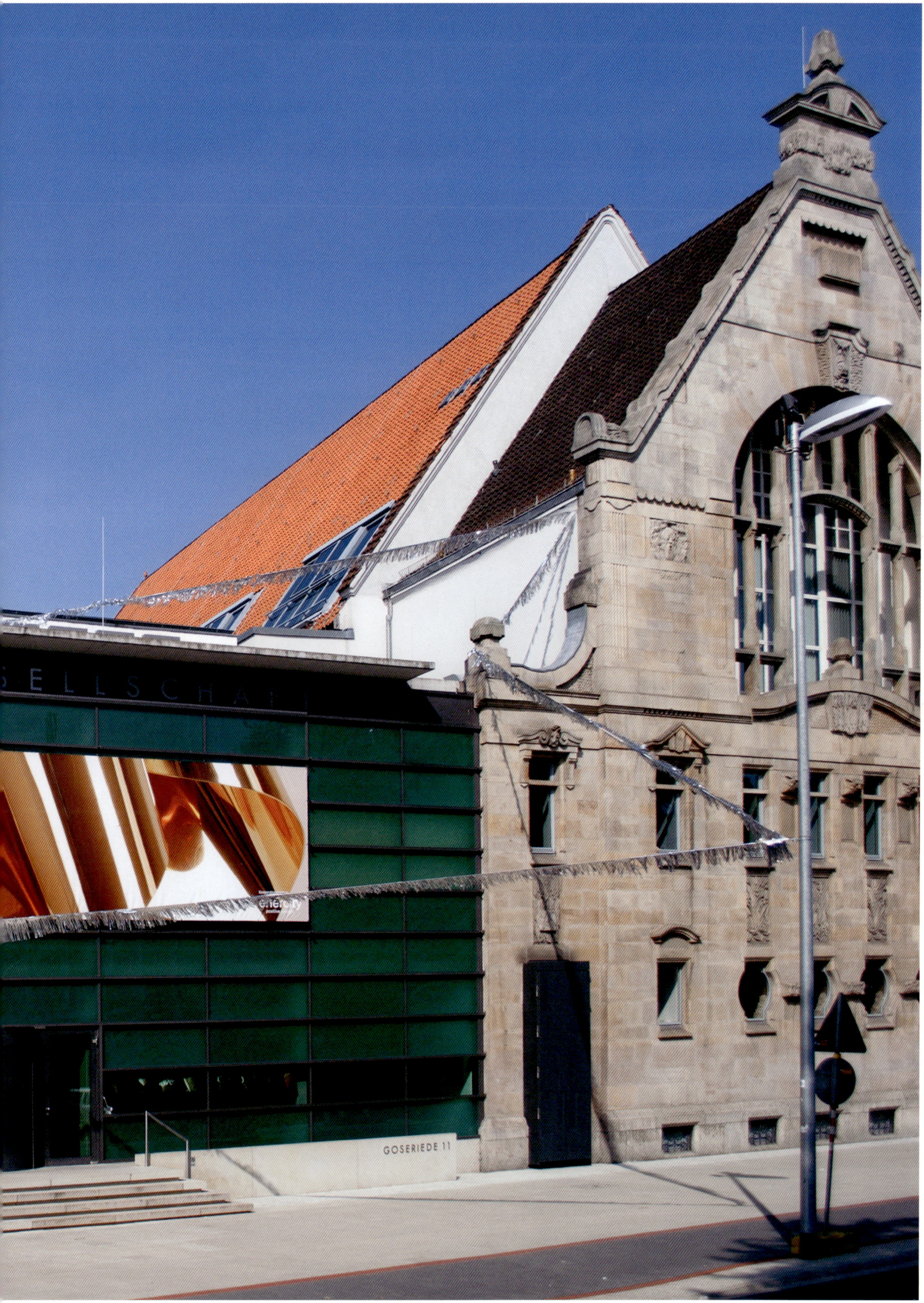
GOSERIEDE 11

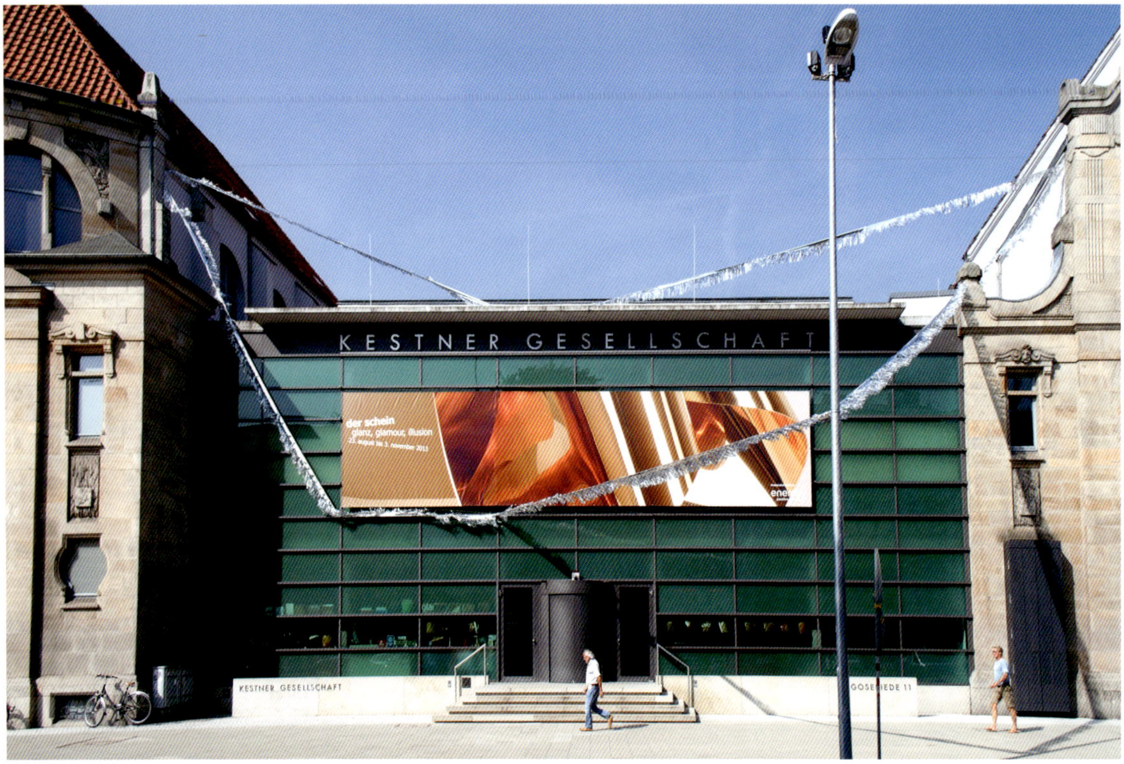
KESTNER GESELLSCHAFT
der schein
glanz, glamour, illusion
KESTNER GESELLSCHAFT
GOSERIEDE 11

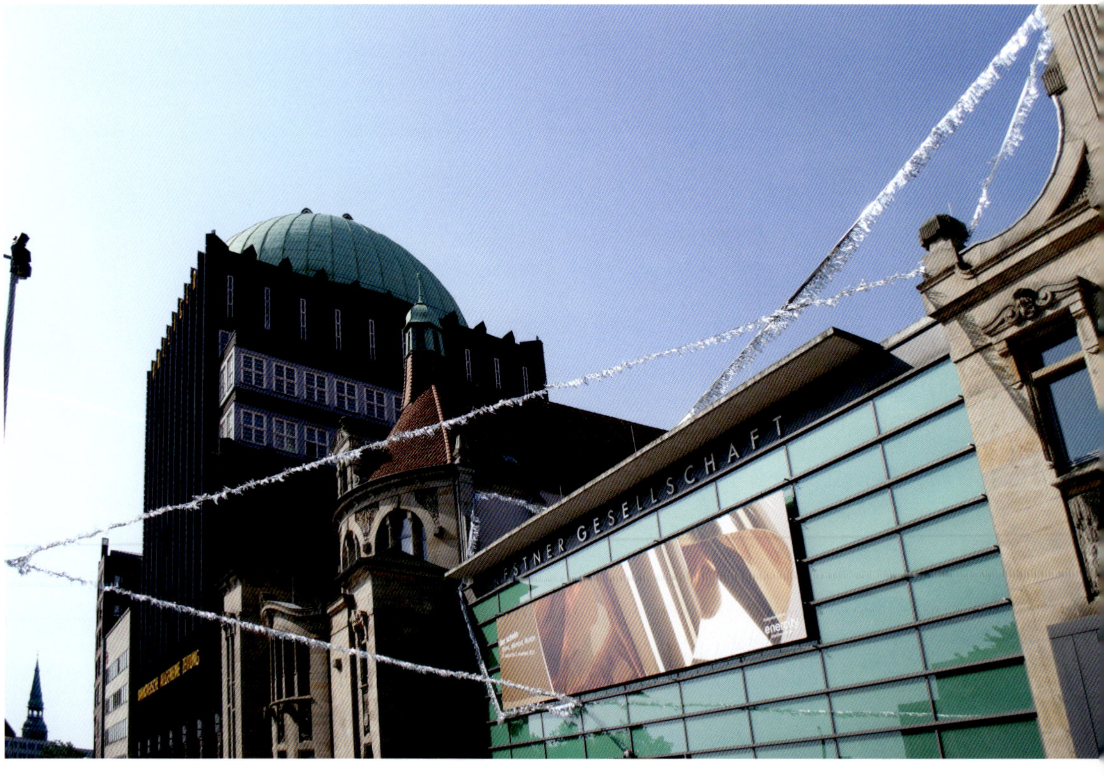
GESELLSCHAFT

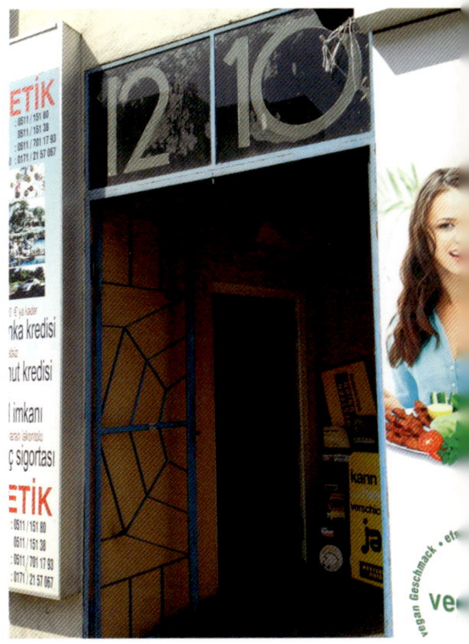

"der schein", kestnergesellschaft Hannover, 2013
Untitled, ca. 5000 x 2500 x 3000 cm, steel, plastic foil, 2013

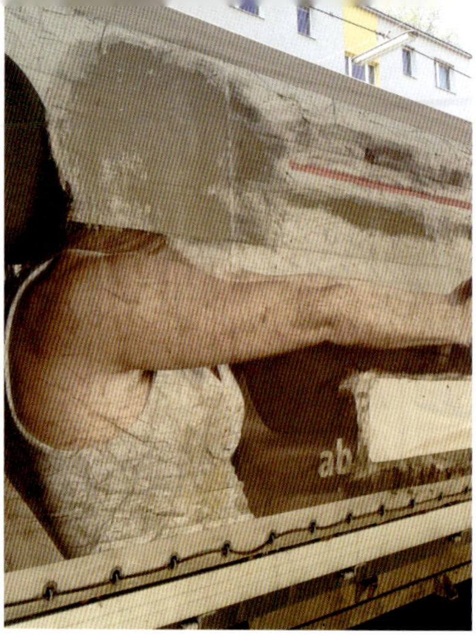

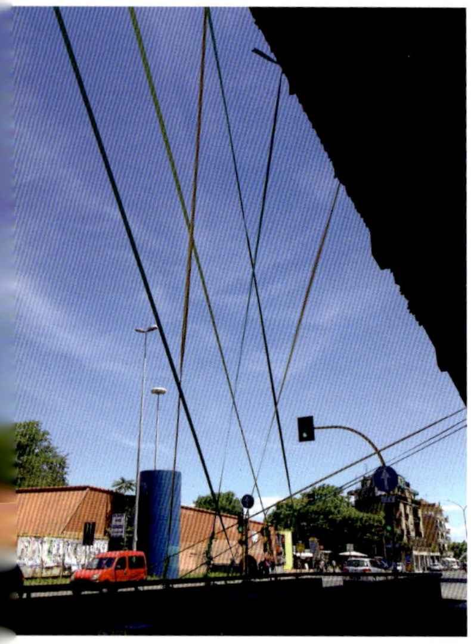

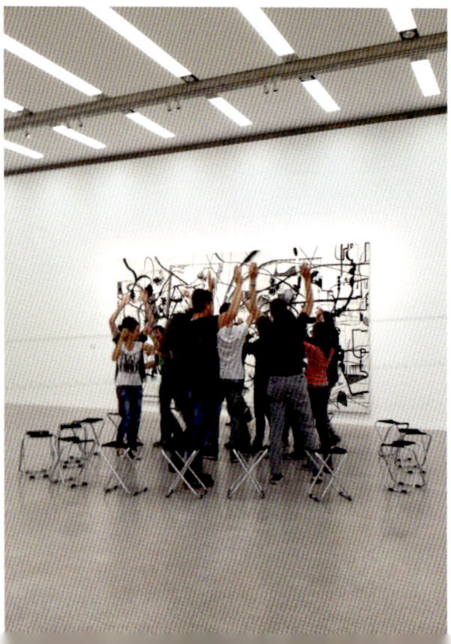

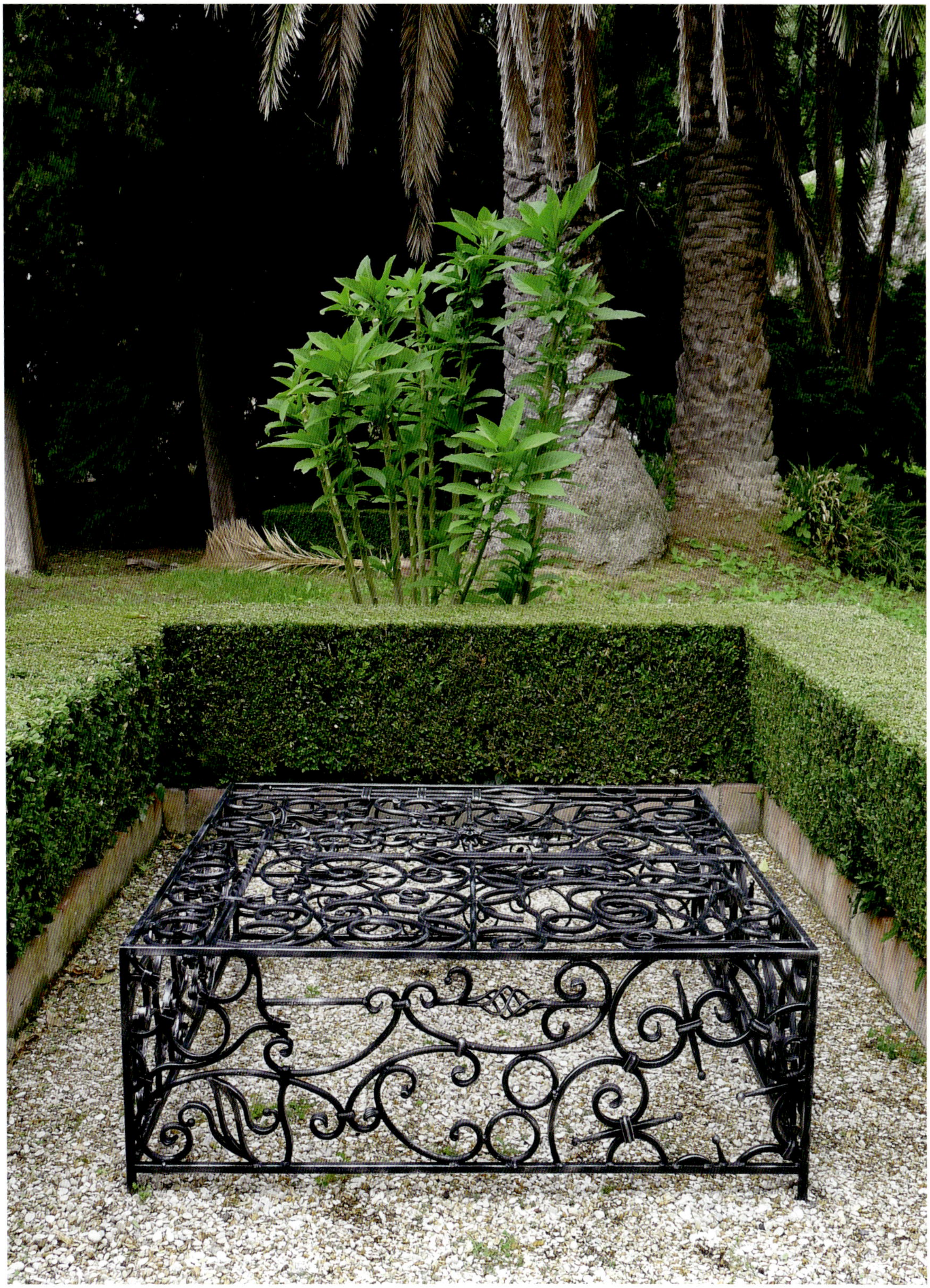

Private Collection Sabina (Italy), 2013
Untitled, 45 x 120 x 120 cm, galvanized iron, lacquer, 2012

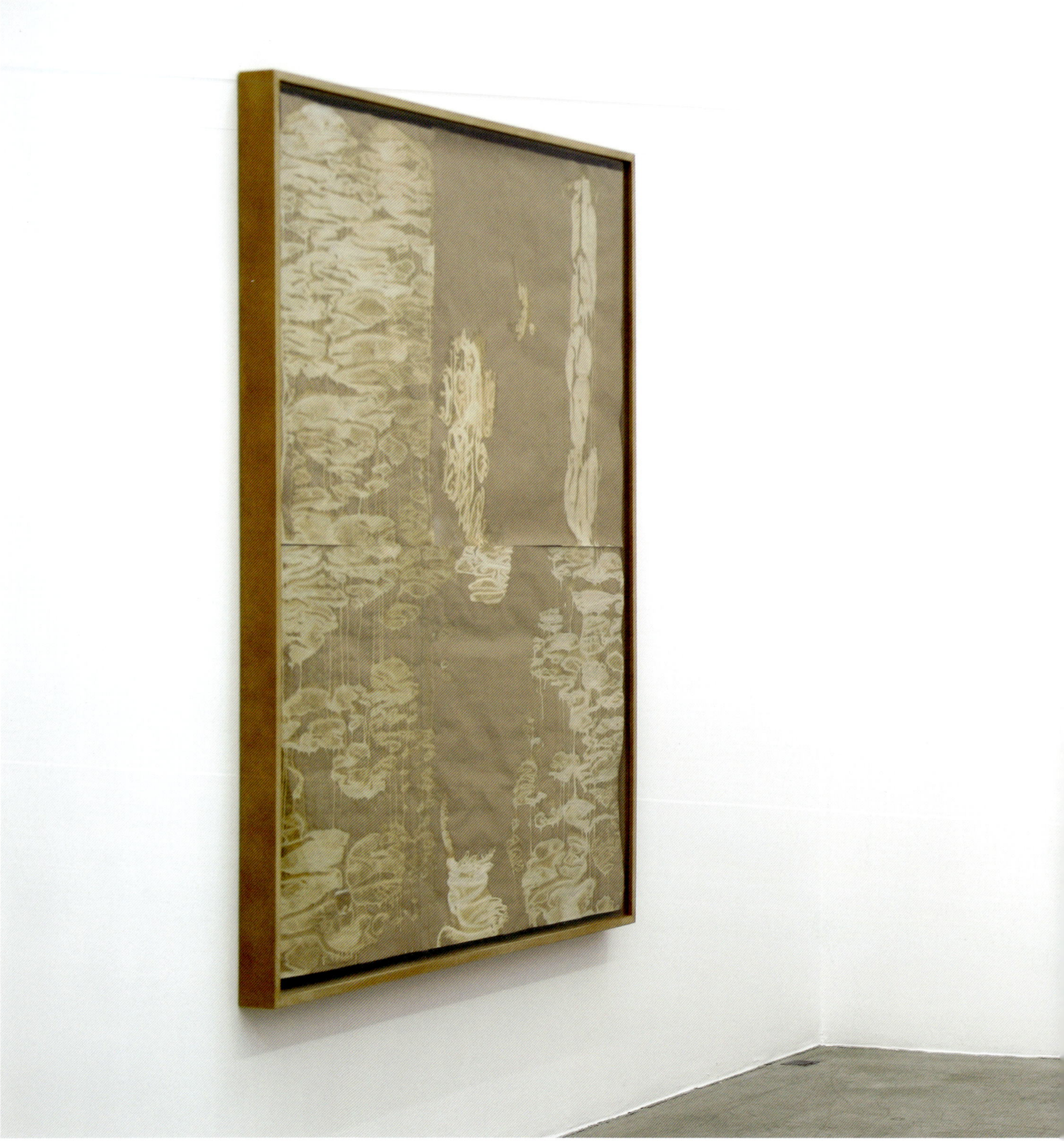

Galerie Johann Widauer, Innsbruck, 2013
Untitled, 180 x 150 cm, MDF, plexiglass, chlorine on paper, tape, 2013

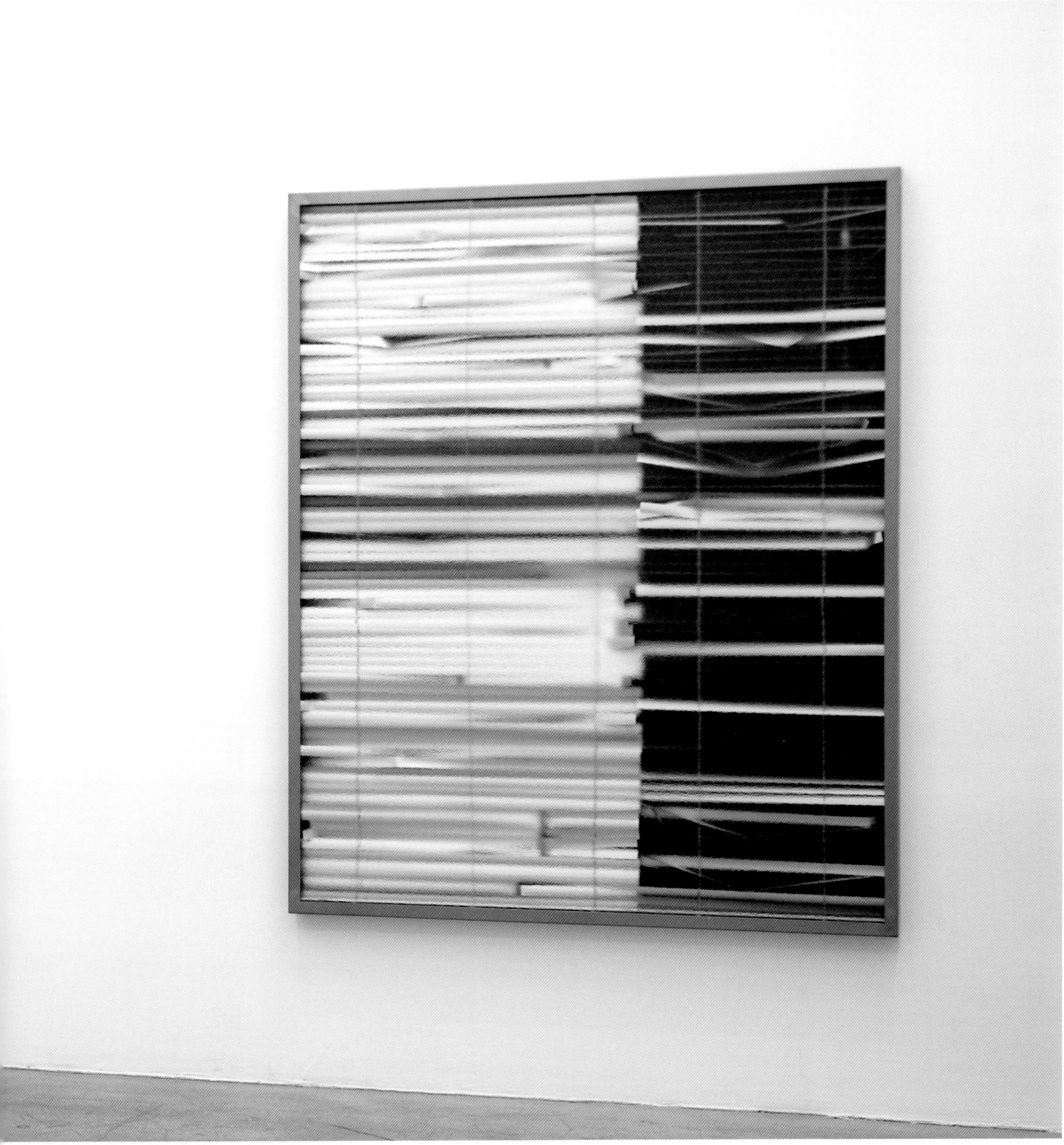

Untitled, 180 x 150 cm, iron, plexiglass, jalousie, 2013

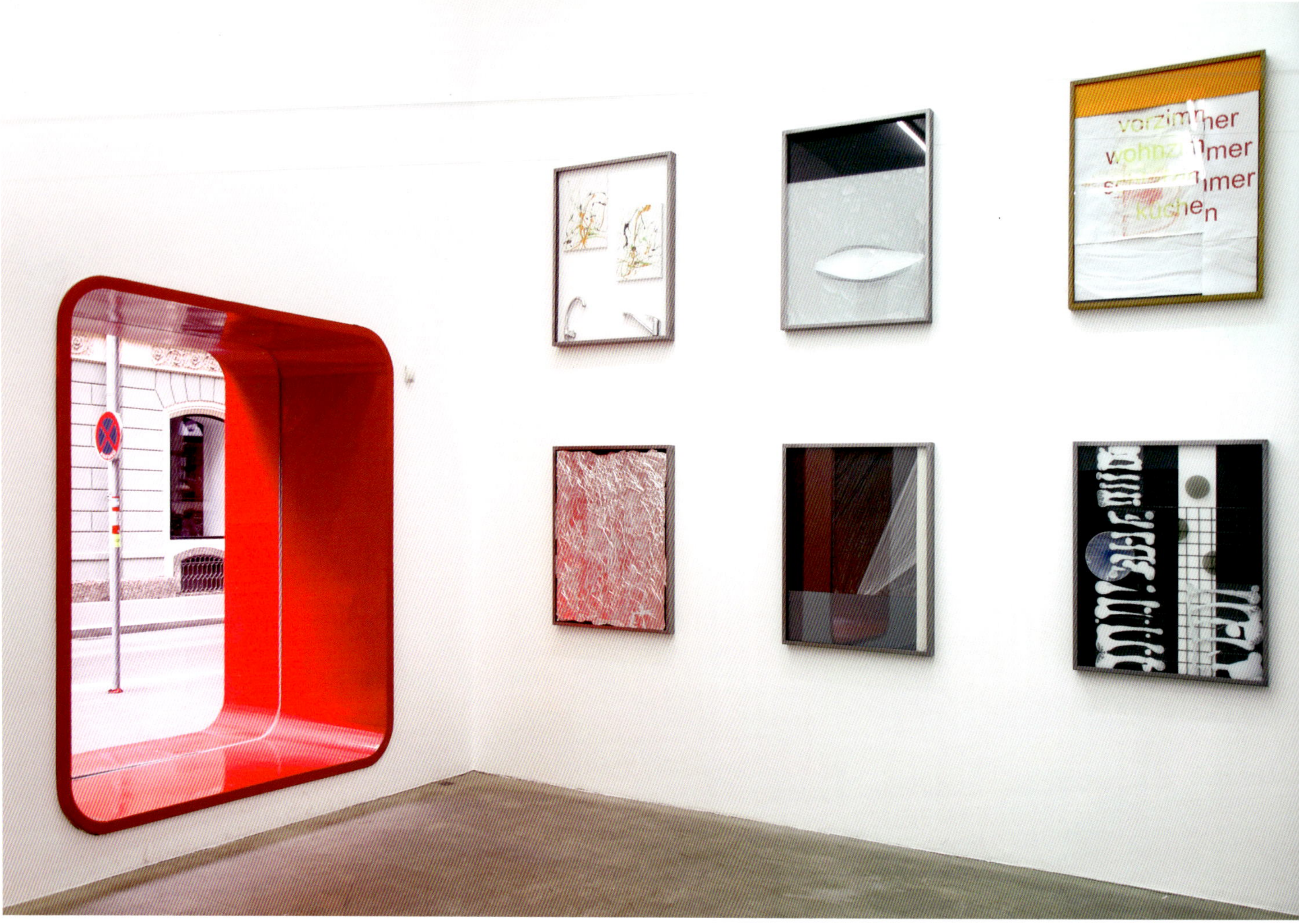

Galerie Johann Widauer, Innsbruck, 2013
Untitled, each 100 x 80 cm, various materials, 2013
right side bottom: Untitled, videos (ca. 6 min, looped, sound), 2012/13

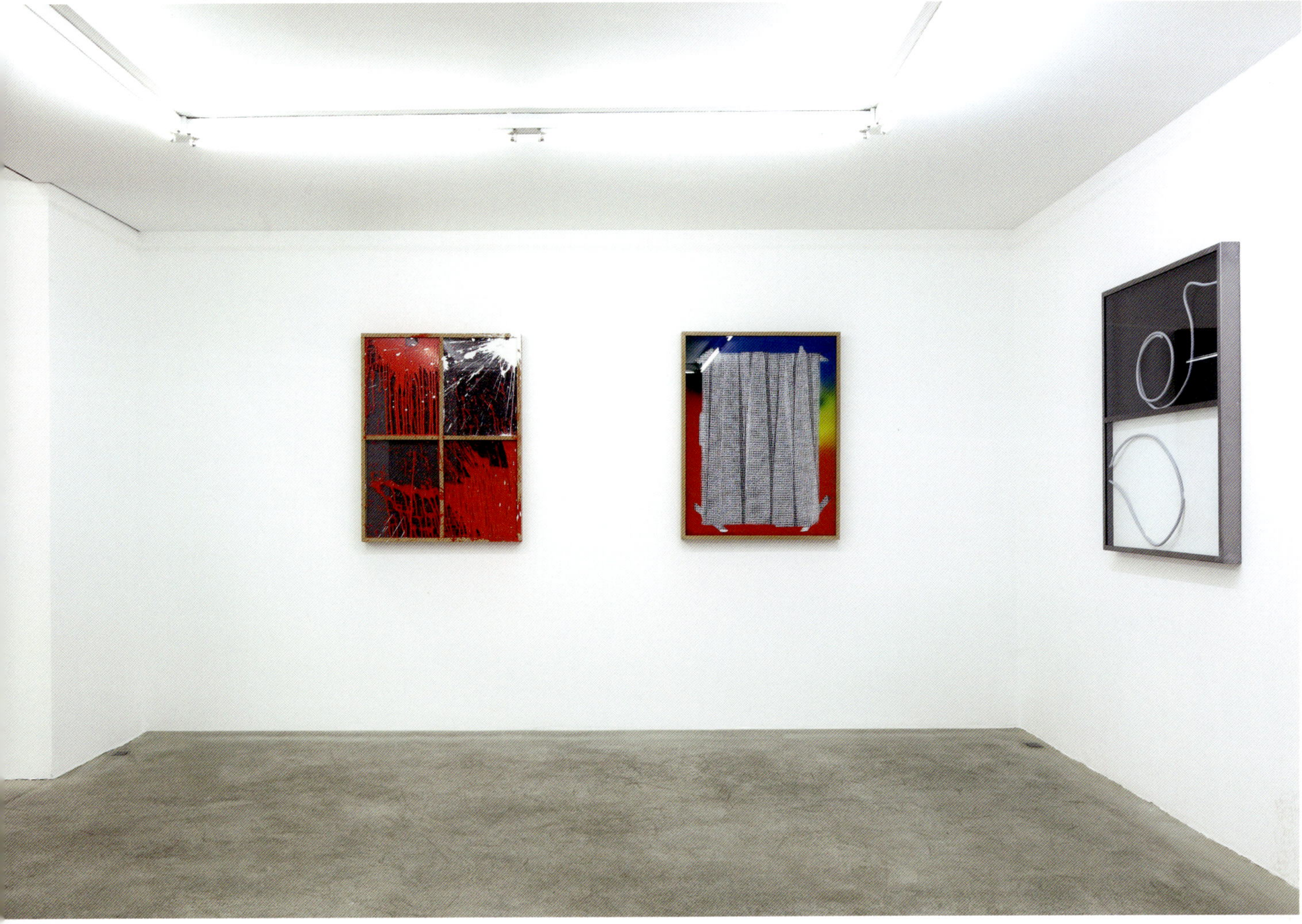

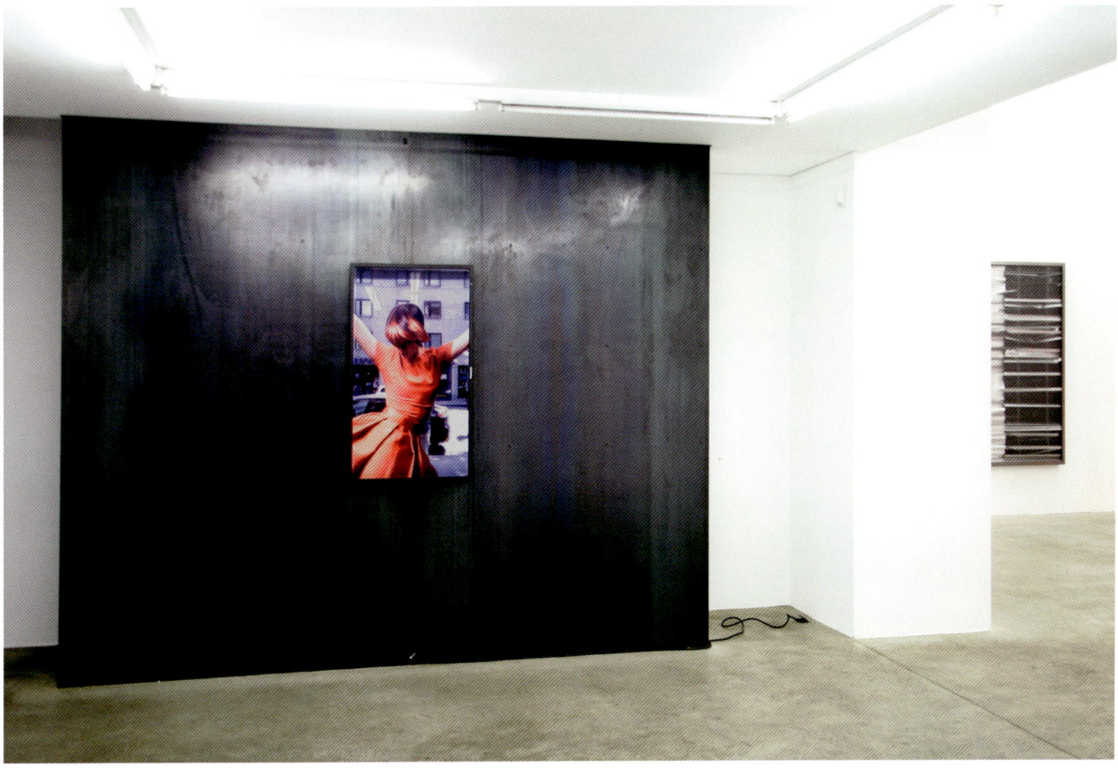

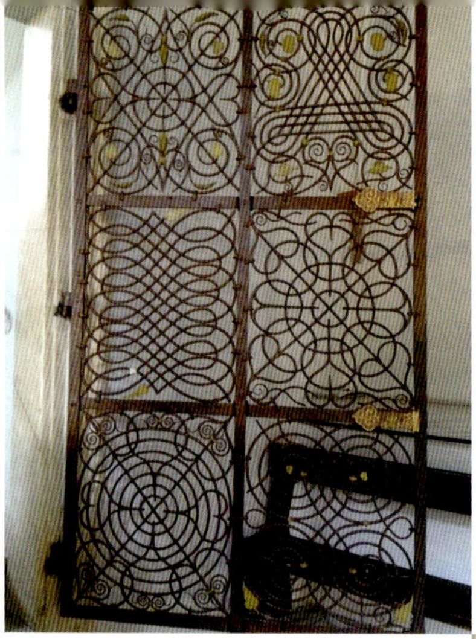
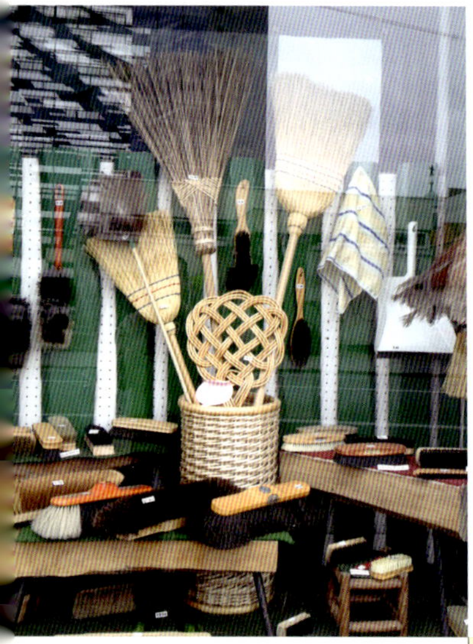
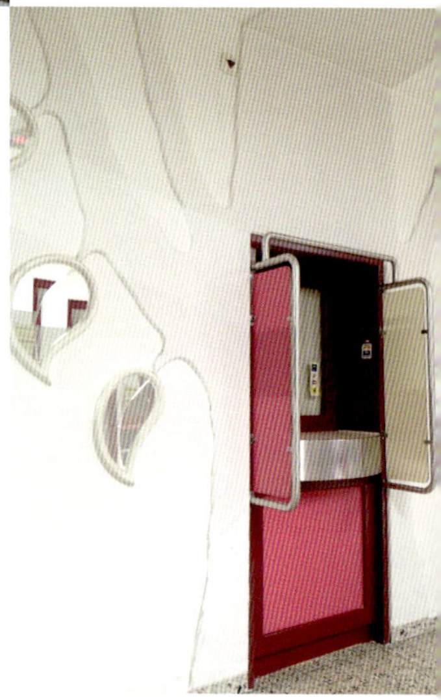
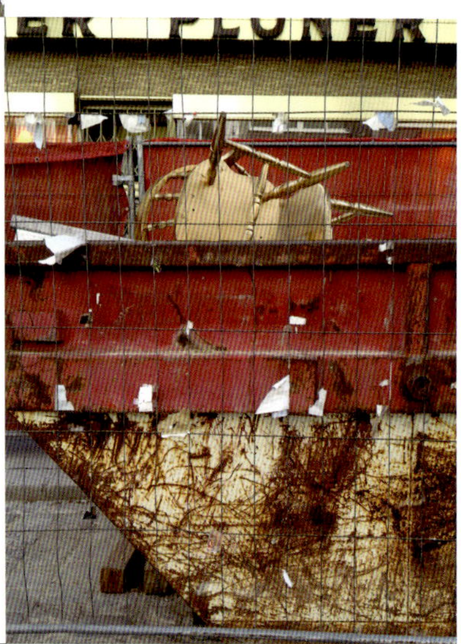
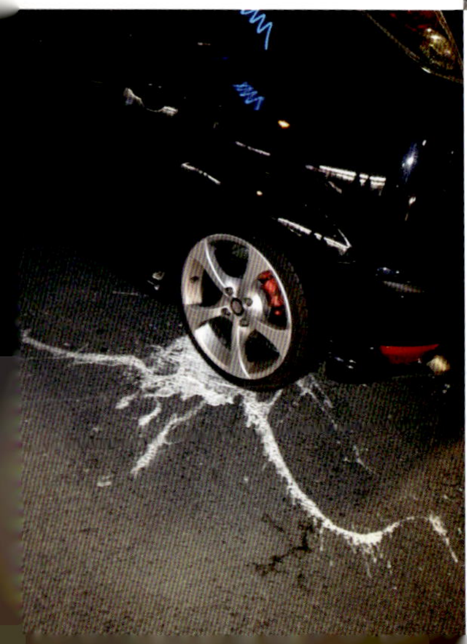
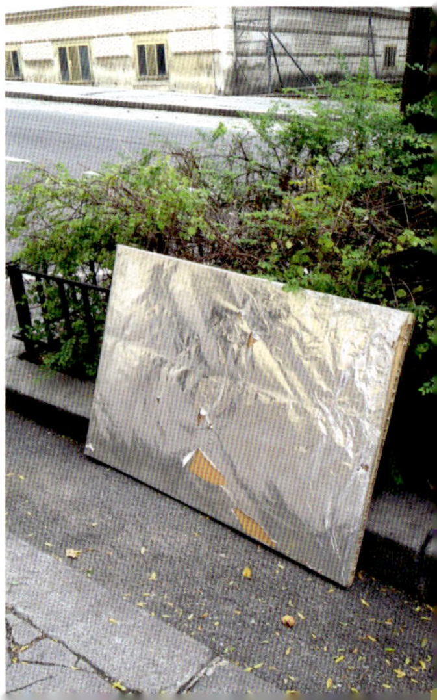

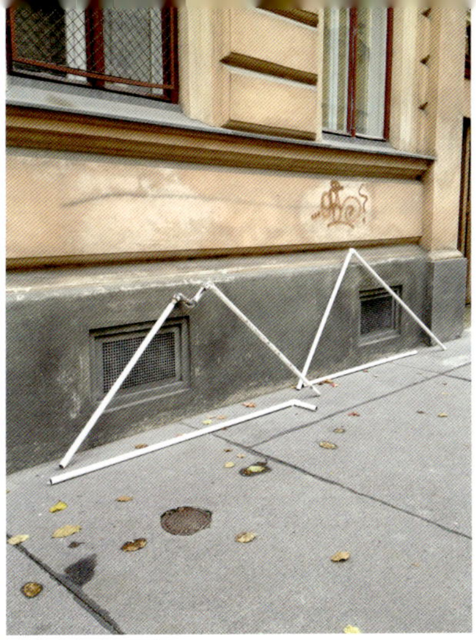

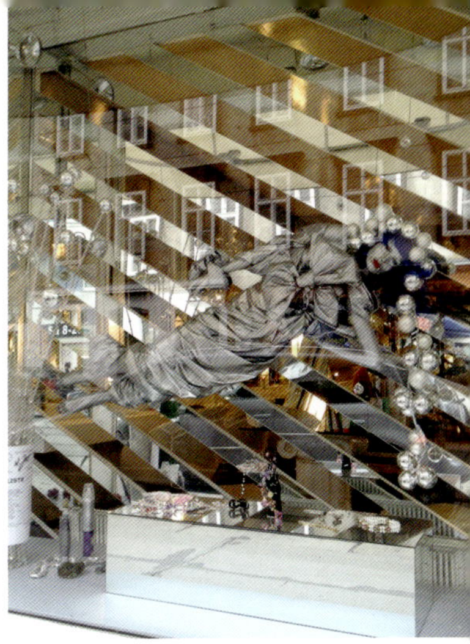

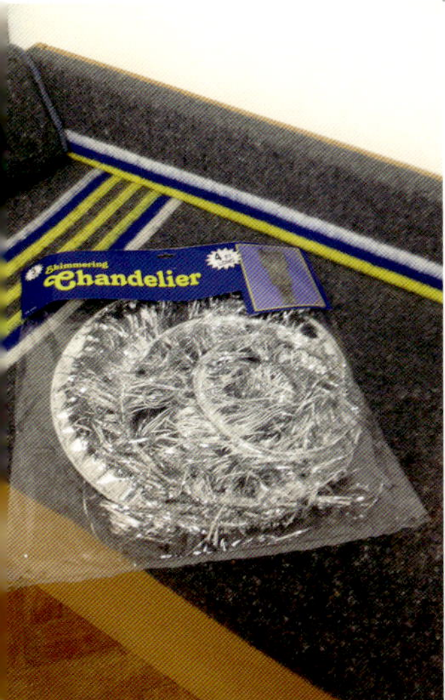
Shimmering
Chandelier

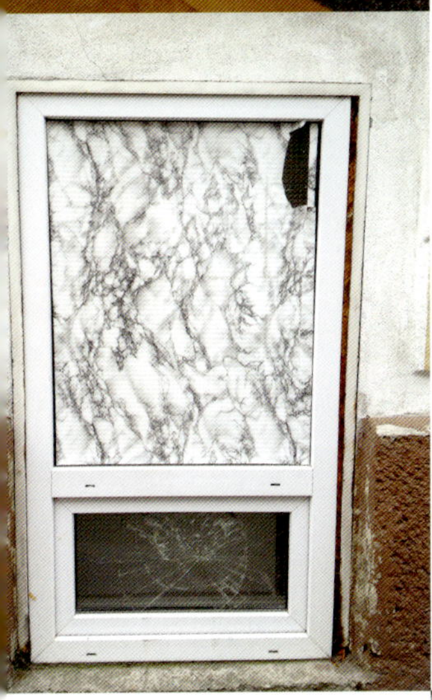

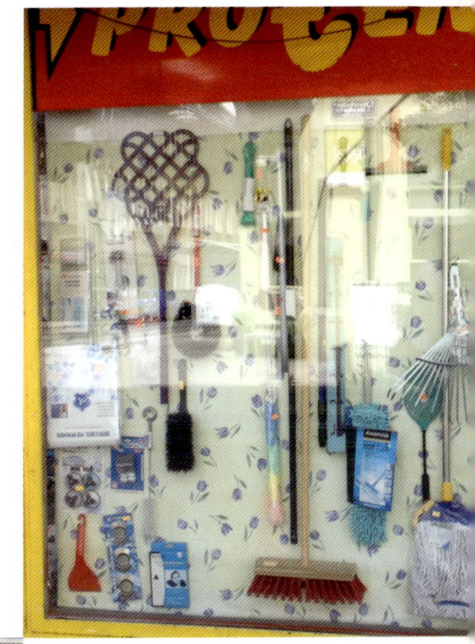

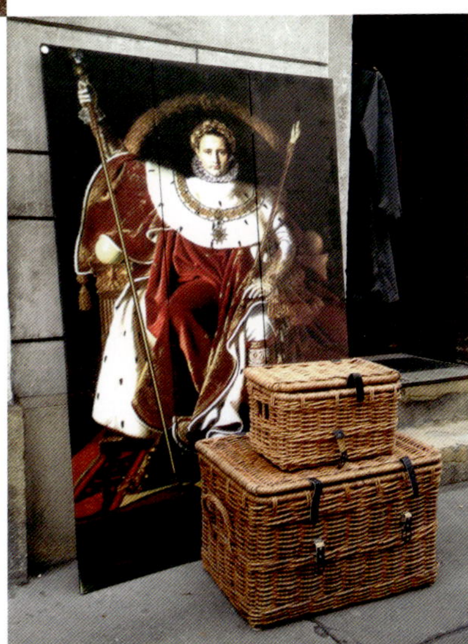

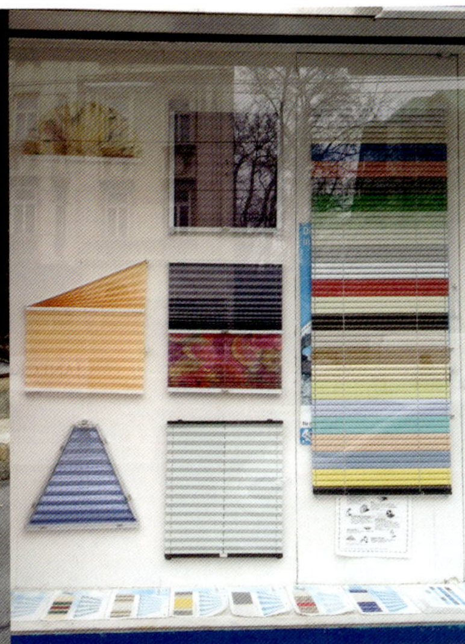

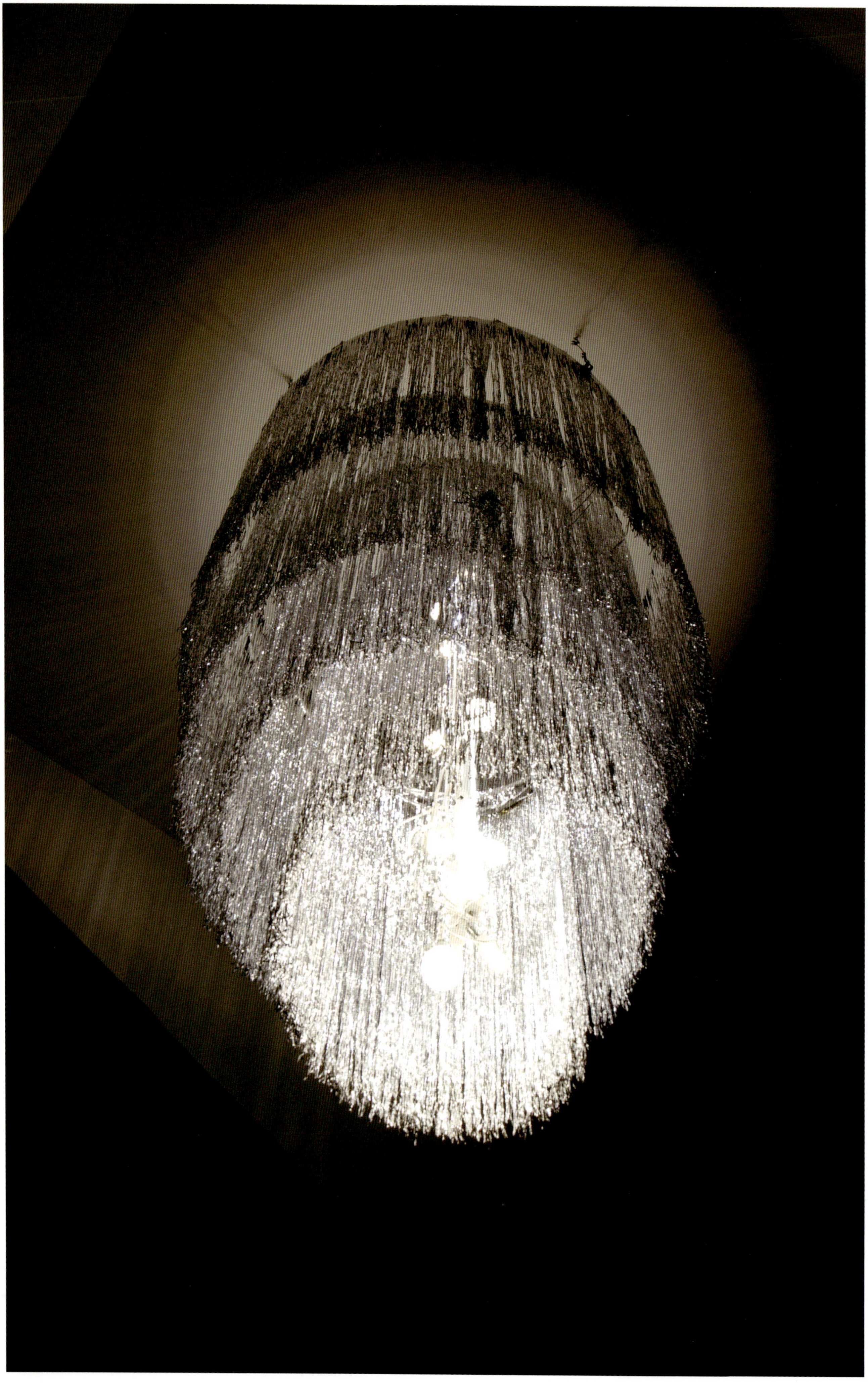

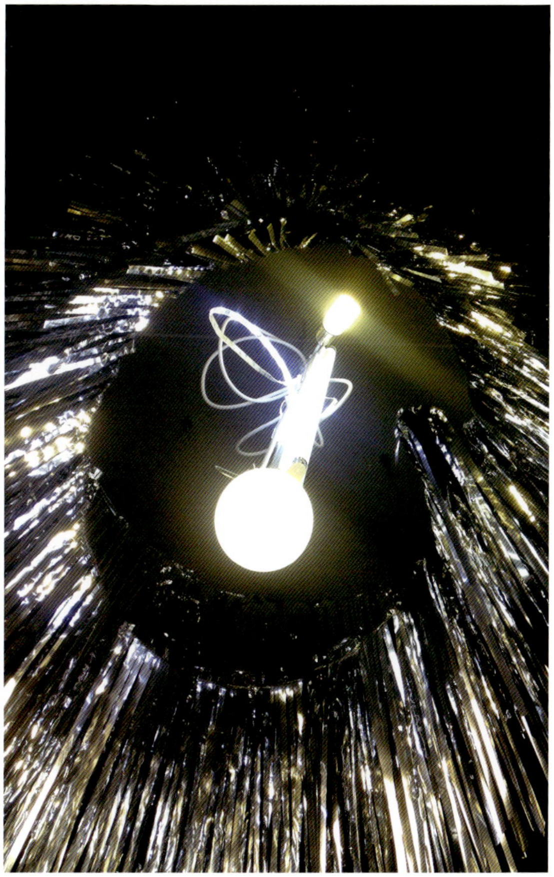 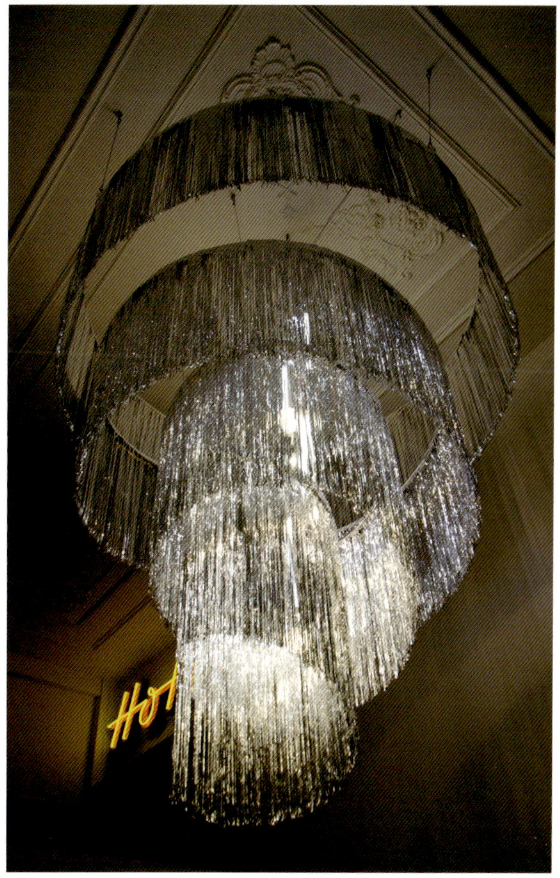

Sofiensäle Vienna, 2014
Untitled, 150 x 100 x 100 cm, iron, plastic foil, various luminous elements, cables, 2014
Untitled, 350 x 300 x 300 cm, iron, plastic foil, various luminous elements, cables, 2013
left page: Untitled, 450 x 200 x 200 cm, iron, plastic foil, various luminous elements, cables, 2014

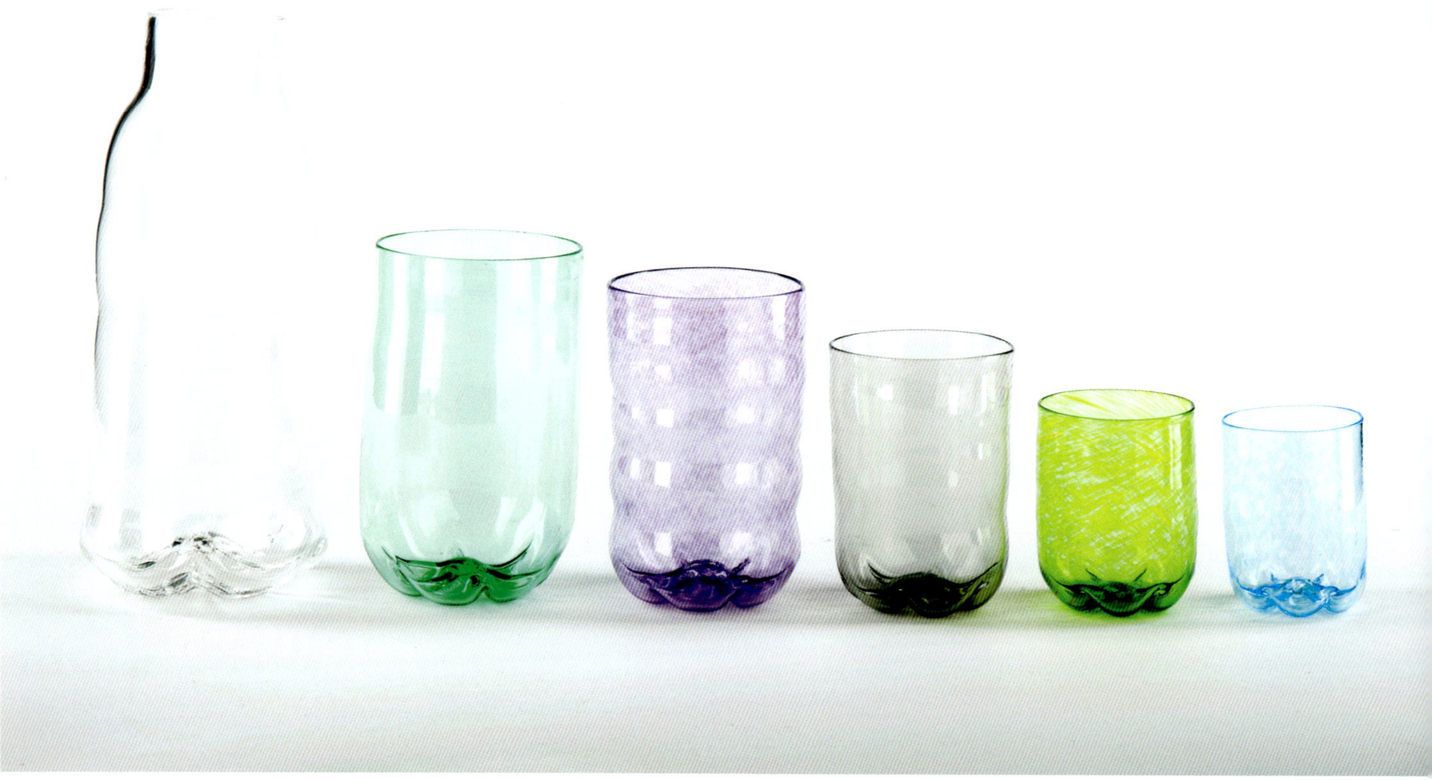

Untitled, Murano glassware handblown by Davide Fuin, 2014
Produced by Golden Ruler Rome

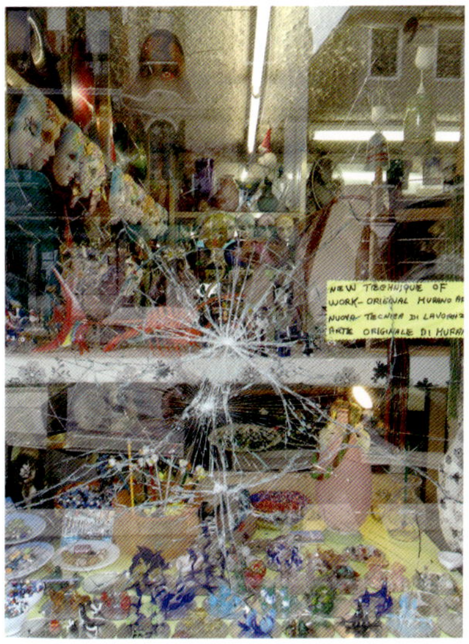
NEW TECHNIQUE OF
WORK - ORIGINAL MURANO
NUOVA TECNICA DI
ARTE ORIGINALE DI

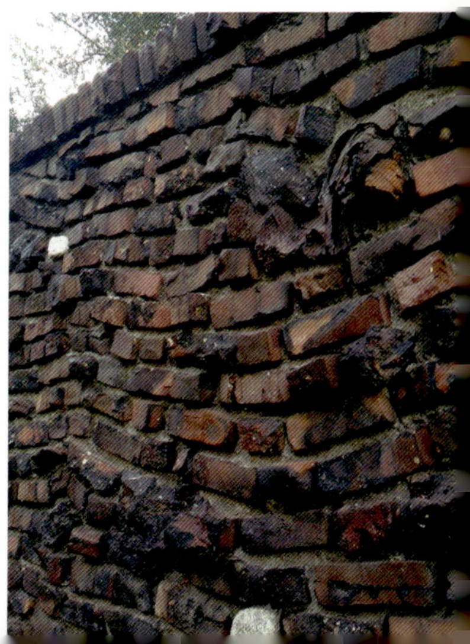

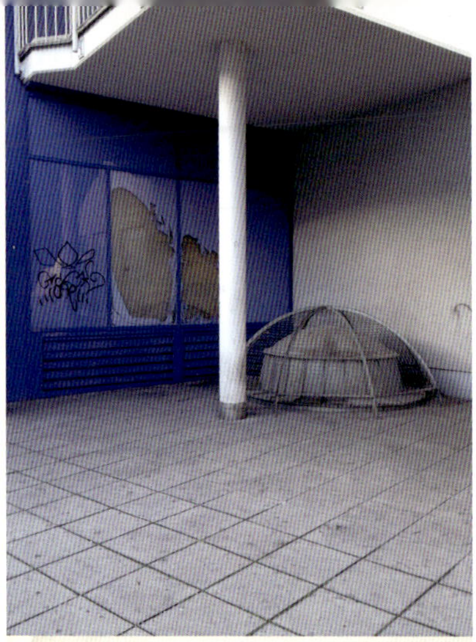

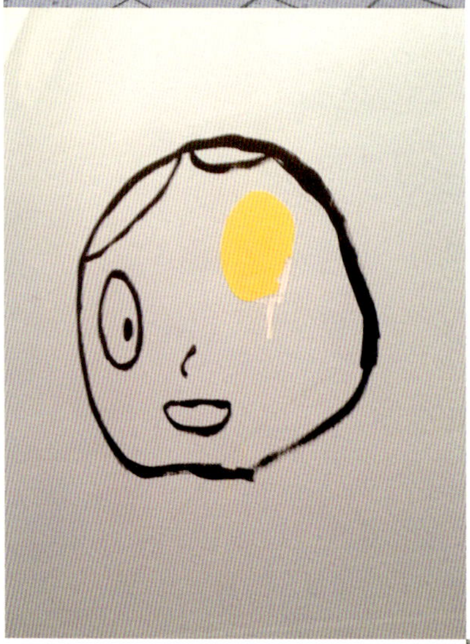

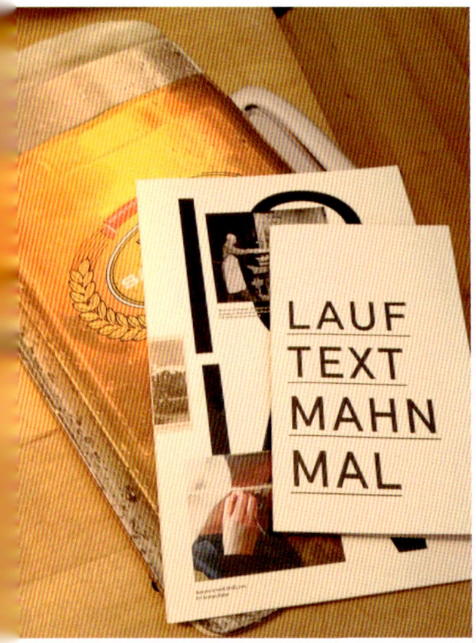
LAUF
TEXT
MAHN
MAL

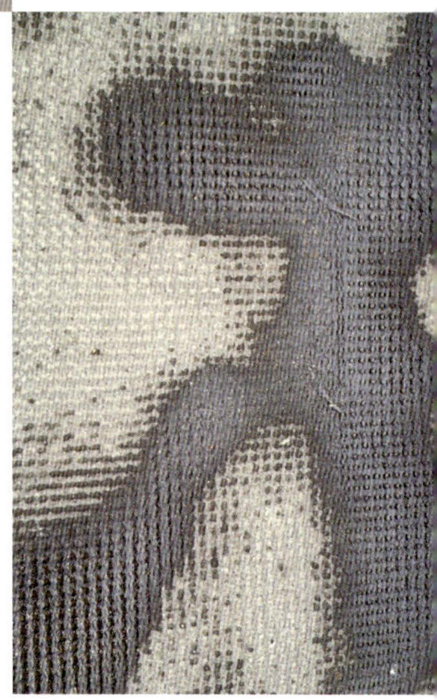

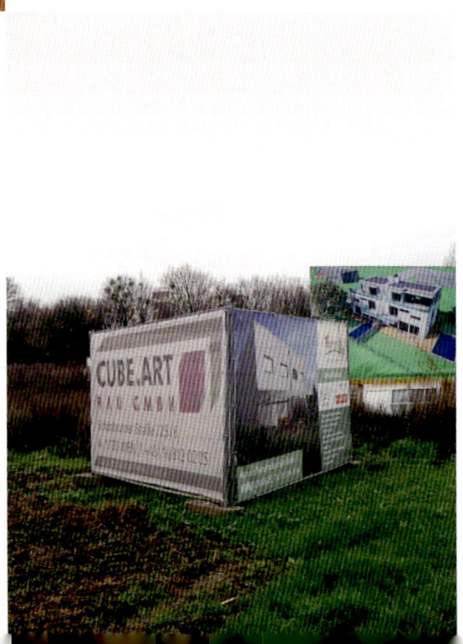
CUBE.ART

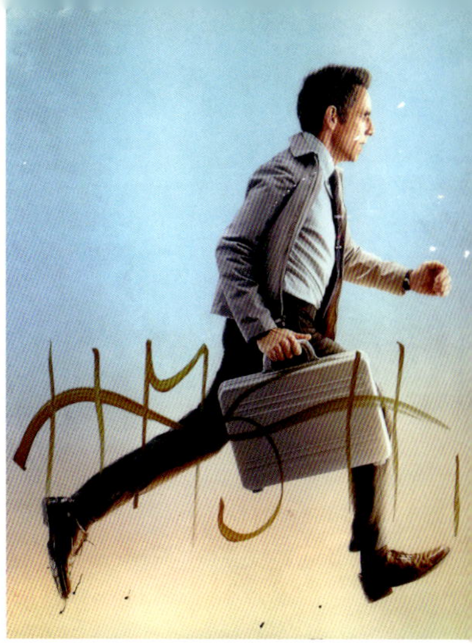

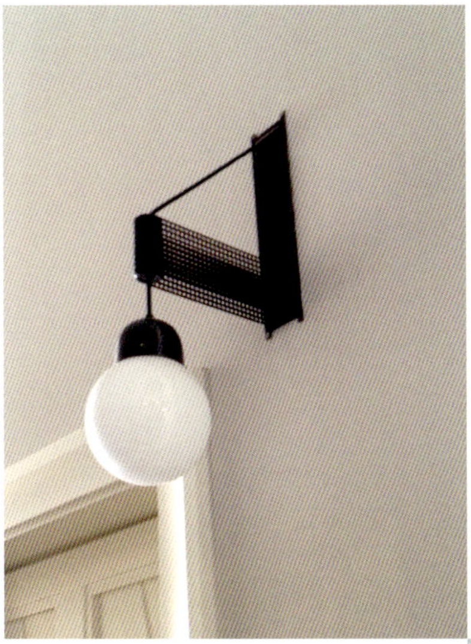

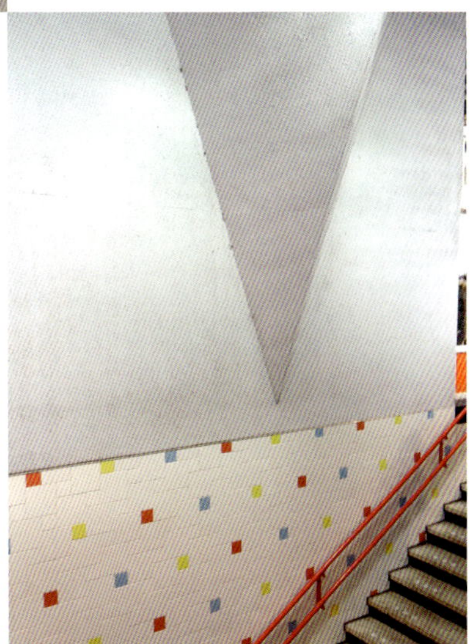

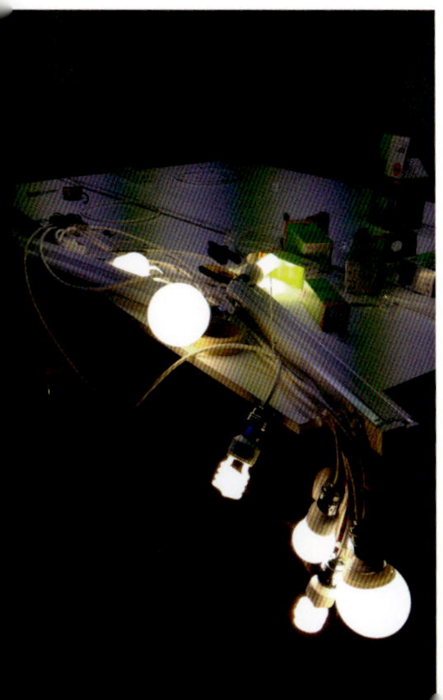

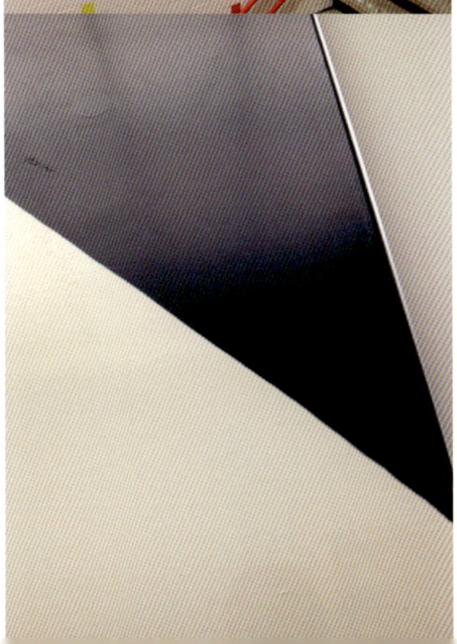

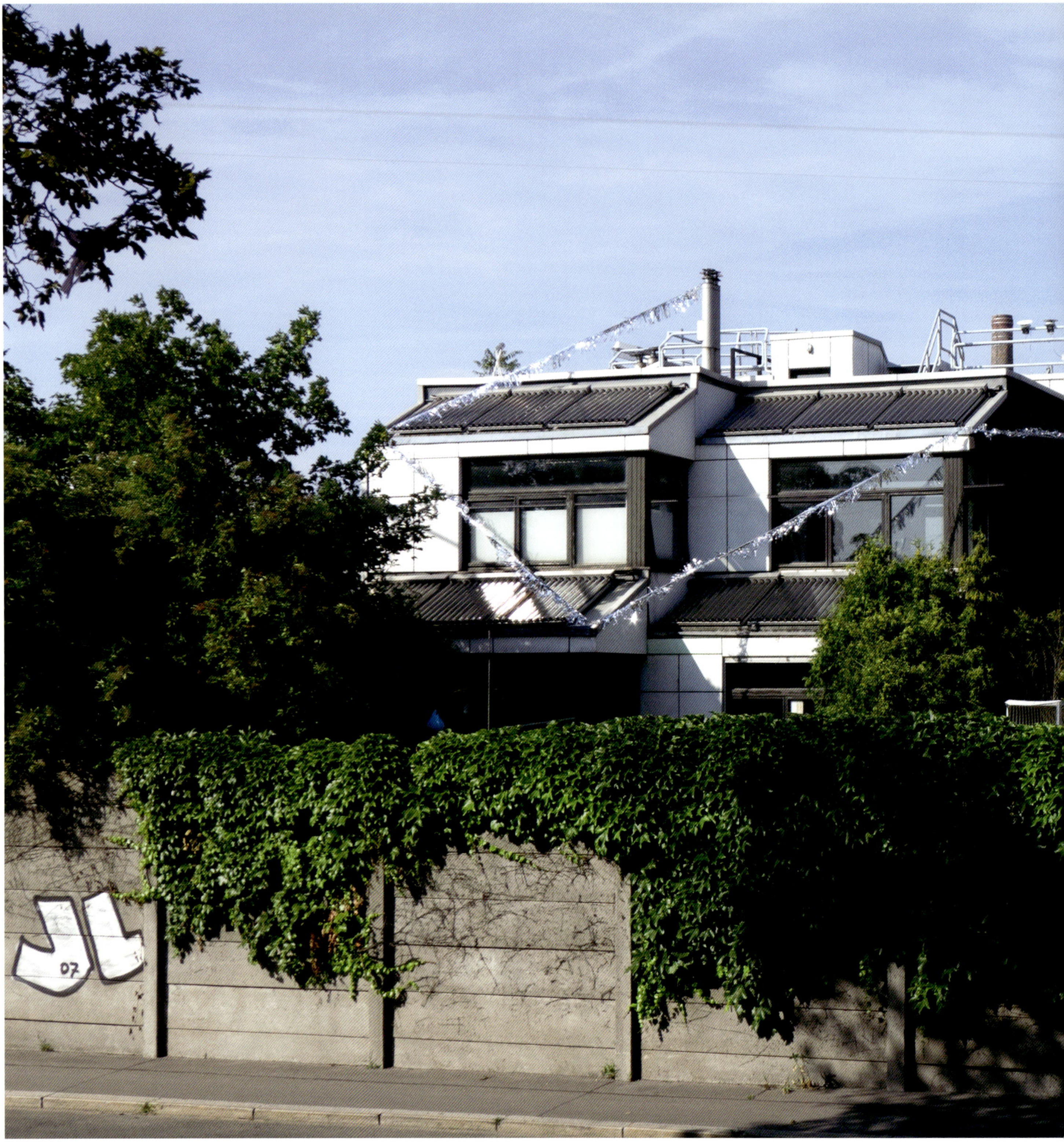
07

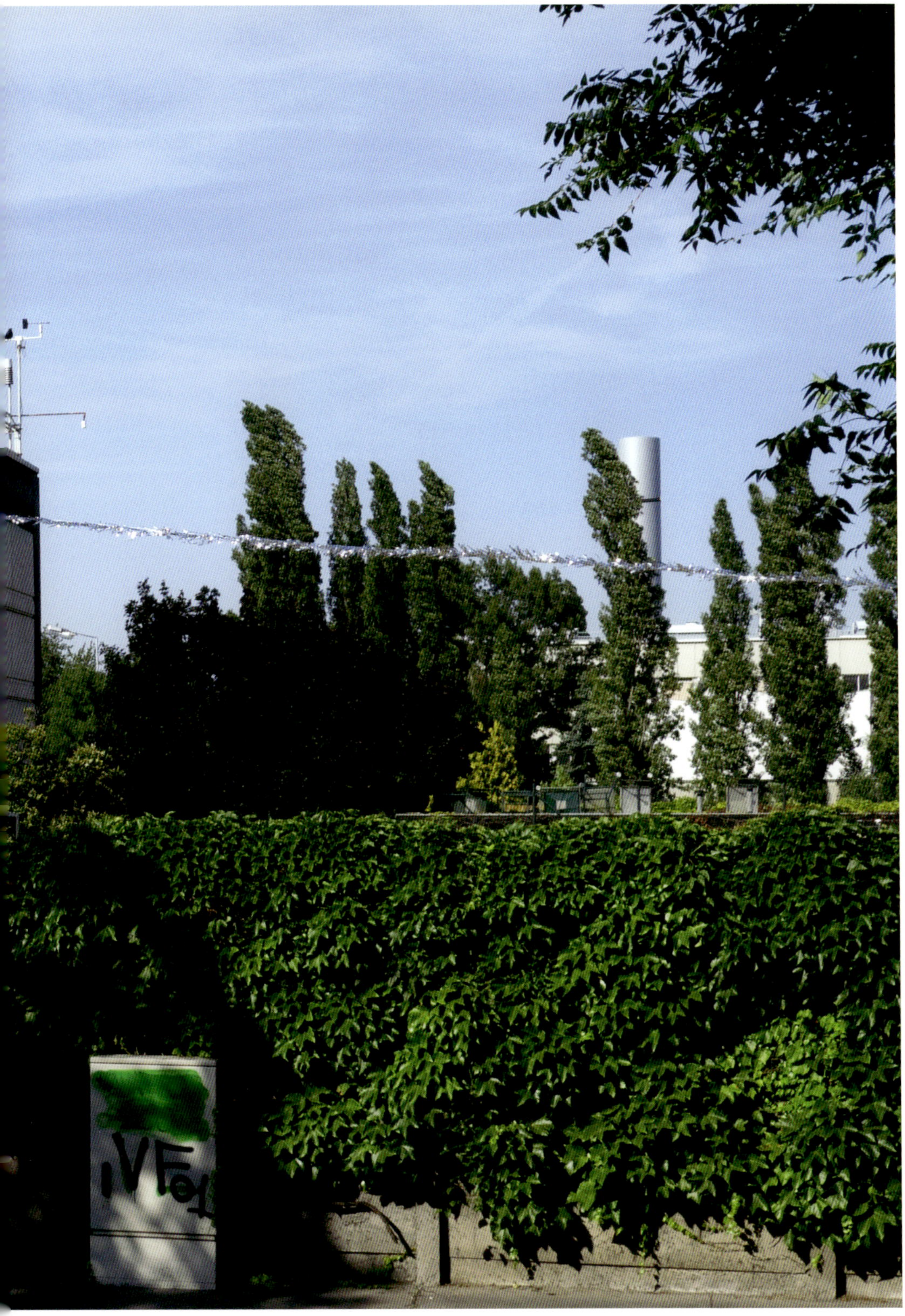

"Arsenale", Sonnenhaus, Vienna, 2014
Untitled, ca. 40 m, steel, plastic foil, 2014

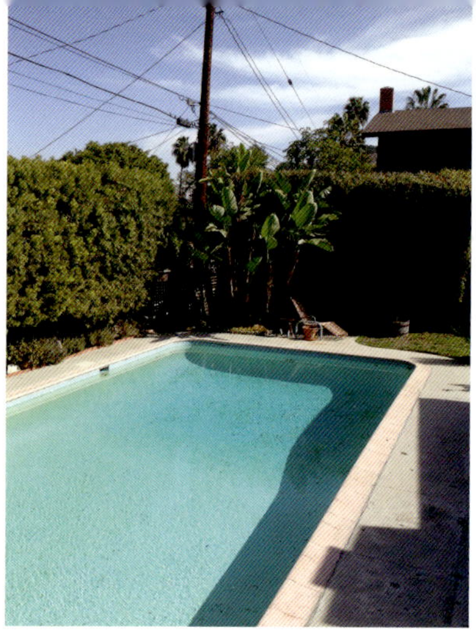

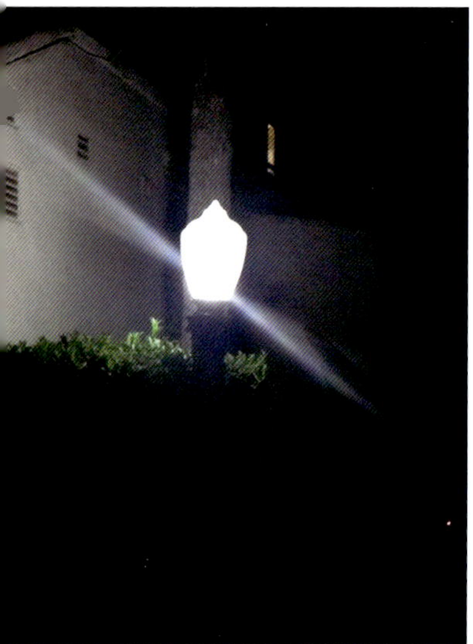

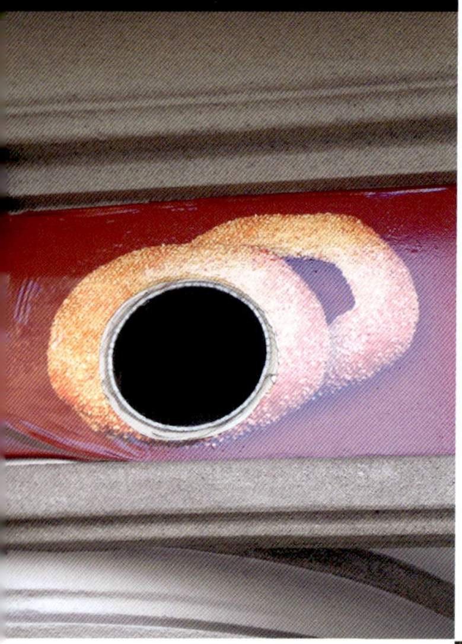

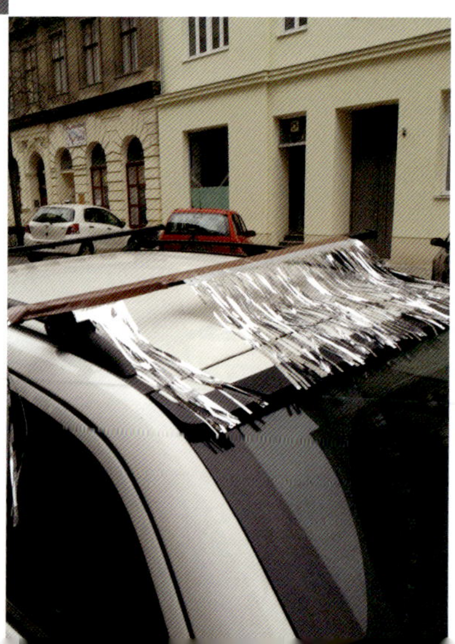

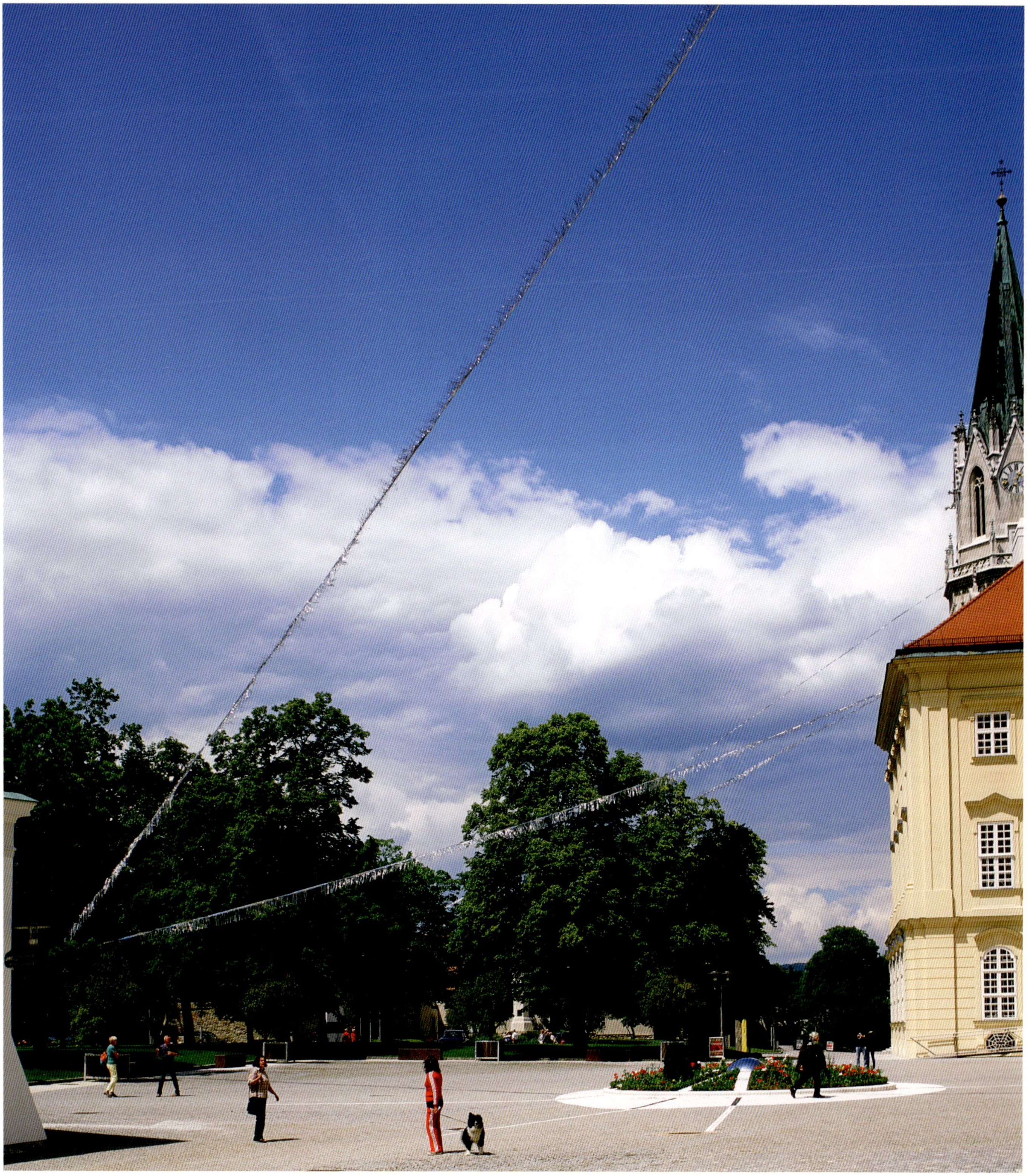

“Hic & Nunc”, Stift Klosterneuburg, 2014
Untitled, ca. 400 m, steel, plastic foil, 2014

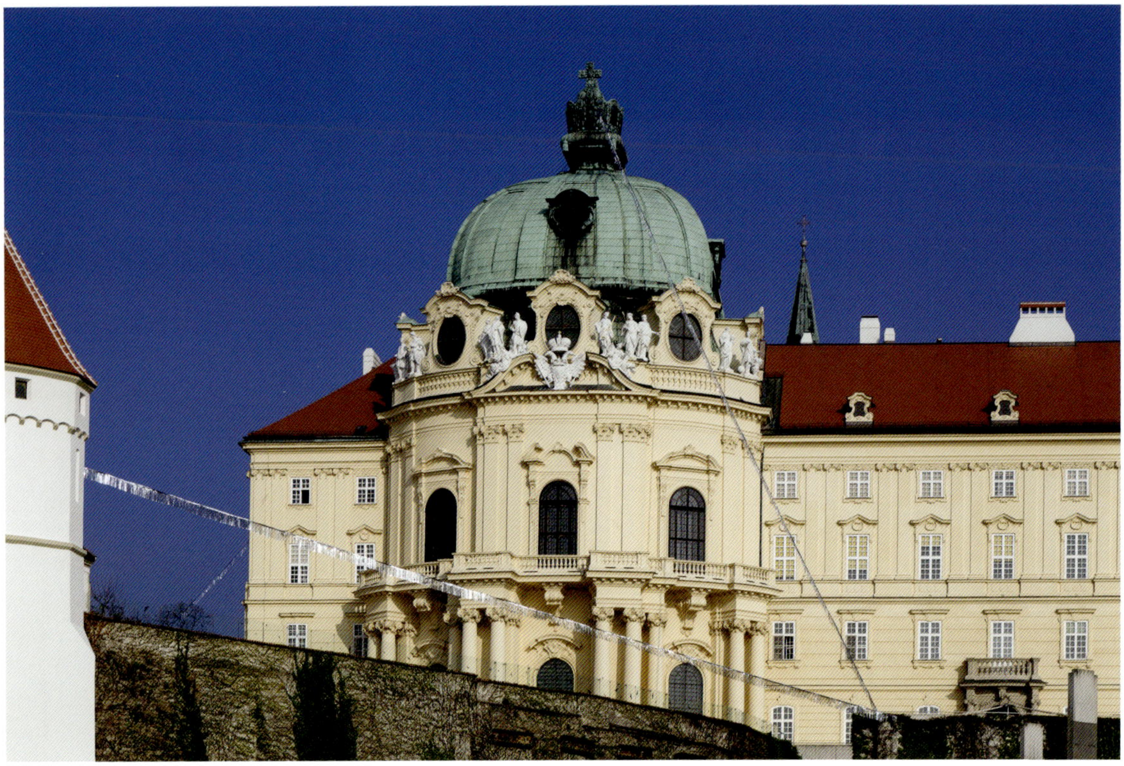

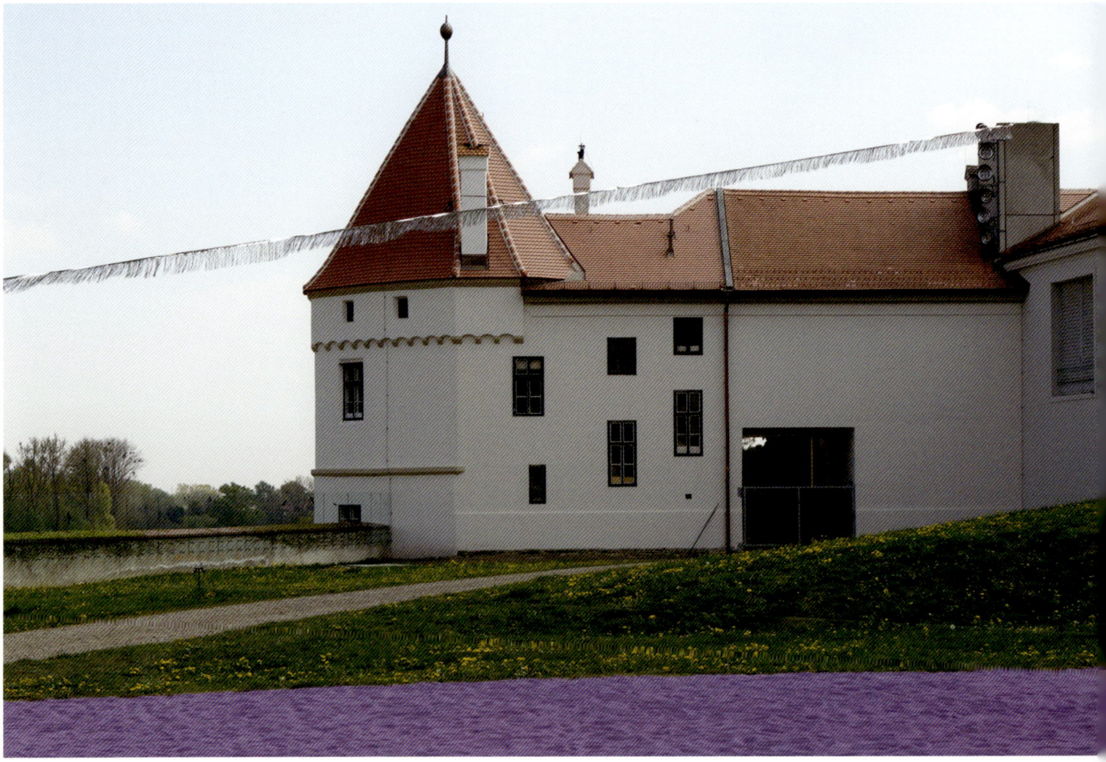

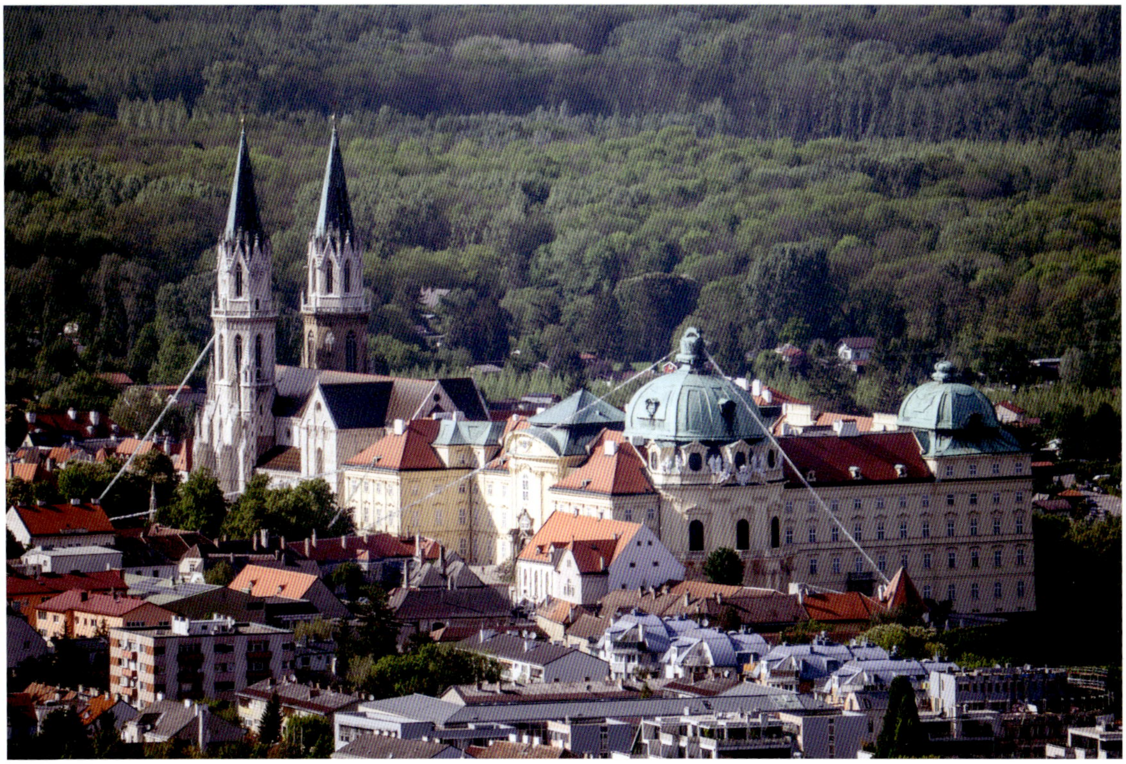

"Hic & Nunc", Stift Klosterneuburg, 2014
Untitled, ca. 400 m, steel, plastic foil, 2014

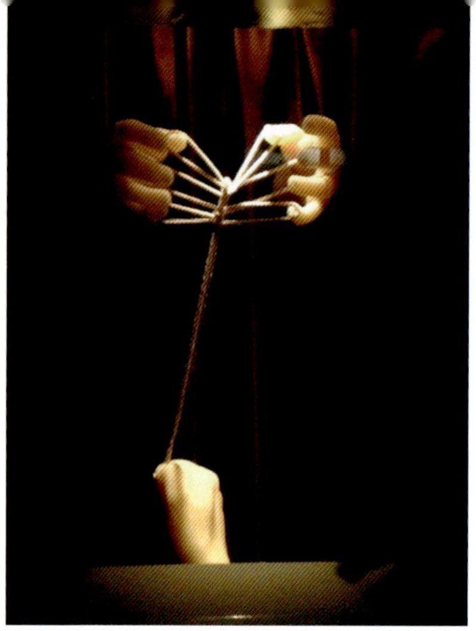

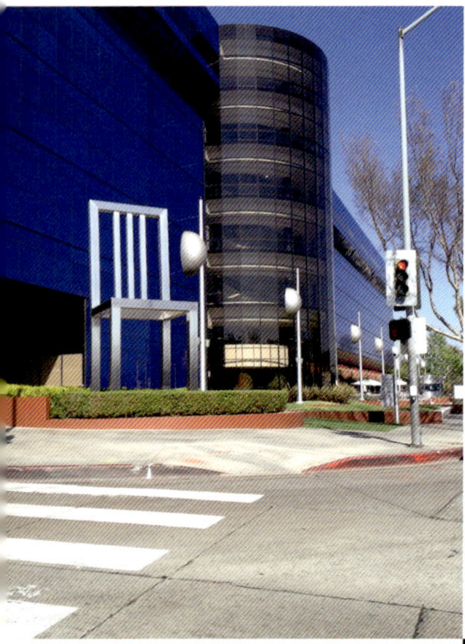

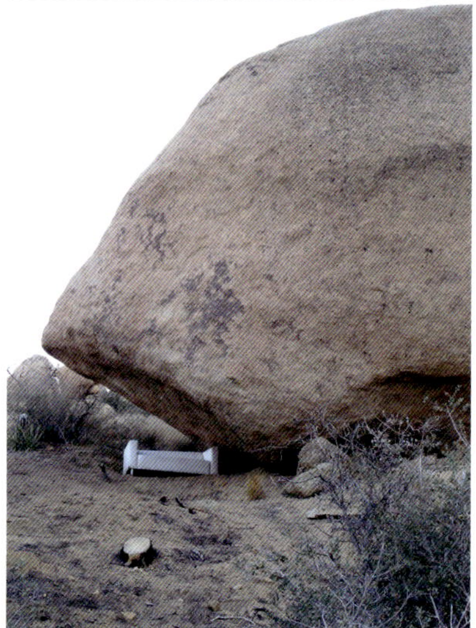

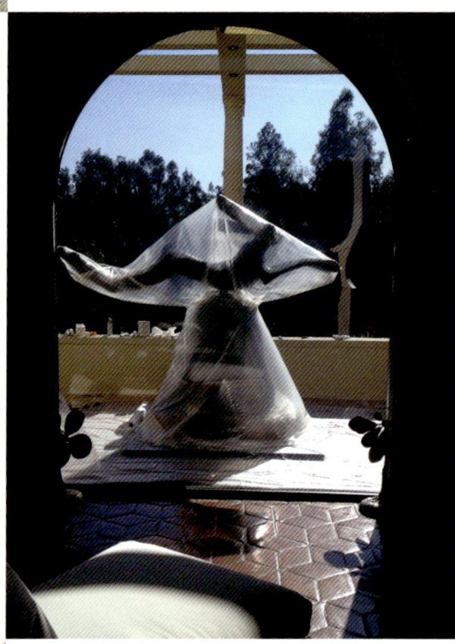

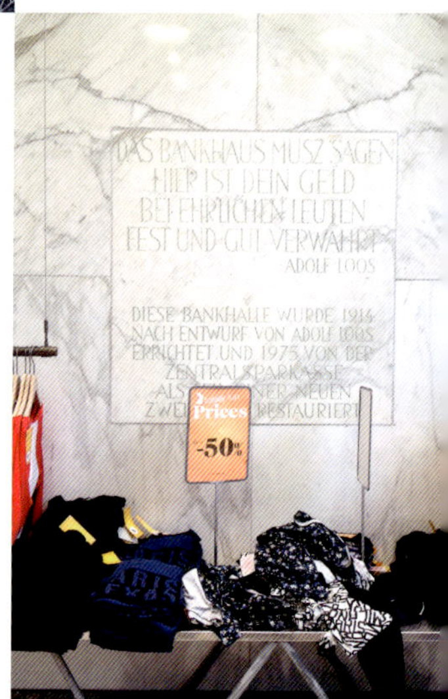
DAS BANKHAUS MUSZ SAGEN
HIER IST DEIN GELD
BEI EHRLICHEN LEUTEN
FEST UND GUT VERWAHRT
ADOLF LOOS
DIESE BANKHALLE WURDE 1914
NACH ENTWURF VON ADOLF LOOS
ERRICHTET UND 1975 VON DER
ZENTRALSPARKASSE
Prices
-50%

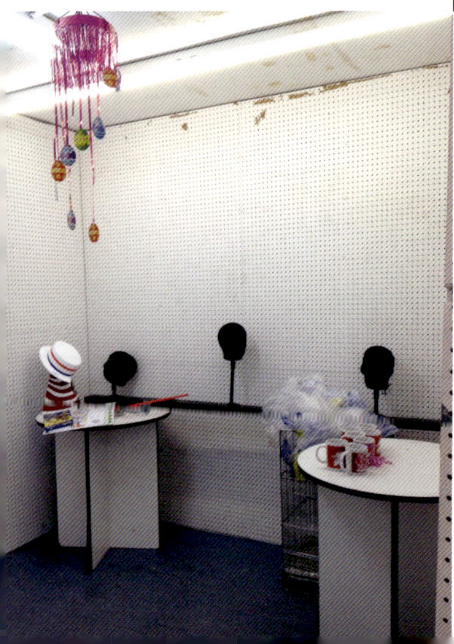

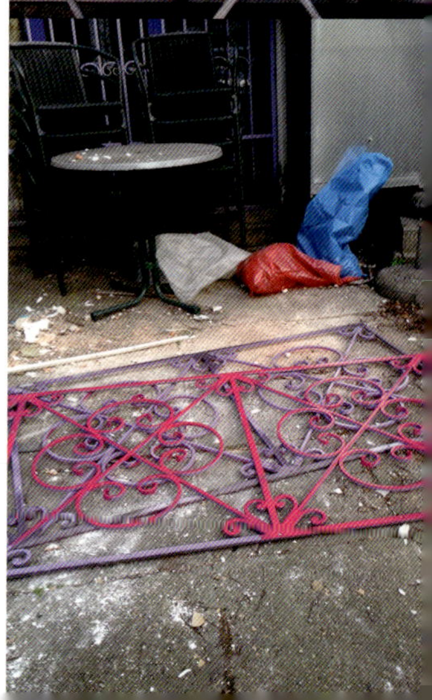

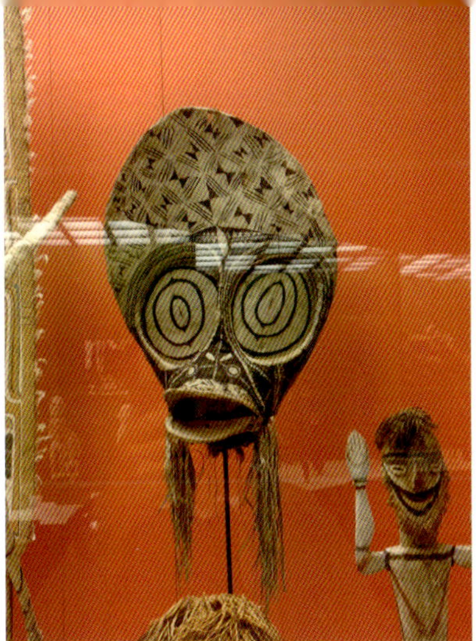

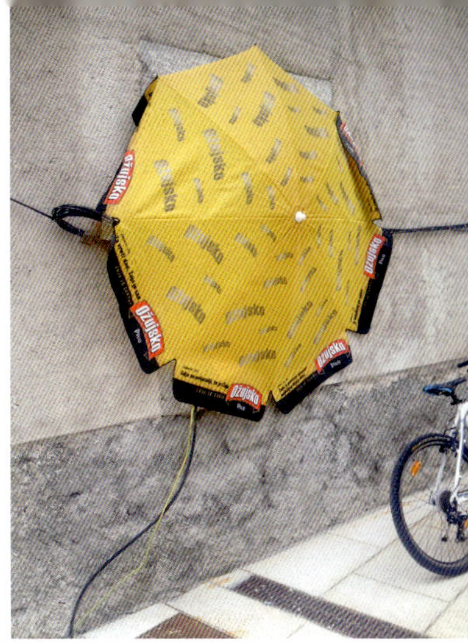

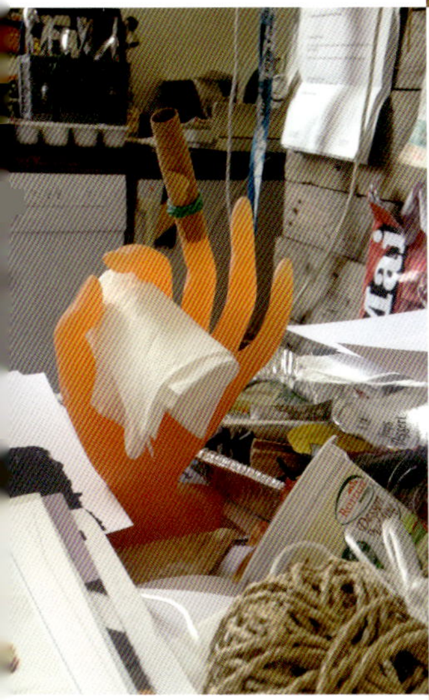

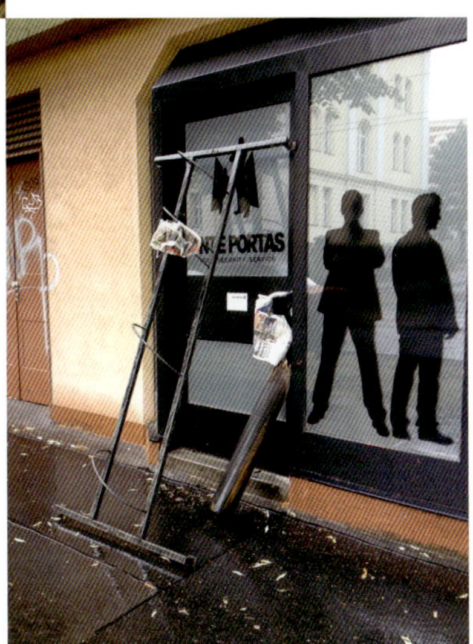

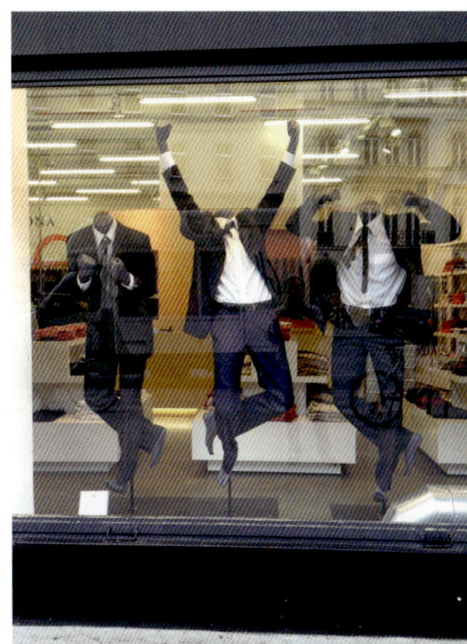

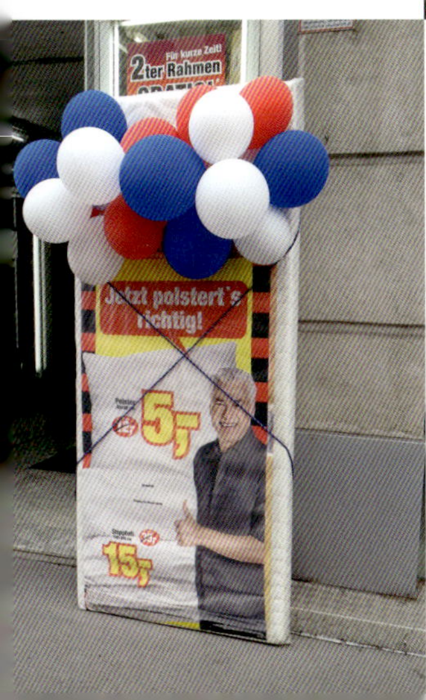
2ter Rahmen
Jetzt polstert´s richtig!

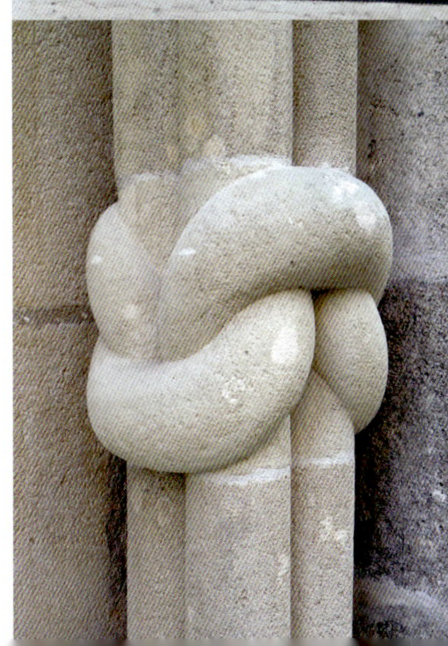

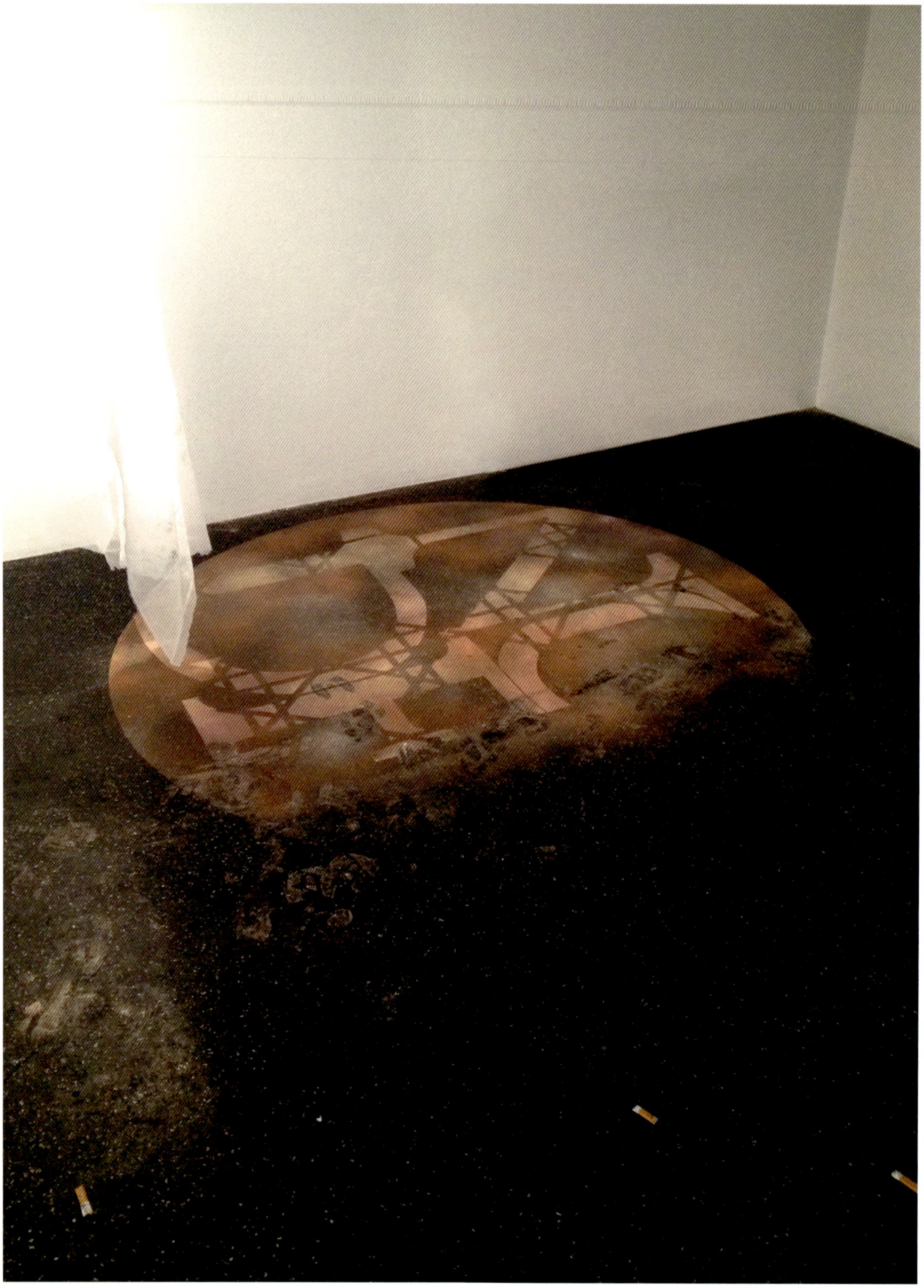

Ve.Sch Vienna 2014 with Axel Koschier and Robert Müller
left page bottom: Untitled, ca. 110 x 120 cm,
make-up on floor and screen, video (ca. 4 min, loop, sound), 2014

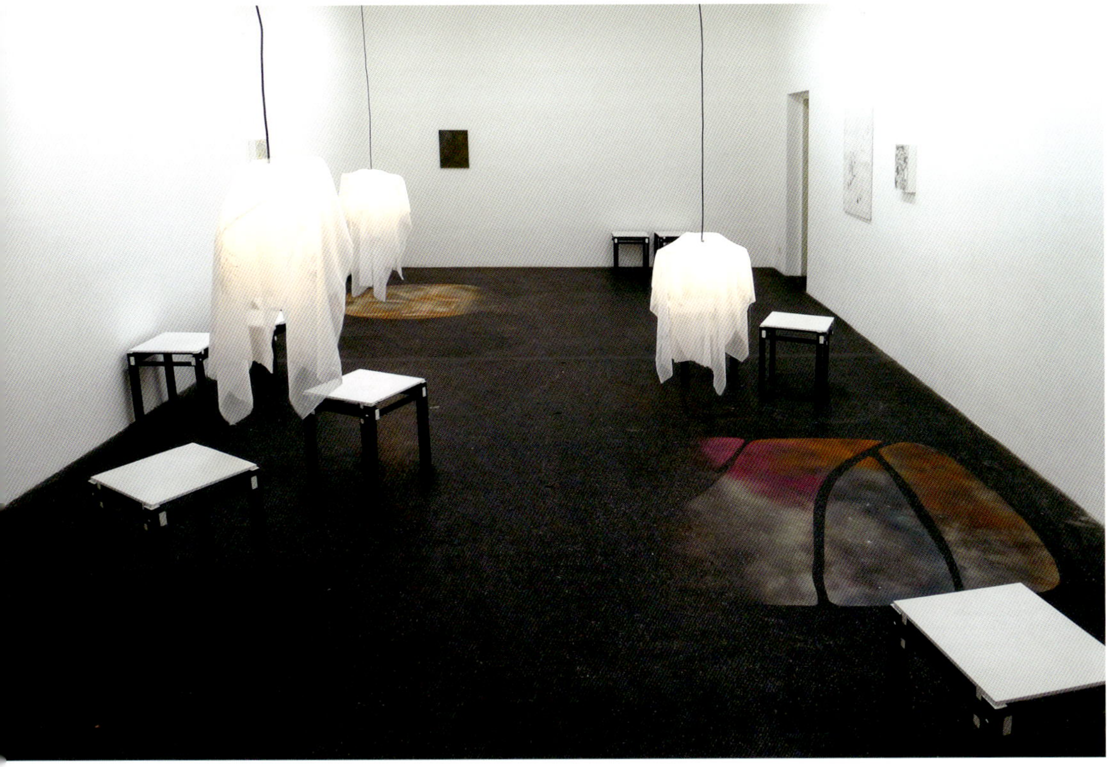

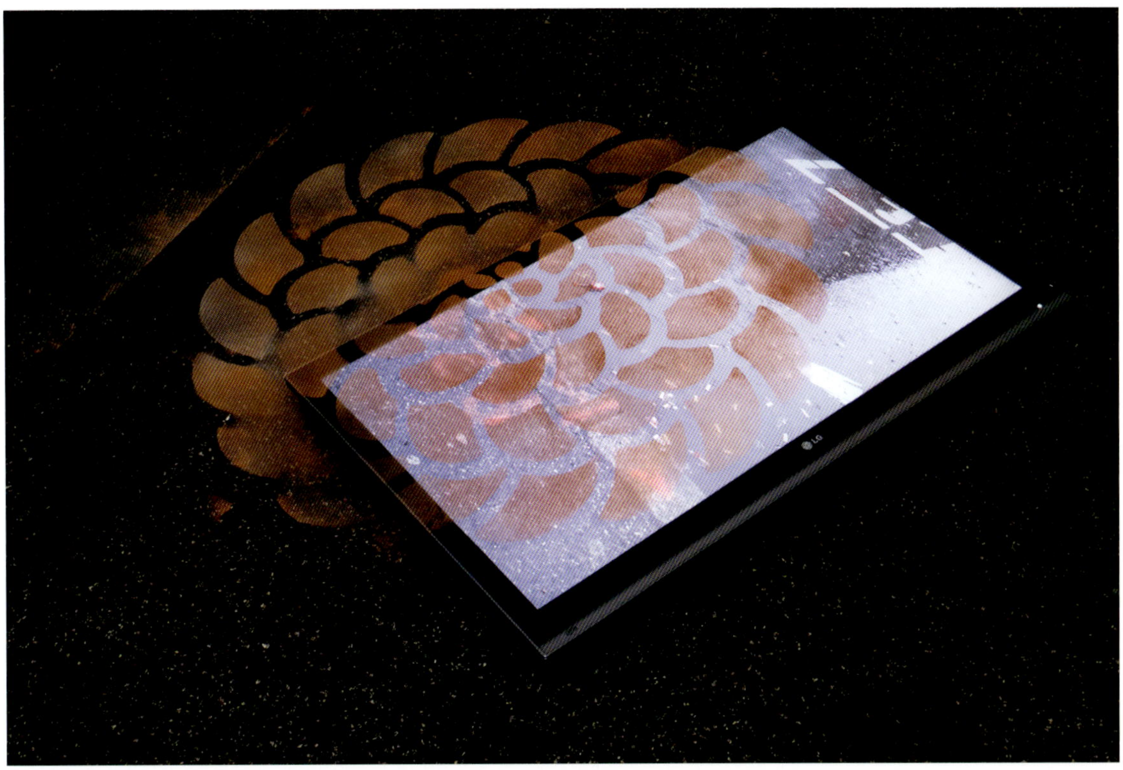

Christian Egger

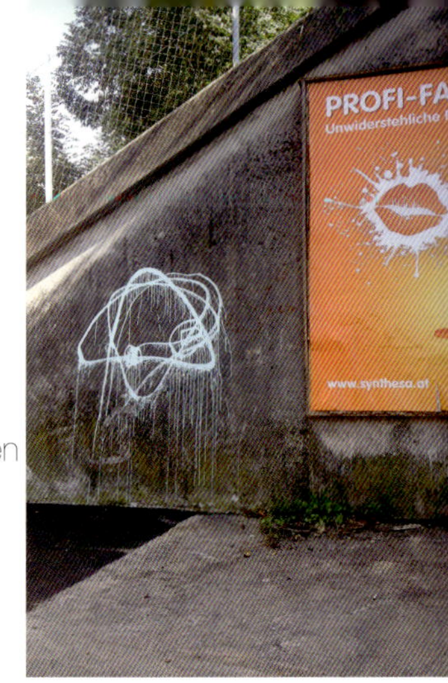

Voluptuous U-Turns on the Streets of Style, Beauty, and Greed

Sich den Arbeiten des Künstlers Manuel Gorkiewicz intensiver zu nähern, bedeutet für mich nun, kuratorische und freundschaftliche Ebenen zu verlassen und zu versuchen, eine vielmehr neutrale Position zu den Arbeiten zu beziehen, und dadurch eher wesentliche Wirkungsebenen der Arbeiten zu erfassen. Aus einer glücklichen Lage heraus, viele der Arbeiten von einem recht frühen Produktionszeitpunkt an zu kennen, ändert sich dennoch der Erkenntnisstand einmal mit dem Sedimentieren der Eindrücke und erneut bei deren Wiederbetrachtung. Eine der Werkreihen, die mich nachhaltig faszinieren und für mich eine demaskierende Wirkung bezüglich des Verhältnisses des/der Betrachter_in zu einem Kunstwerk transportieren. Gerade hinsichtlich des in dieser Gegenwart stets dominanten Drucks zur Selbstdarstellung, zur eigenen medialen Verbreitung des eigenen Gesichts und zu dessen Rund-um-die-Uhr-Präsentation im Einklang mit einer erfolgreichen Darstellung eines Tuns, nach dem größtmögliche Nachfrage bestehen soll, bei zeitgleicher Ables- und Ausstellbarkeit eigener maximaler Zufriedenheit darüber. Ich spreche hier von den Make-up-Bildern des Künstlers, die er mit Farbpigmenten handelsüblicher Make-up-Produkte malt. Im Auftrag kommt es zur Repräsentation des Farbproduktes durch sich selbst (Farbe als Farbe), die in ihrer eigentlichen Verwendung zur kosmetischen Optimierung der Schönheit des Menschen, vornehmlich von Personen weiblichen Geschlechts, oder generell Maskierungen des Femininen dient. Er entführt die Präsentation in der ebenfalls designten und praktisch-einfachen Make-up-Verpackung und das dortige Inszenierungspotential an dafür nicht vorgesehene Orte wie Museumsinnen- wie Museumsaußenwände, zu Galerie- und Offspace-Böden, wobei das Farbpuder hierbei teilweise auch über Bildrahmen, Fotodrucke und horizontale Bildschirmoberflächen hinaus verläuft. Dadurch werden höchst interessante Fragen nach Inhalt, der Darstellung von Dingen und Ideen, die man gemeinhin noch mit Malerei verbindet, aufgeworfen. Die Arbeiten stellen das aber eben nicht dar, sie verweisen auf eine funktionale Ästhetik über ein komplexes Dazwischen, das auf einer Ausstellungswand alleine eigentlich nicht eingelöst werden kann, es gleicht einer endlosen wie verführerischen Falle. Dass die Betrachter_innen mit dem Gesichtsfeldausschnitt genau auf die zu ihrer Behübschung und Verzierung entwickelte und maximierte Farbpalette sehen, ist ein unendlich starker Effekt und bewirkt die Umkehrung einer Bildbetrachtungssituation, quasi ein Kosmetik-Selbstporträt und eine Readymade-Hommage ihrer Verpackung und eine Wiederaufführung des in sie geflossenen Produktdesign-Know-hows. Zumal mit dem Gesicht, und nur mit dem Gesicht (den Augen) in beiden Fällen, die direkte Kontaktaufnahme mit den Arbeiten möglich ist. Und das Gesicht darüber hinaus ganz verschiedene Kontexte berührt und eben auch archaische Konnotationen hat – der Kopf als höchster Punkt des Körpers, der eine ganze Gedankenwelt, den Sitz des Geistigen, einen Ort für Dialog, Austausch, Kontakt etc. repräsentiert. Beim Betrachten ist er nun mit Untersuchungen des eigenen Aussehens, den Hilfsmittel von dessen Optimierung und der dafür entwickelten Farbpalette konfrontiert, an einem Ort, der üblicherweise der geistigen Auseinandersetzung mit künstlerischen Arbeiten unabhängig vom eigenen Äußeren gilt.

„Die eine Sorte Nahrung, die ein Mädchen nur immer hungriger macht, die Auslagen, die Bilder von Auslagen, die Vorstellungen von Auslagen, die Überprüfungen an sich und den anderen im Lichte der Auslagen, die Vergleiche, die neuen Aussagen, denn an den Veränderungen der Auslagen merkt man die Zeit.

Denn immer muss und will man wissen, was die nächste Auslage zeigen wird. Denn sie darf sich nicht mit etwas Vorstellbaren decken, sie muss immer, jedes Jahr, ganz und gar neu sein."[1]

Sehe ich diese Bilder von der Eröffnung, für die ich mich selbst hübsch oder ausgehtüchtig gemacht habe, wird der Kontrollblick auf die richtige Nutzung der eigenen Palette provoziert. Diese Bilder treffen einen analogen Nerv. Noch eine Spur wirksamer und altruistischer als Fragen, die mit den Social Media bei Diskursen, auf aktuelle Malerei angewandt, einhergehen und die Betrachtung von Bildern und den Austausch darüber heute so belasten. Diese Bilder erinnern die Betrachter_innen nicht nur, wie sehr man selbst damit beschäftigt ist, ein genehmes Bild von sich anzufertigen und fortwährend nachzubessern, sondern auch daran, wie unbarmherzig unabgeschlossen dieser Prozess im Kapitalismus bleiben muss. Oder ist es gar einfach das Ergebnis so langen Starrens auf eine weiße Wand, bis sich diese des eigenen Make-ups bediente und man ungläubiger Zeuge eines räuberischen Deals würde? Im Ernst, es handelt sich hierbei um recht schonungslos entlarvende Reflexionen über die Identitätsfragen gewidmete Zeit, etwa vor Spiegeln, über subjektive Einschätzungen zur Wahrnehmung der eigenen Person und der Möglichkeits-Phantasien im Einnehmen einer anderen, weit glamouröseren, einfach herbeizuschminkenden Erscheinung. Die zeitlos bösen Pointen des Karikaturisten und Malers Ad Reinhardt in der Serie „How to Look at ..." erhalten in den Settings des Künstlers eine Reflexionsebene, die sich selbst als potentiell schön und harmlos gibt. Darin zeigt ein Mann mit Hut lachend auf ein abstraktes Bild und kommentiert es mit „Ha Ha what does this represent?".
Daraufhin personalisiert sich das Bild und fragt zurück: „What do you represent?". Darunter folgt der Absatz: „An abstract painting will react to you if you react to it. You get from it what you bring to it. It will meet you half way but no further. It is alive if you are. It represents something and so do you. You, SIR, ARE A SPACE, TOO." Der Auftrag der Kosmetikfarben, wie diese in ihren Behältern lauern und, nur sachte aufgetragen, auch leicht jene Bildschirmoberflächen bedecken, die heute alleine wiederzugeben vermögen, wie man sich selbst wahrnehmen will.

„Das Ich, will sagen der ‚Akt der Reflexion in sich selbst', muss stets ‚etwas Absolutes außerhalb seiner selbst setzen', währenddessen es erkennt, dass dieses Etwas nur ‚für es' existieren kann, das heißt, in Bezug auf die Endlichkeit und den genauen Anschauungsmodus des Ich."[2]

Das ortsspezifische Anbringen und die Reaktion auf die örtlichen Gegebenheiten erweitern die Lesbarkeit der Make-up-Interventionen des Künstlers zusätzlich. Der Kosmetikfarbkreis über dem Eingangsbereich einer Wiener Künstler_innenbar (Pro Choice, 2012) definierte jenen nicht nur, sondern ermahnte sanft, dass mit dem Betreten die eigenen Schönheitsvorbereitungen wirkend würden. Zwei einen Flur säumende Wände (Galerie im Taxispalais, Innsbruck, 2012) bemalte der Künstler so, dass sich bei dessen Begehung ein Effekt der umgebenden Unausweichlichkeit der übergroßen und monumentalen Überführungen der eigentlich in kleinen Dosen aufbewahrten Farbe spürbar einstellte. Die punktuellen Bilder im und am Künstlerhaus in Graz (2013) erfüllten im Inneren des perfekten White Cube das ausstellungsthematisch intendierte Thema und „verließen" die Leinwand (Chat Jet. Painting ‹Beyond› The Medium), während es an der Außenseite aussah, als wollte sich das Haus selbst für einen besonderen Auftrittsmoment in Schminktipps üben, dabei die Ideen von der Wand als Haut eines Hauses sprichwörtlich rückkoppelnd.

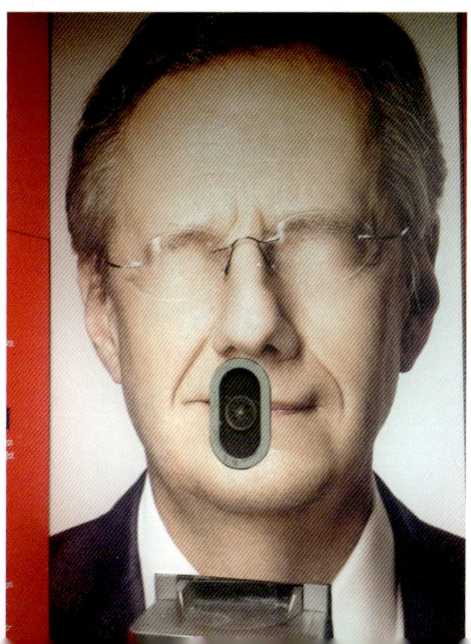

Es ist ein weit verbreitetes Charakteristikum heutiger künstlerischer Praxen, sich auf Bildproduktionstechniken einer technisch avancierten Massenkultur zu beziehen und diese zu verfremden, zu überhöhen oder zu unterwandern. Die Künstler_innen thematisieren diese neuen und konkurrierenden Bildproduktionsverfahren an Orten, die für die Präsentation zeitgenössischer bildnerischer Kunstprodukte vorgesehen sind, mit dem dort verhandelten Kunstanspruch. In vielen Fällen zeigt sich dabei das industriell und technologisch avancierte Bild als verweisende Bezugsgröße zu einer draußen mächtigen Film-, Fernseh- und digitalen Simulationsindustrie, oft nur symbolisch wiederholt und unkritisch. Die Arbeiten Gorkiewiczs schälen das eine oder andere Zusatzproblem heraus, mit den leichten Mitteln und Strategien des Glamourösen, der stilistischen Übertreibung, zarter Ironie, dem Freilegen der theatralischen und androgynen Potentialität jeglicher Umgebungen, der beiläufigen Inszenierung der Triumphe der Oberflächeneffekte über Künstlichkeit und Bedeutung. So stößt der Künstler nicht nur auf die zentralen Probleme der Malerei heute, sondern zeigt zudem auch, wie sehr sich diese unseren Problemen bereits angeglichen präsentieren.

„Aber heute, wo die Arbeit und die Zeit derart mit der Zeitlichkeit der digitalen Netze verwoben sind, die rund um die Uhr aktiv sind, ist ihr Arbeitsmodus ungleich immanenter respektive auf viel direktere Weise partizipatorisch. Was dabei wegfällt, ist der Luxus einer klar abgegrenzten zeitlichen und räumlichen Distanz zwischen der Zeit und dem Ort ihrer Herstellung und der Nichtzeit beziehungsweise dem Nichtort der Infonetze, in denen Erstere außer Kraft gesetzt scheinen. Also wird sie Teil dieser Grenzverwischung, verfolgt und belauert sich und beginnt sich dabei sorglos mit ihrem eigenen Selfie zu verwechseln."[3]

[1] Jutta Koether, *f.* (Graz: Edition Bleich Rossi, 1987), herausgegeben von Isabelle Graw, Daniel Birnbaum, Institut für Kunstkritik, Frankfurt am Main: Sternberg Press, 2015.

[2] Sylvain Portier, *Fichte et le dépassement de la „chose en soie*: 1792–1799, Paris: Éd. L'Harmattan, 2006, S. 54.

[3] John Kelsey, „Das Sextleben der Malerei", in: *Painting 2.0: Malerei im Informationszeitalter*, Ausst.-Kat. Museum Brandhorst, München (2015/16), München: Prestel Verlag, 2006, S. 270.

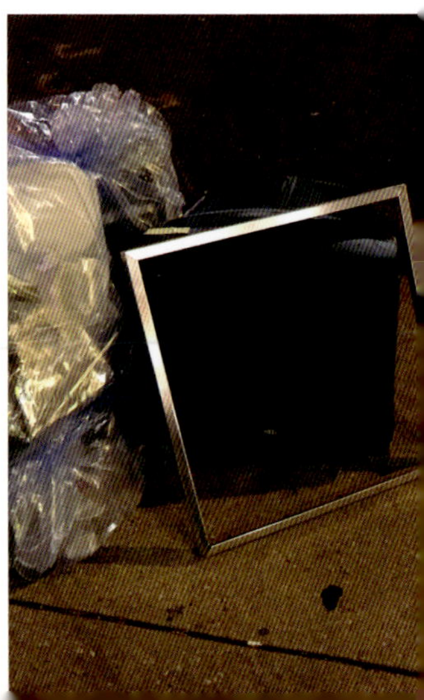

Christian Egger

Voluptuous U-Turns on the Streets of Style, Beauty, and Greed

Taking a more intensive look at the work of artist Manuel Gorkiewicz requires me to recuse myself as curator and friend, and to adopt instead a neutral position on the work through which to capture its more significant levels of impact. Being in the fortunate position of having known much of the work from a fairly early point in its production, this level of insight nonetheless changes, first through a sedimentation of impressions, and then again through their reconsideration.

One series that has long fascinated me consists of the artist's makeup paintings, which he creates with color pigments used in commercially available makeup products. These pieces convey an unmasking effect regarding the relationship between observer and artwork, all the more so in light of the currently dominant pressure to promote oneself – to publicize one's own face and present it around the clock – in line with a successful display of activity for which there should be the greatest possible demand, accompanied by a clearly visible show of maximal self-satisfaction. In its application, the pigment comes to represent itself (color as color), which when used as intended, serves to cosmetically optimize the beauty of above-all female persons or to generally mask the feminine. Hijacking their standard mode of presentation in carefully designed and practical make-up packaging, as well as the theatrical potential contained therein, he spirits it off to unintended places, like the interior and exterior walls of museums or the floors of galleries and art spaces, the powdered pigments partly extending beyond picture frames, photo prints, and horizontal display screens. The most interesting questions this raises regard content, concerning the representation of things and ideas that are generally still associated with painting. And yet the work depicts something else entirely – it refers instead to a functional aesthetic by means of a complex intermediary state that cannot really be redeemed on an exhibition wall alone; as such it is like an endless and seductive trap. The viewer's field of vision is directed precisely toward a color palette developed and maximized for her or his own beautification and adornment. The result is an incredibly strong effect, causing an inversion of the viewing situation – essentially a cosmetic self-portrait and readymade homage to its packaging, a restaging of the product design expertise that went into developing it. This is all the more so because it is through the face, and only through the face (the eyes), that direct contact with the work is possible. Moreover, the face also touches on a wide variety of contexts and even has an archaic connotation – the head as the highest point of the body, representing a whole world of ideas, the seat of spirituality, a place for dialogue, exchange, contact, etc. In the process of viewing, the face finds itself confronted with explorations of its own appearance, the tools of its optimization, and a color palette developed especially for that purpose, but in a setting usually devoted to the spiritual contemplation of artistic works entirely independent of one's own appearance.

"The one sort of nourishment that only makes a girl ever hungrier, the display windows, the pictures of display windows, the thought of display windows, the inspection of ourselves and others in the light of the display windows, the comparisons, the new statements – for in the changes to the display windows we notice the passage of time. For we always need and want to know what the next display window will show. For they must not be like anything that can be imagined; they must always, every year, be completely and entirely new."[1]

Seeing these paintings at the opening, for which I made myself pretty or at least fit to be seen in public, provokes a quick inspection to make sure I have applied my personal palette correctly. The paintings strike an analog nerve. They are somewhat more effective and altruistic than the questions that accompany the discourses in social-media on contemporary painting, which make viewing and discussing paintings so difficult today. These paintings remind the viewer not only of how preoccupied we are with creating and continually touching up a pleasing image of ourselves, but also of how mercilessly incomplete this process must remain under capitalism. Or is it simply the result of staring too long at a white wall, until it has helped itself to our own makeup, leaving us as an incredulous witness to that predatory deal? In truth, we are faced with rather unsparingly revealing reflections on the time we devote to issues of identity, in front the mirror, for example, with subjective assessments of how we are perceived; as well as fantasies of assuming a different and far more glamorous appearance through the mere application of makeup.

In his series *How to Look at Modern Art*, cartoonist and painter Ad Reinhardt couches his timelessly malicious punch lines in settings through which they assume a level of reflection that presents itself as potentially nice and harmless. In one, a man with a hat points laughingly at an abstract painting, commenting: "Ha Ha, what does this represent?" Coming to life, the painting responds by asking: "What do you represent?" The caption below reads: "An Abstract Painting will react to you if you react to it. You get from it what you bring to it. It will meet you half way but no further. It is alive if you are. It represents something and so do you. You, SIR, ARE A SPACE, TOO."

"The gentle application of cosmetic colors, the way they lurk in their containers, lightly covers those display-screen surfaces that today alone are able to reproduce the way we wish to perceive ourselves. "The ego, that is to say, the 'act of reflection in itself,' must always 'place something absolute outside of its own self,' while recognizing that this something can only exist 'for it,' that is, in relation to the finiteness and the precise perspectival mode of the ego."[2]

The site-specific application and responsiveness to the given situation further enhances the readability of the artist's make-up interventions. A cosmetic color circle above the doorway of an artist-run art space/bar in Vienna (Pro Choice, 2012), not only defined the entrance, but also served as a gentle reminder that one's own beauty preparations would go into effect upon entering. Two walls flanking a corridor in (Galerie im Taxispalais 2012) were painted by the artist in a way that, when walking between them, made palpable an effect of enveloping inevitability through the oversized and monumental transference of colors normally found stored in tiny cases. For the Künstlerhaus Graz exhibition "Chat Jet – Painting ‹Beyond› The Medium" in 2013, the artist scattered paintings in and around the building. Within the perfect white-cube interior, the paintings embodied the exhibition's thematic intention and "left" the canvas, while on the exterior wall they gave the suggestion that the entire building was practicing make-up tips for some special public appearance, creating a literal feedback loop with the idea of walls as architectural skin.

It is a common feature of contemporary artistic practice to reference, distort, exaggerate, or undermine the image production techniques of a technically advanced mainstream culture. Artists address these new and competing image production processes in spaces designated for the presentation of contemporary artistic production, with all their attendant claims to artistic legitimacy. In many cases, however, the industrially and technologically advanced image, as a reference parameter for an externally powerful film, television, and digital simulation industry, proves to be a merely symbolic and uncritical reiteration. Gorkiewicz's work, however, carves out a number of additional problems through the easy means and strategies of the glamorous, using stylistic exaggerations and delicate irony, exposing the theatrical and androgynous potentiality of every environment, and casually enacting the triumph of surface effects over artificiality and meaning. In doing so, the artist not only touches upon the central problems of painting today, he also reveals the degree to which they are already present, aligned with our own problems.

"But now that the work and time of painting have become so immersed within the 24-7 temporality of digital networks, it can only operate in an immanent and immediately participatory way, without the luxury of any clearly demarcated temporal or spatial gap between the proper time and place of its own work and the no-time and nonplace of info networks that seem to abolish these. So it involves itself in boundary confusion, haunting and stalking itself, happily confusing itself with its selfie."[3]

[1] Jutta Koether, *f.* (Graz: Edition Bleich Rossi, 1987), Frankfurt am Main: Sternberg Press, 2015.
[2] Sylvain Portier, *Fichte et le dépassement de la „chose en soie": 1792–1799*, Paris: Éd. L'Harmattan, 2006: 54.
[3] John Kelsey, "The Sext Life of Painting," *Painting 2.0: Expression in the Information Age*, exhibition catalog Museum Brandhorst, Munich (2015/16), Munich: Prestel Verlag, 2006: 270.

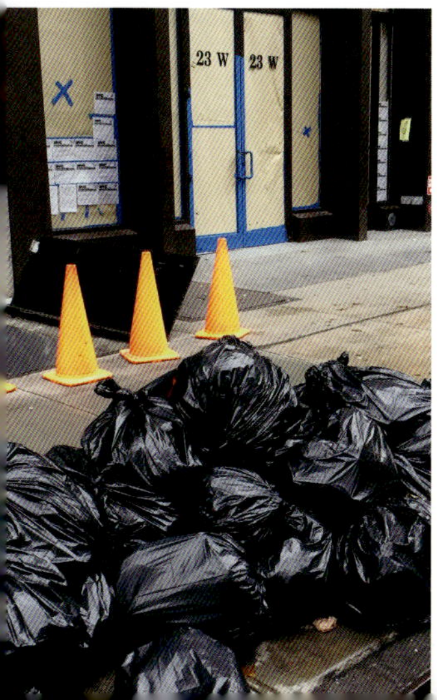

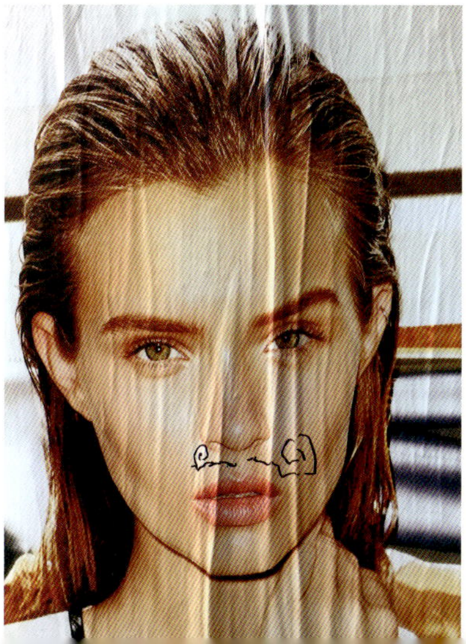

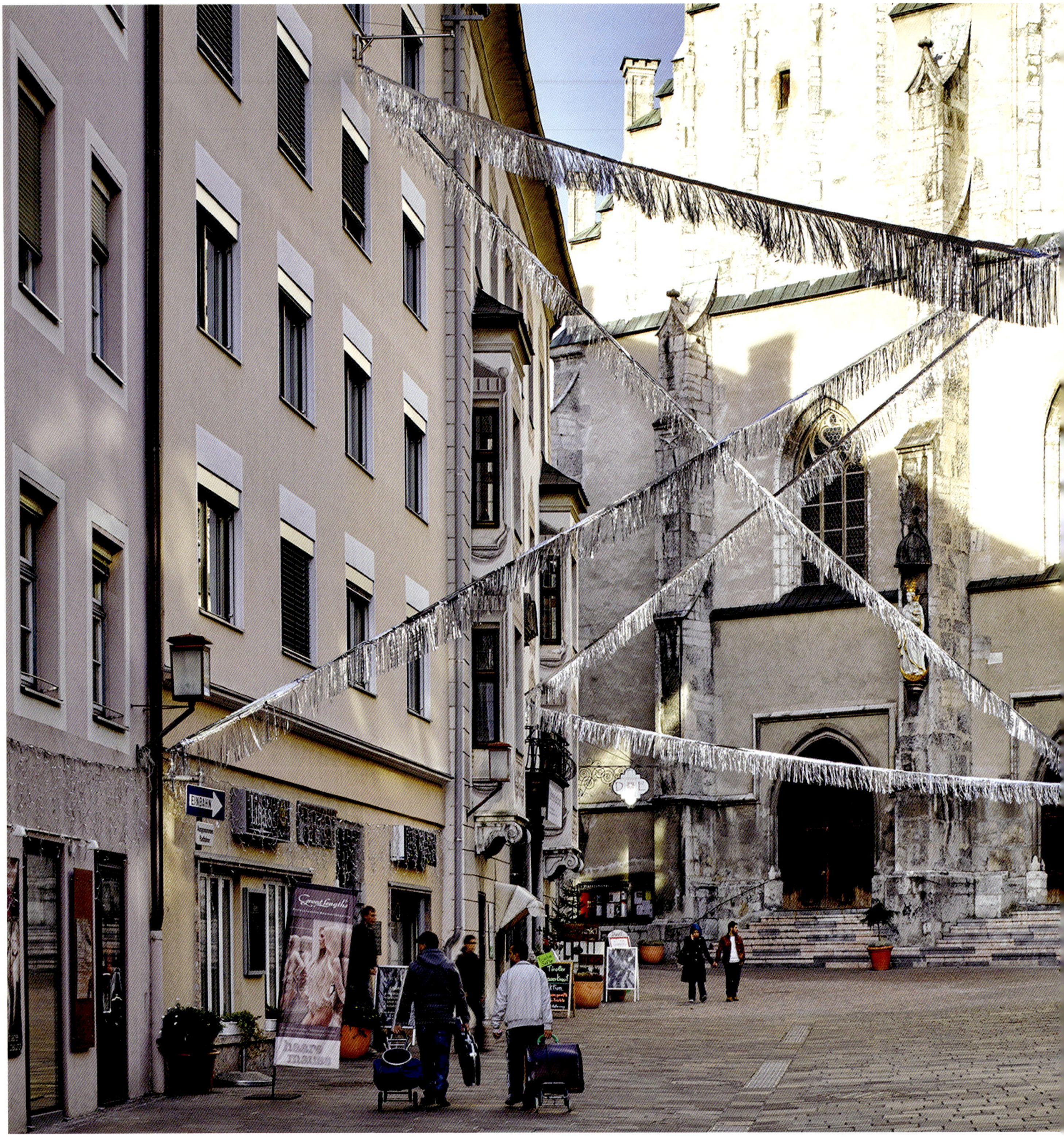
EINBAHN

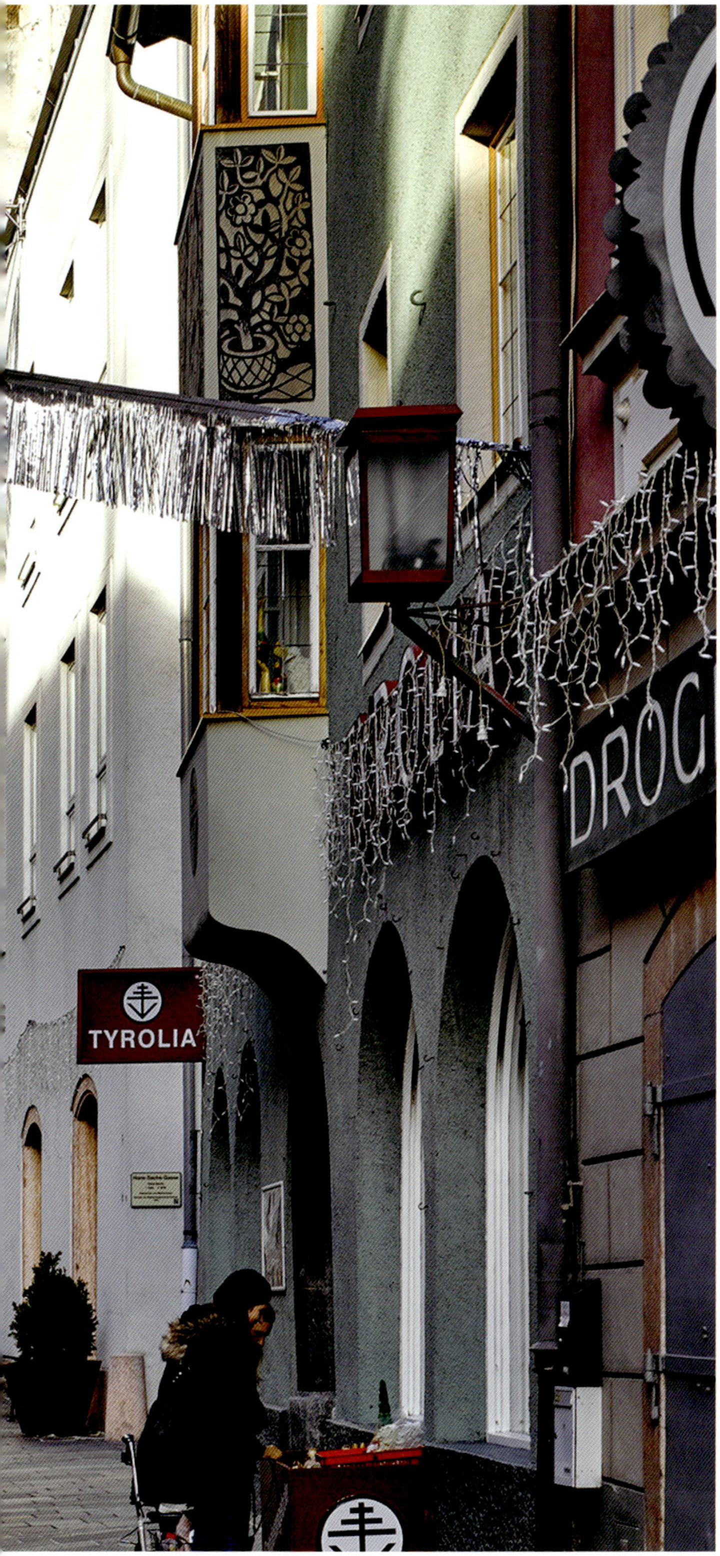

"Vogelsbergeriana", Galerie der Stadt Schwaz, 2014
Untitled, ca.150 m, steel, plastic foil, 2014

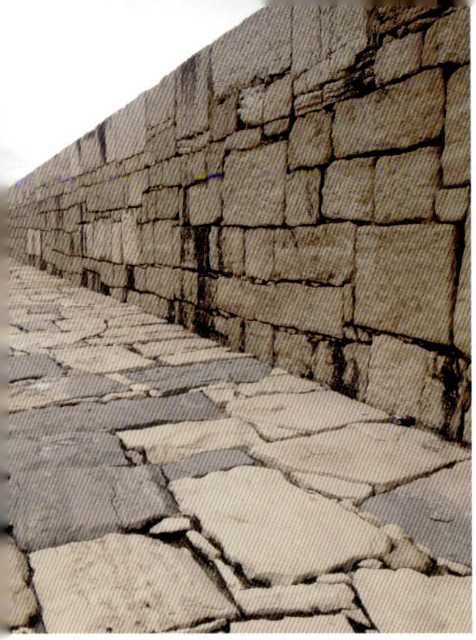
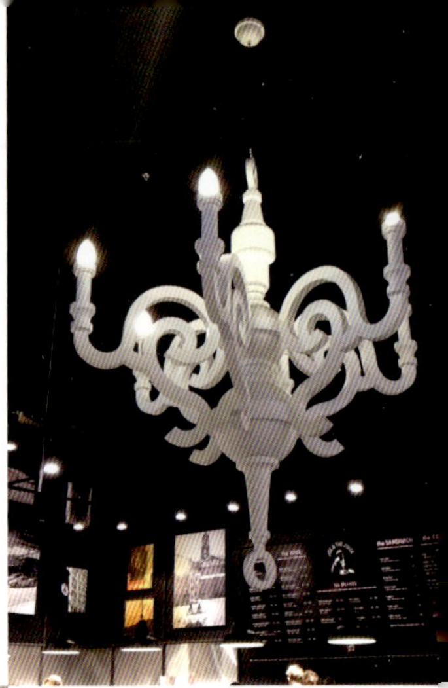
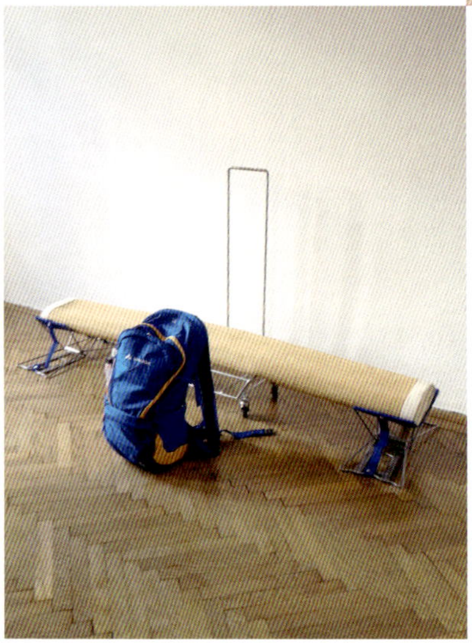
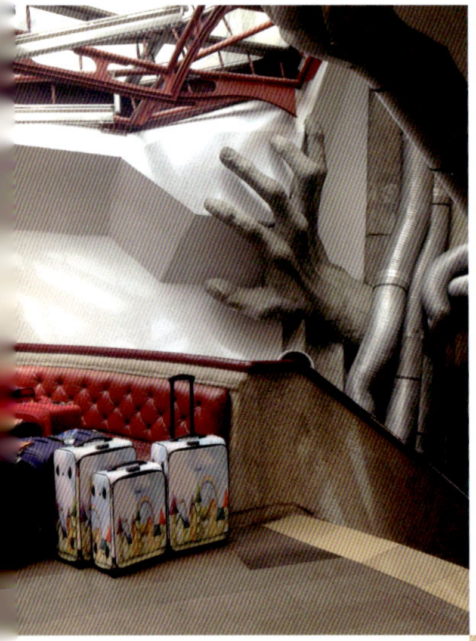
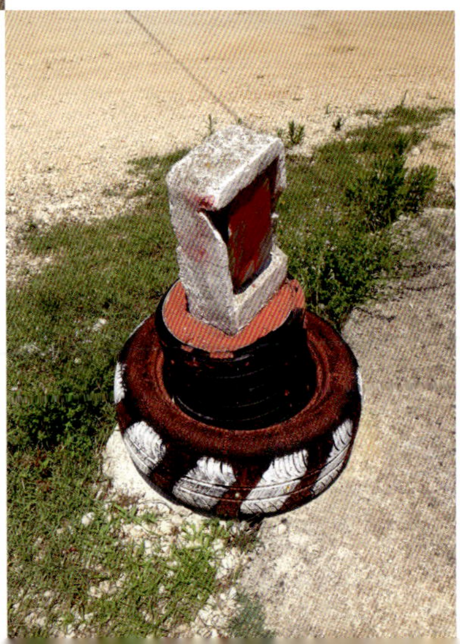
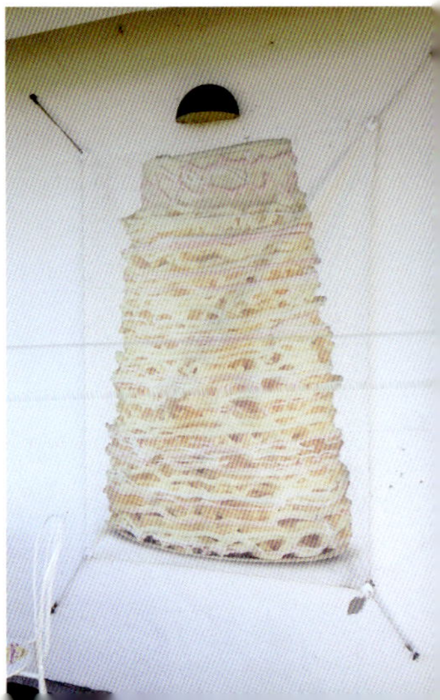

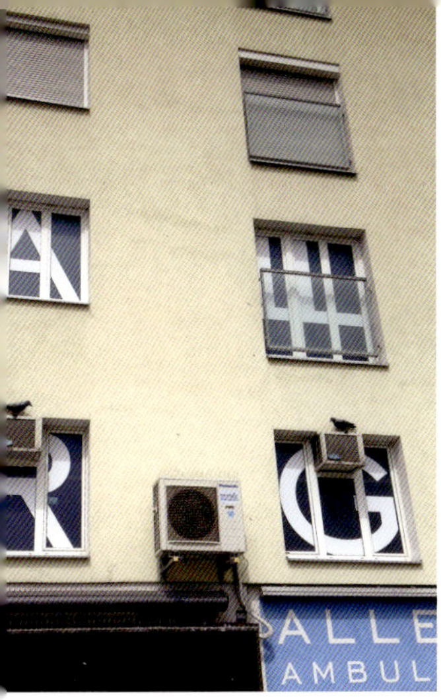
ALLE
AMBUL

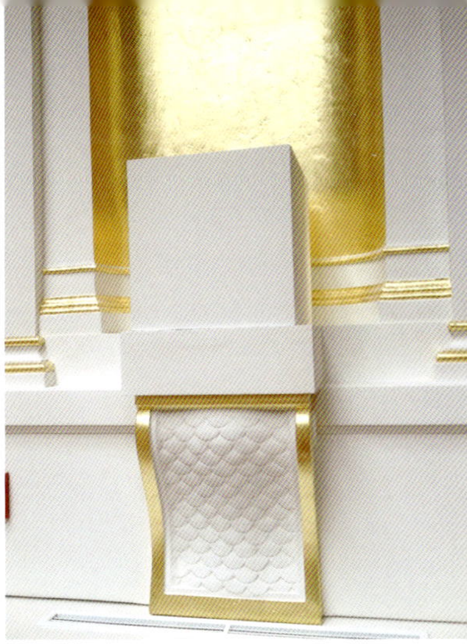

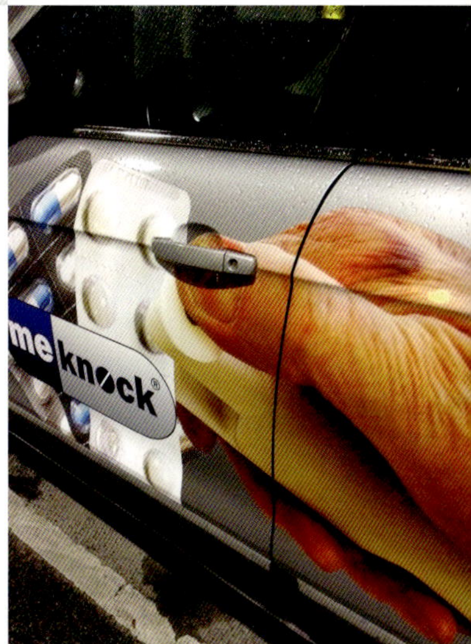
meknock®

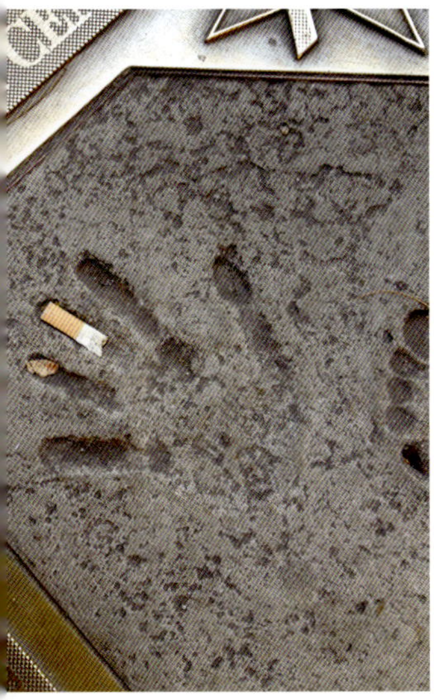

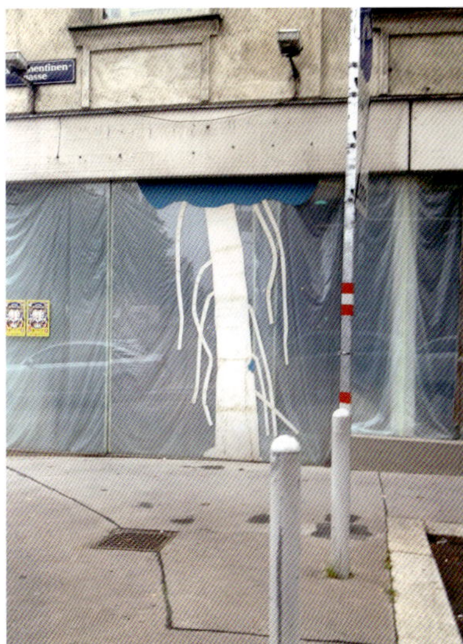

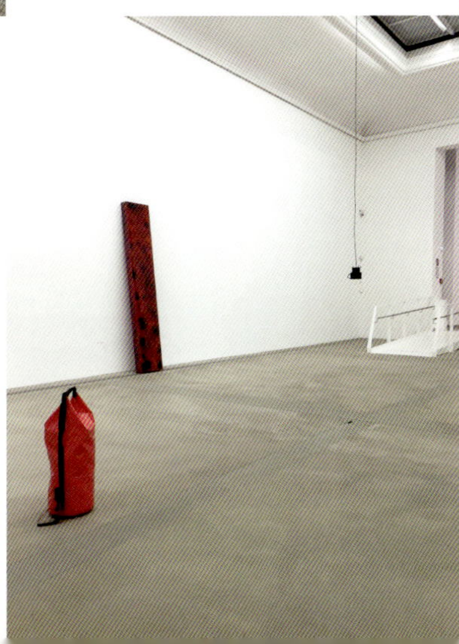

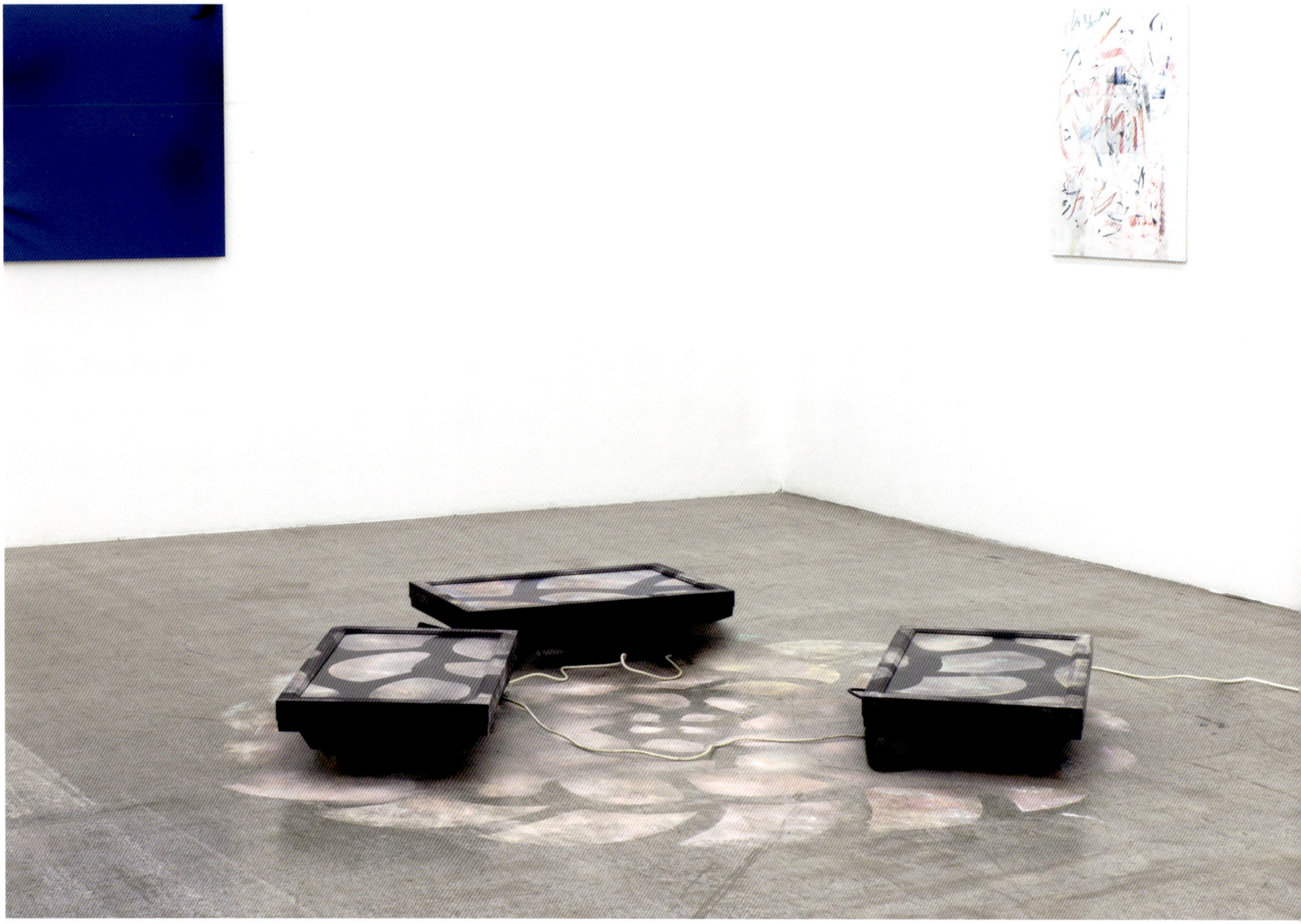

“Was die Wange rötet, kann übel nicht seyn”, Kerstin Engholm Gallery, Vienna, 2015

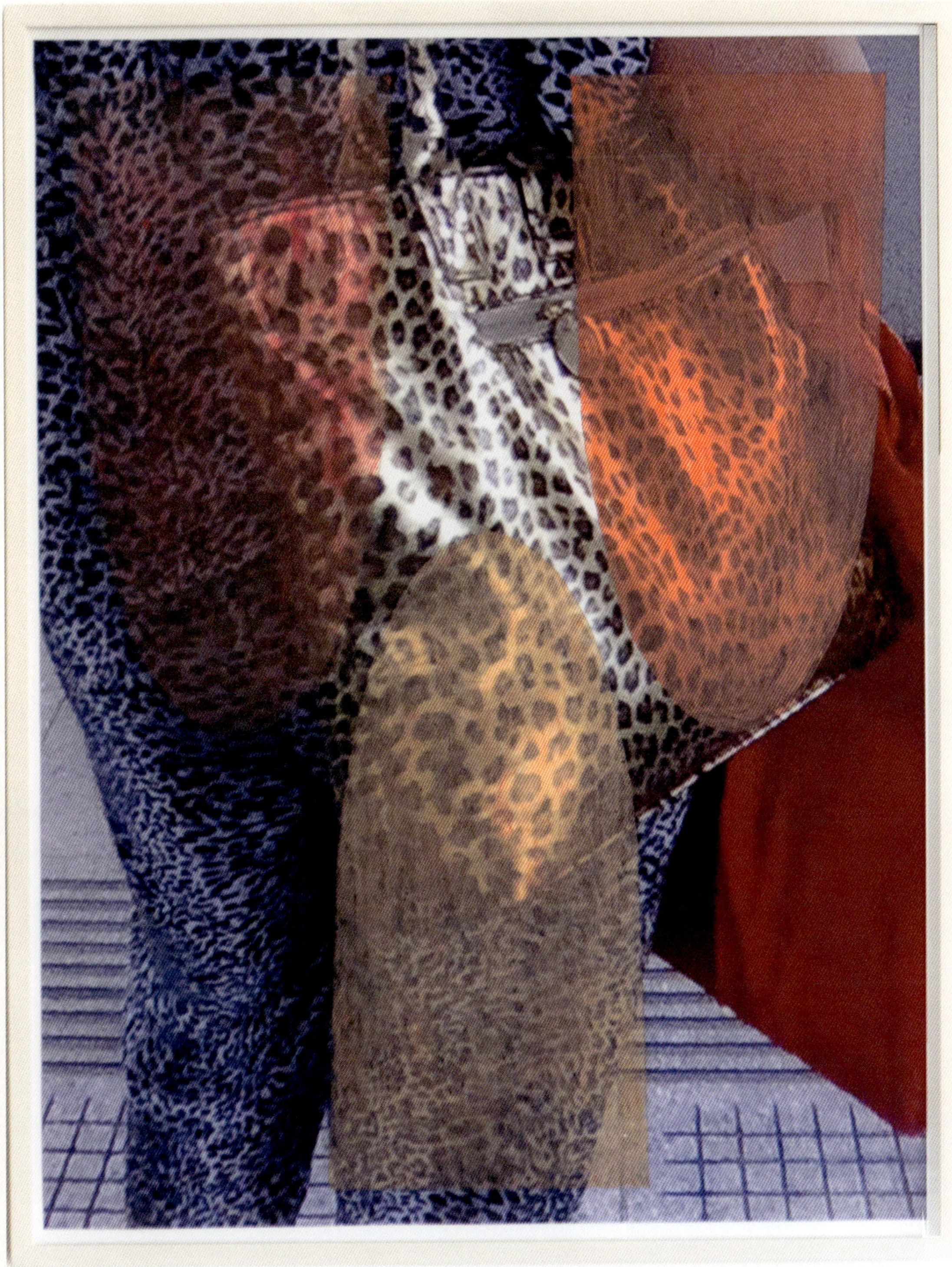

Untitled, 65 x 50 cm, lipstick on inkjet print, 2013
left page: Untitled, 240 x 240 x 10 cm, make-up on 3 monitors and floor, videos (ca. 3 min, looped, sound), 2015

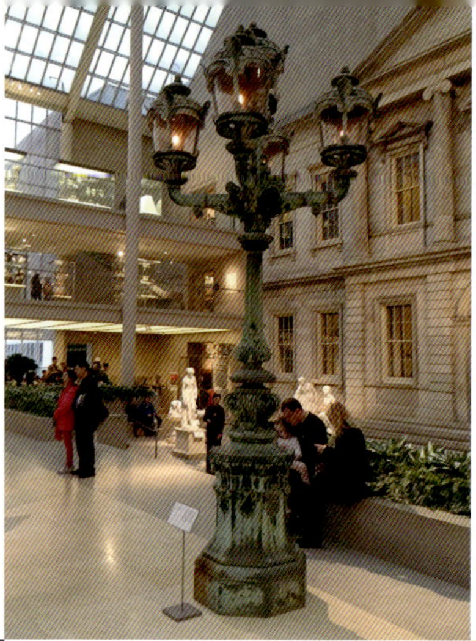

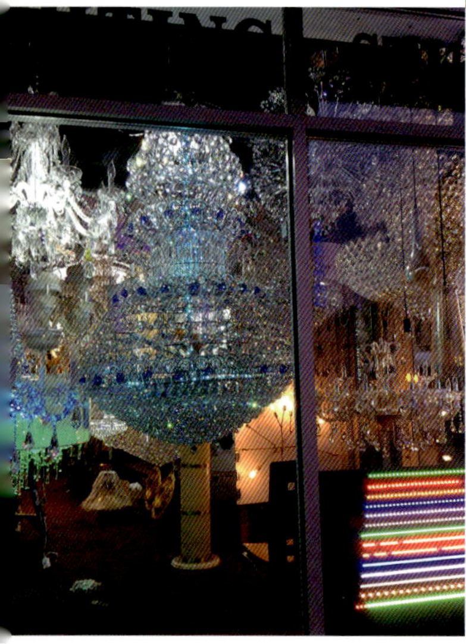

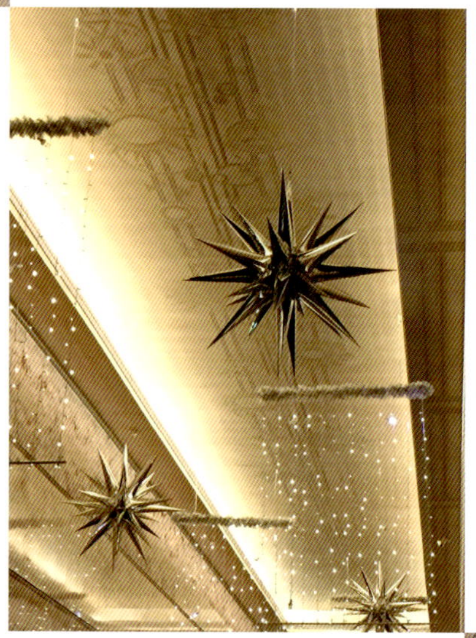

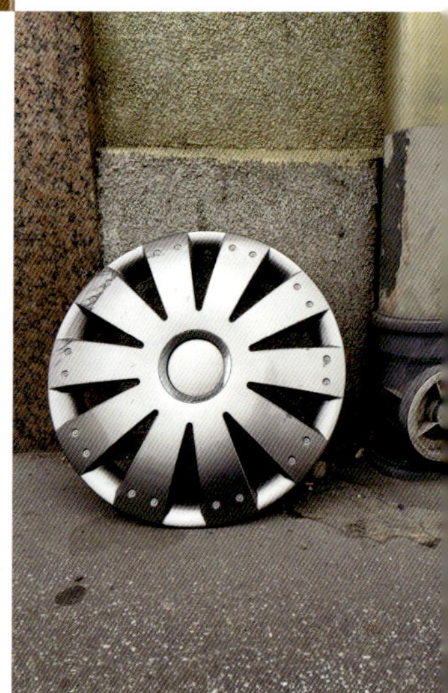

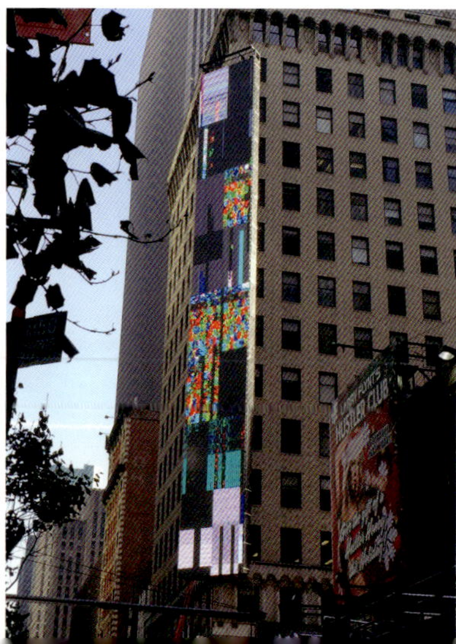

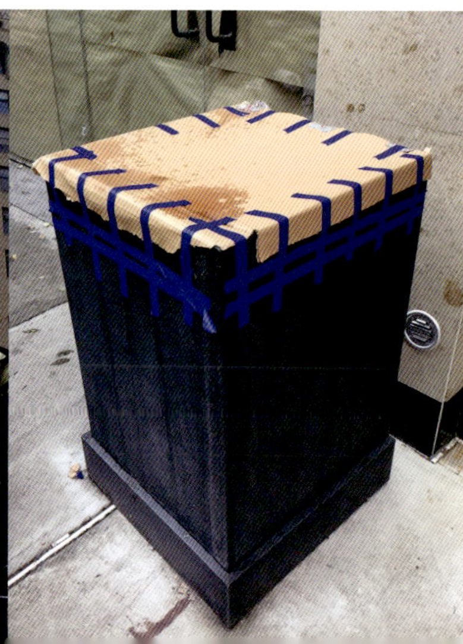

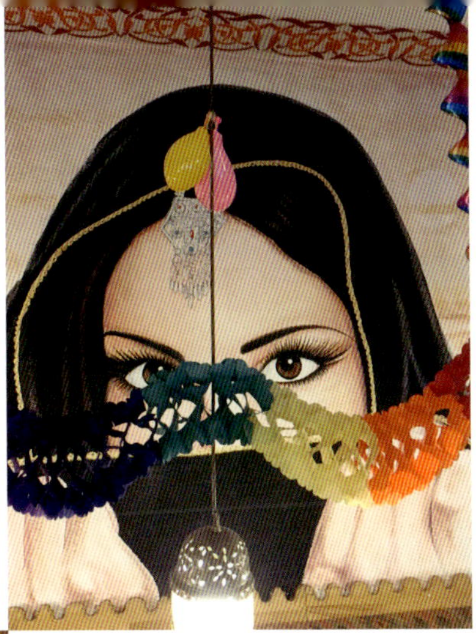

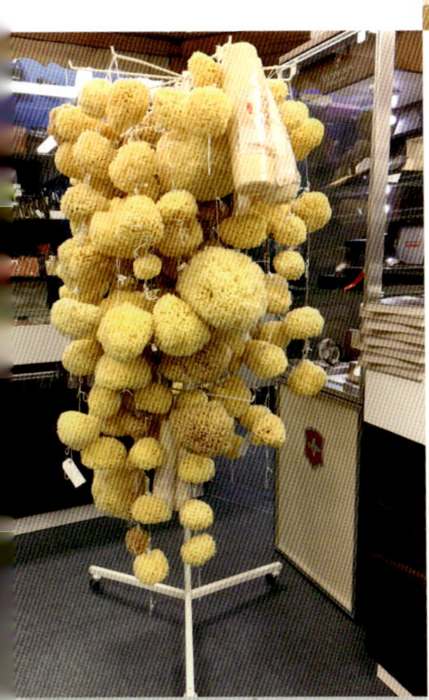

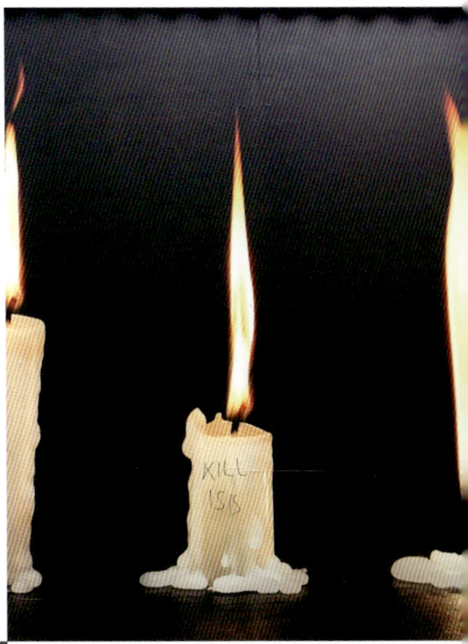
KILL
ISIS

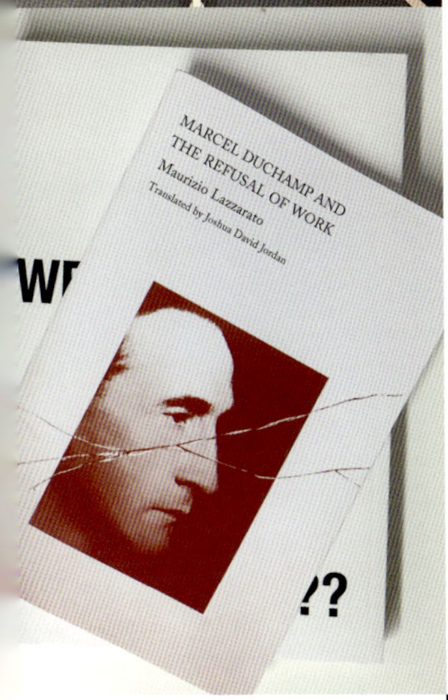
MARCEL DUCHAMP AND
THE REFUSAL OF WORK
Maurizio Lazzarato
Translated by Joshua David Jordan

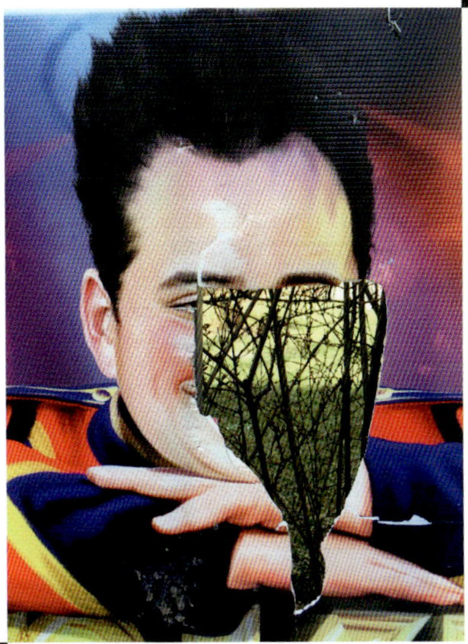

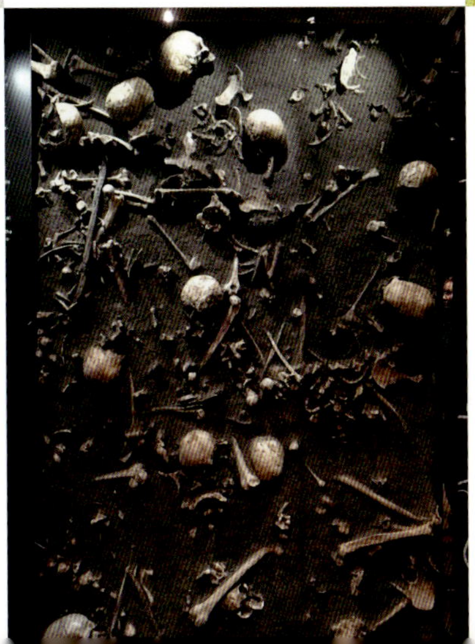

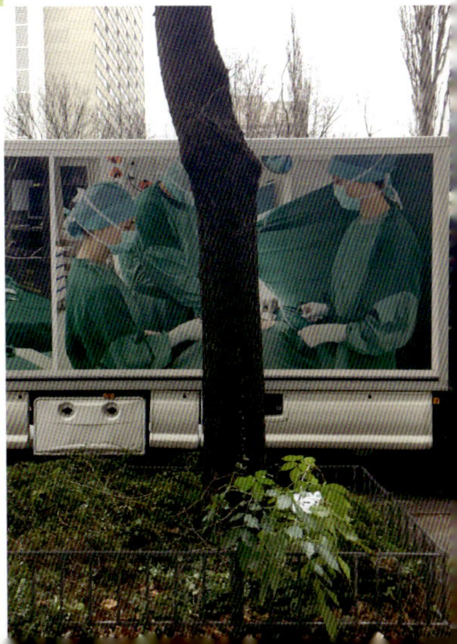

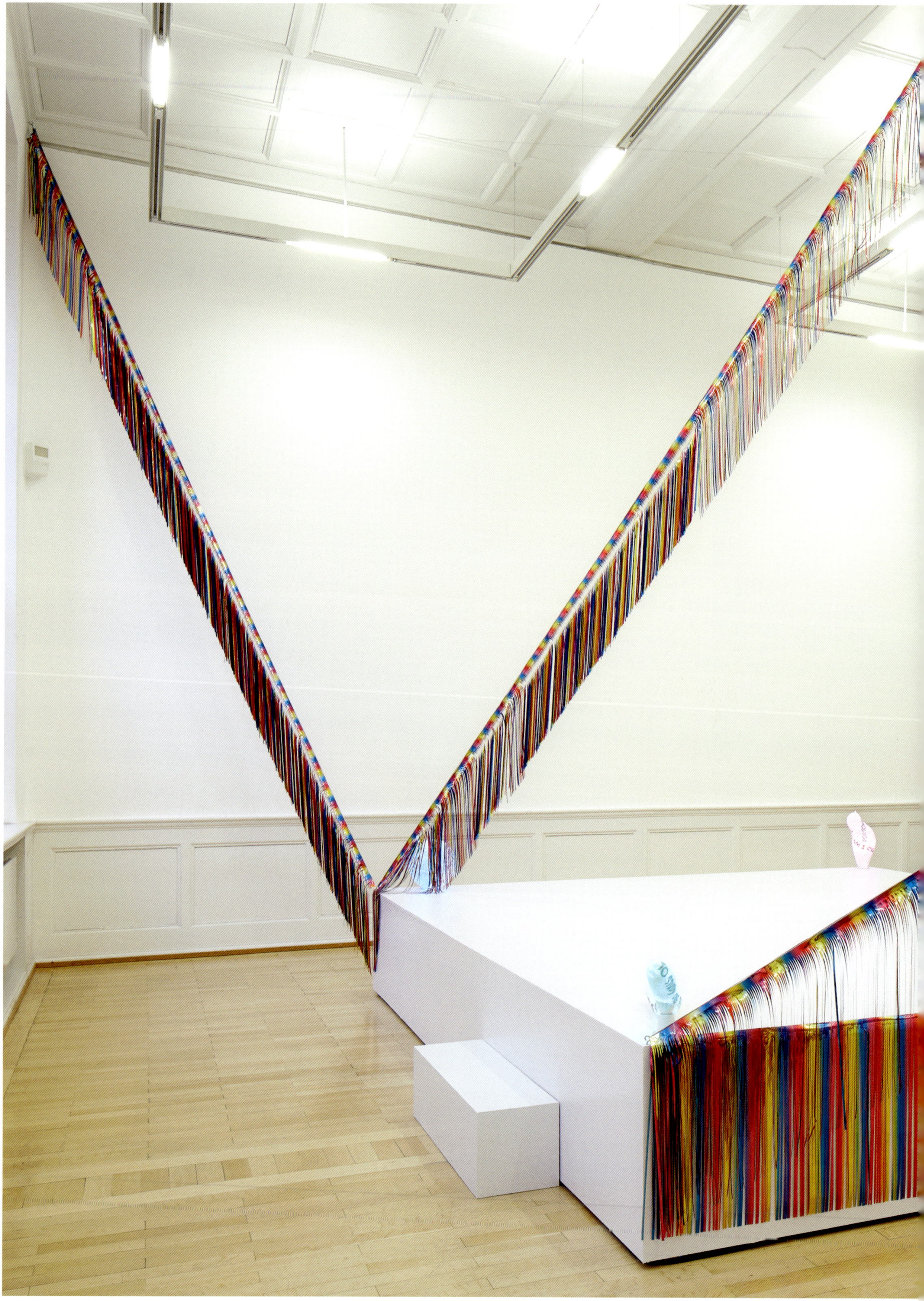

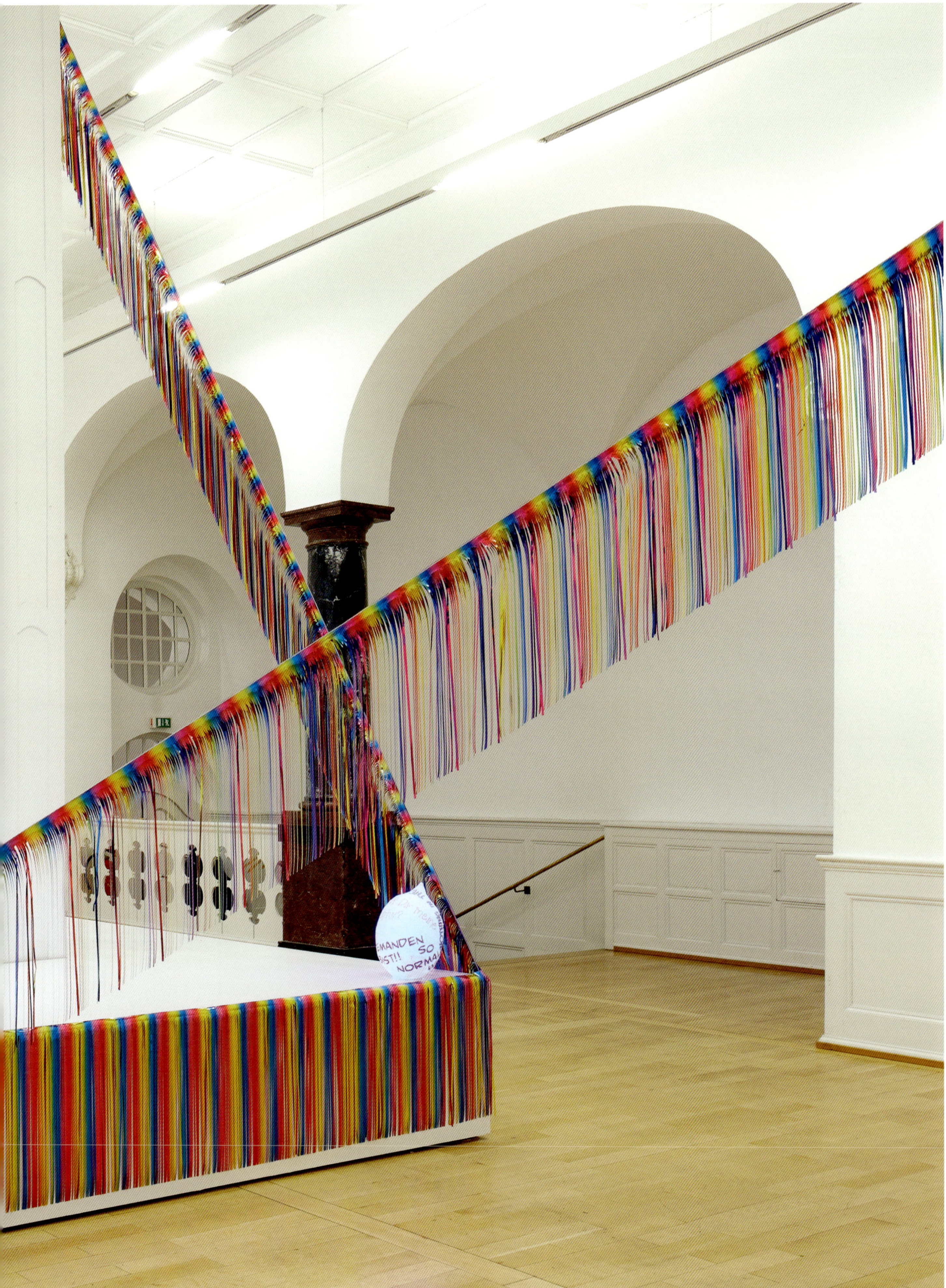
SO

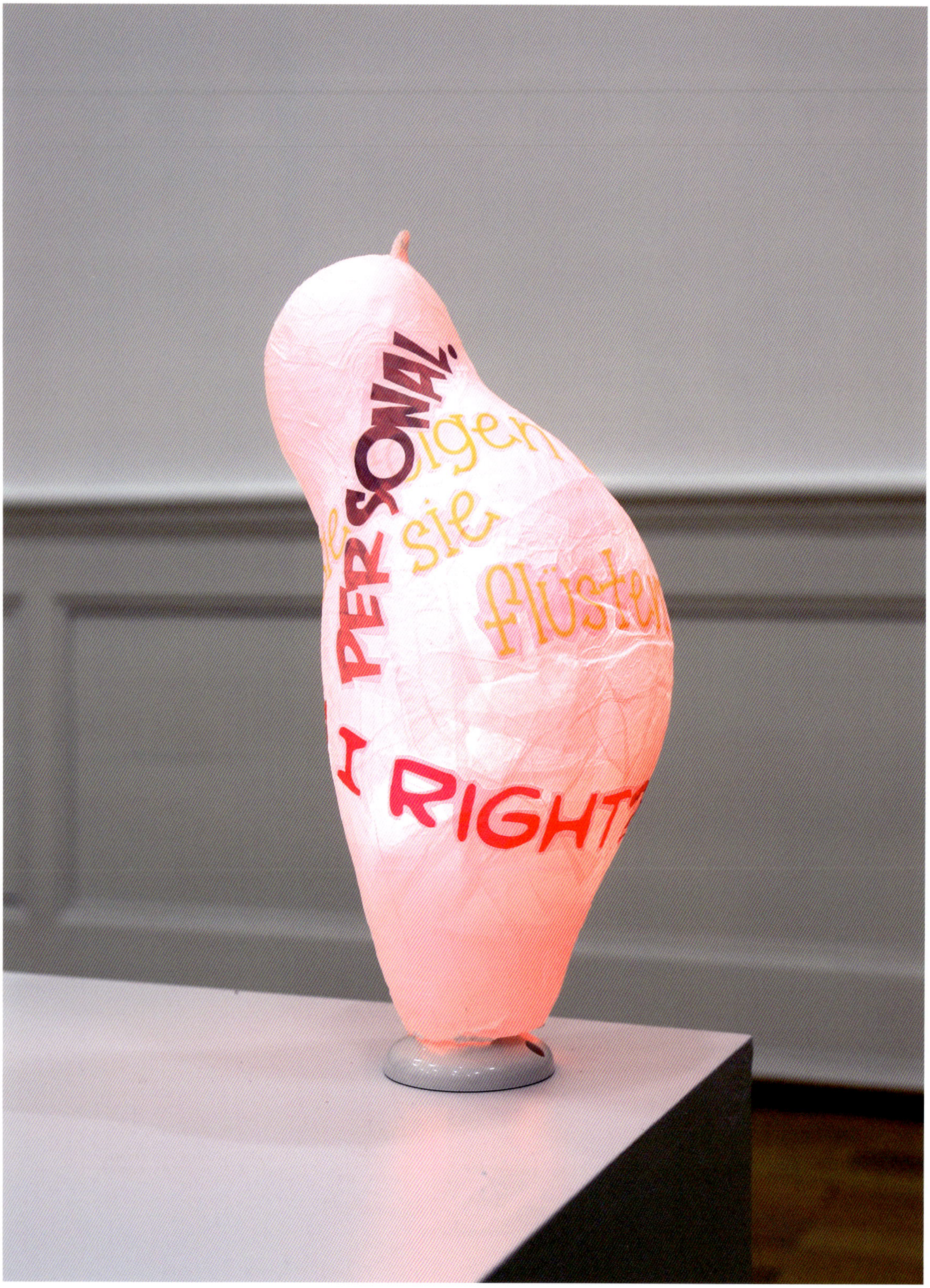

"Kerstin Cmelka mit Manuel Gorkiewicz, Mario Mentrup, Hanno Millesi und Mandla Reuter"
Badischer Kunstverein, Karlsruhe, 2015

p. 102 & 106 : Untitled, mixed media, 2015
this page: Untitled, ca. 35 x 15 x 10 cm, paper, laser print, LED, 2015
right page top: Untitled, ca. 35 x 20 x 20 cm, paper, laser print, LED, 2015
right page bottom: Untitled, ca. 20 x 8 x 65 cm, paper, laser print, LED, 2015

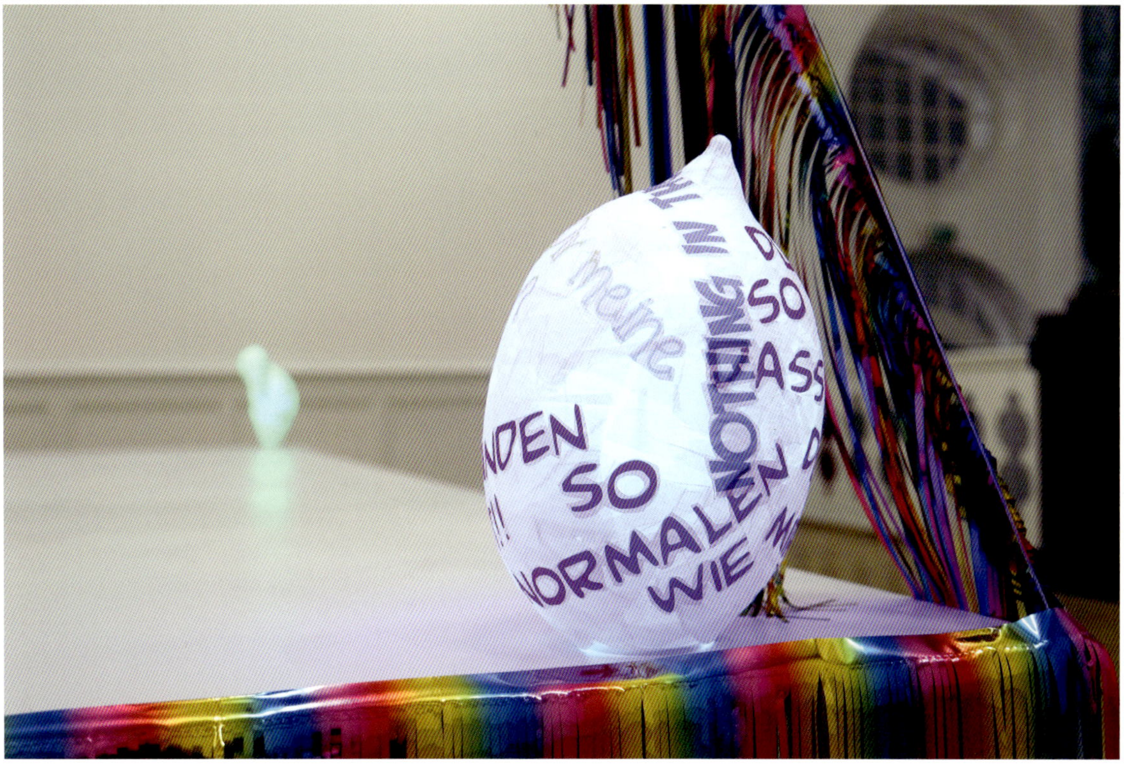

meine
NOTHING IN
SO
SO
NORMALEN
WIE

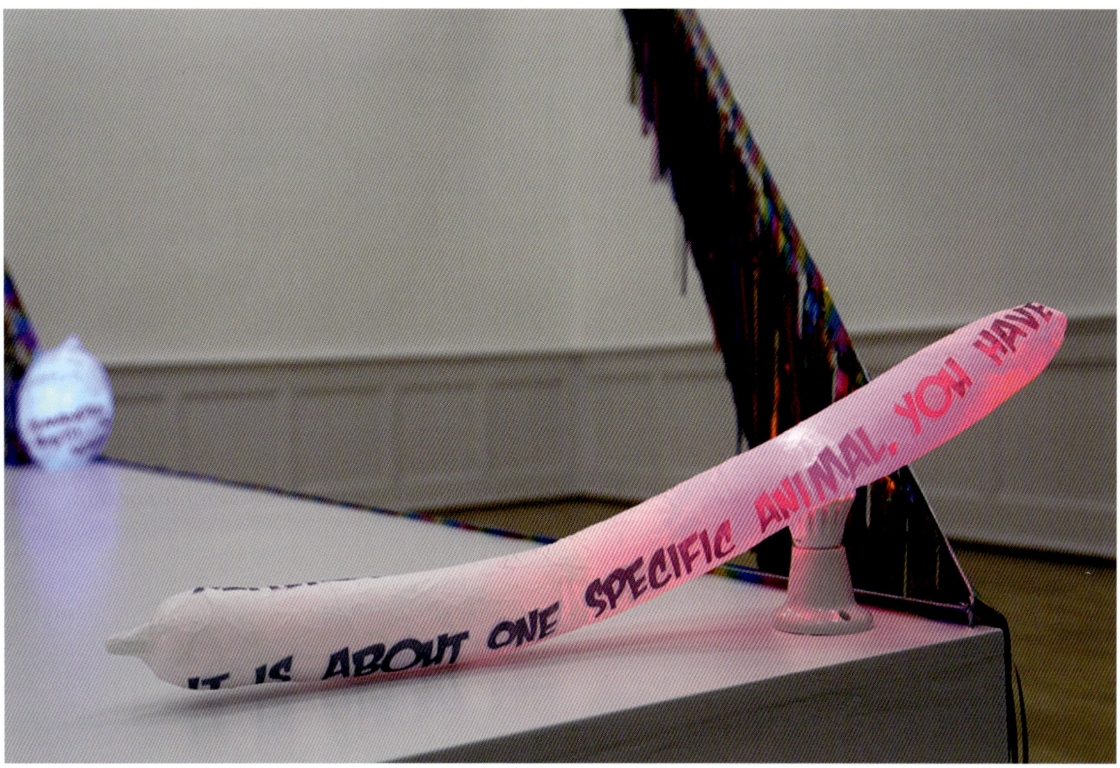

IT IS ABOUT ONE SPECIFIC ANIMAL. YOU HAVE

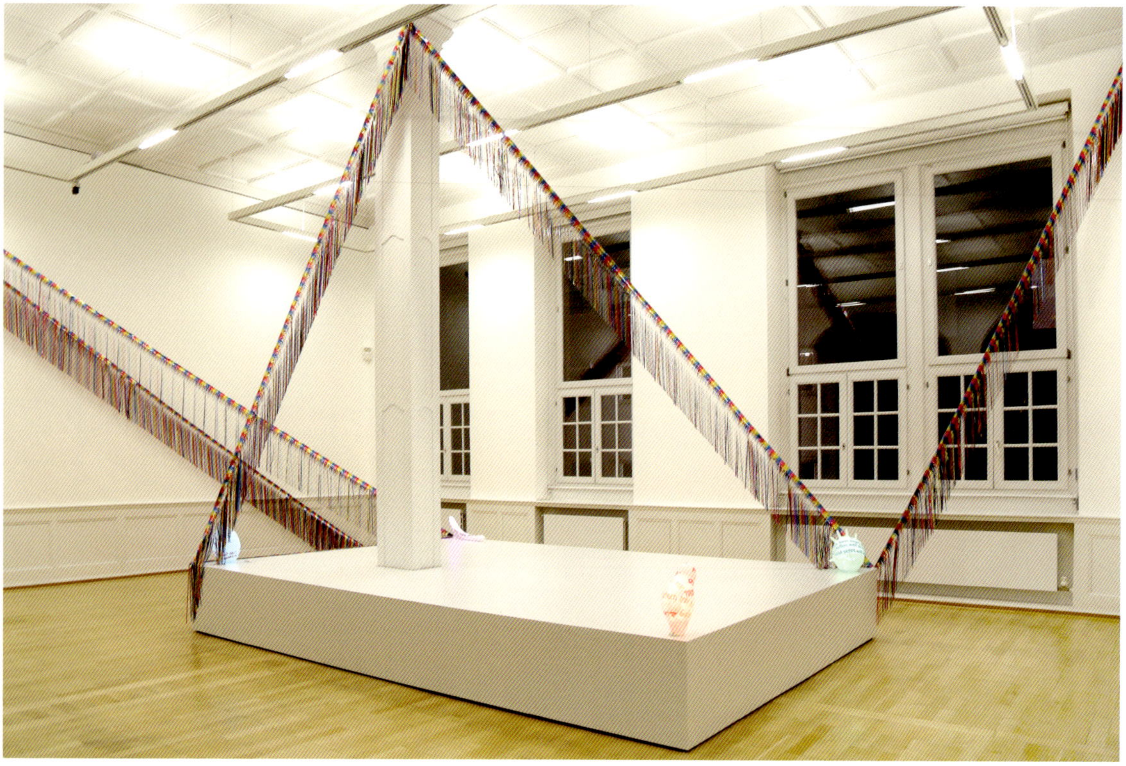

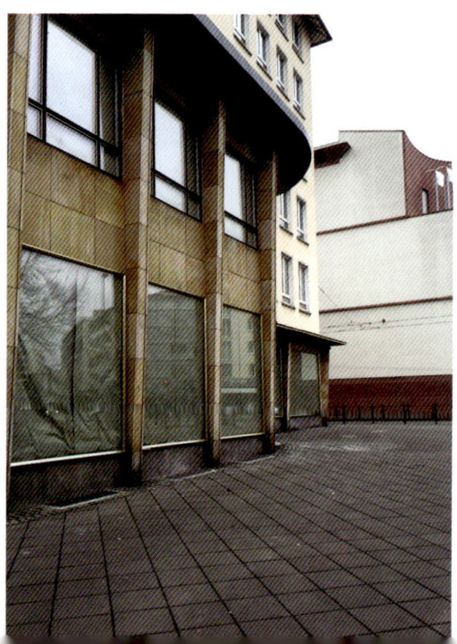

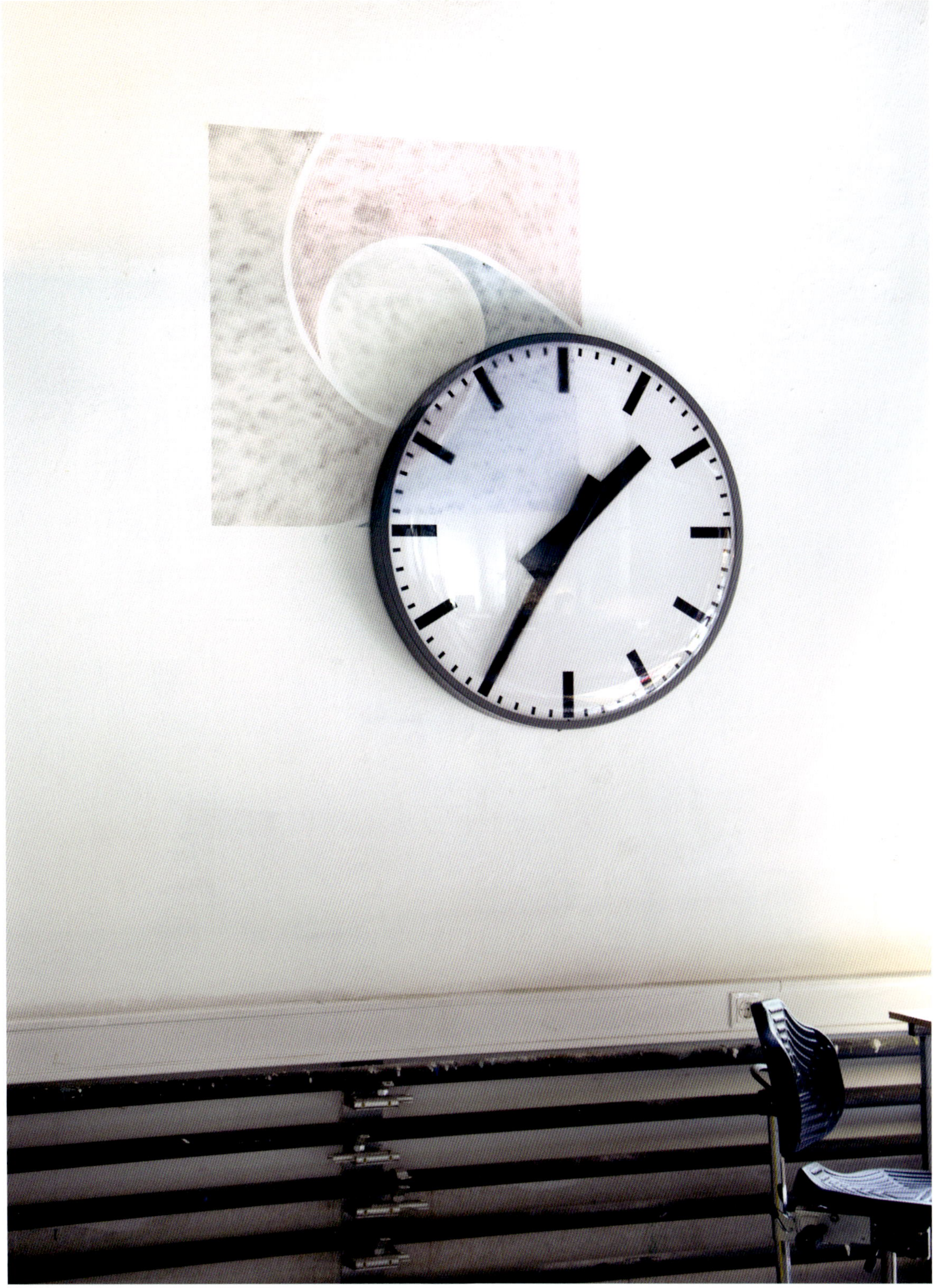

"Semperdepot" Near My Desk, Vienna, 2015
Christian Mayer and Manuel Gorkiewicz
ca. 130 x 130 cm, make-up, skin cream, clock (Vienna mean solar time), 2015

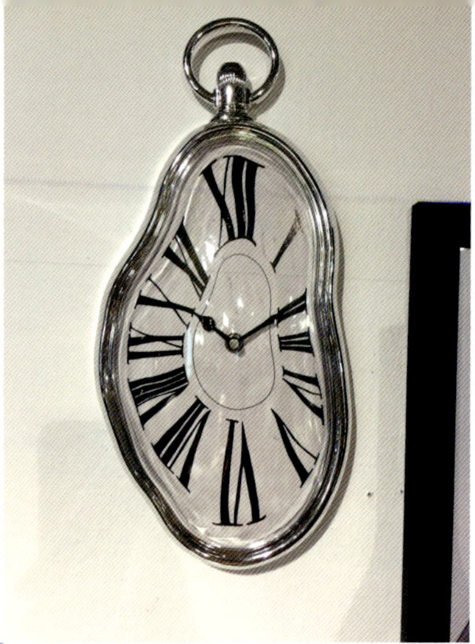

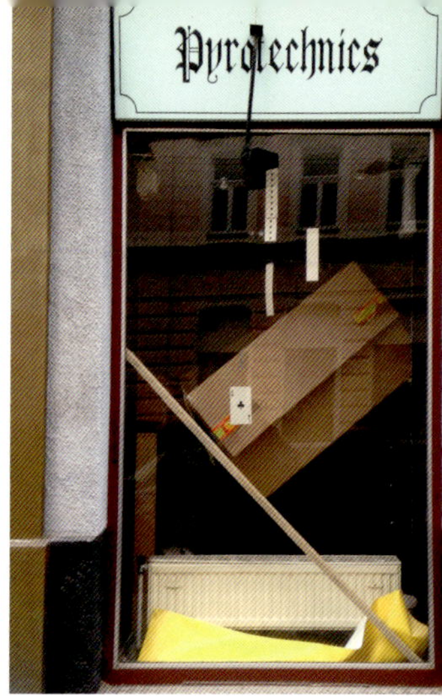
Pyrotechnics

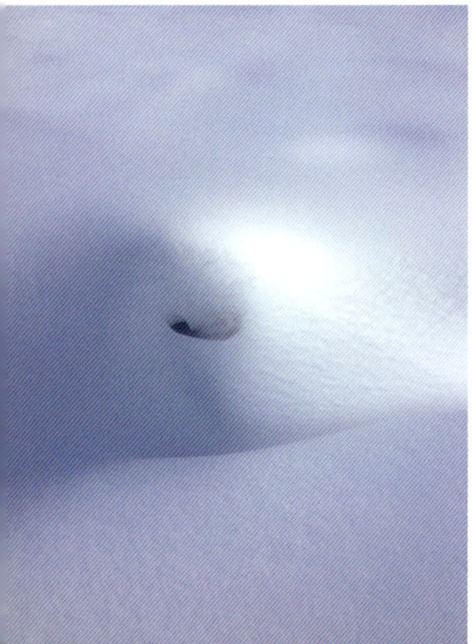

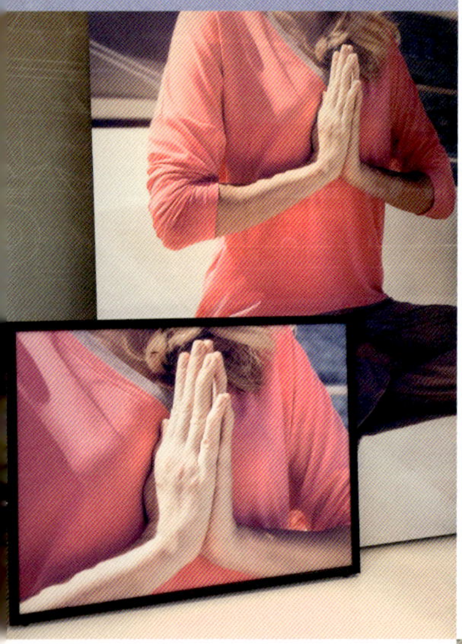

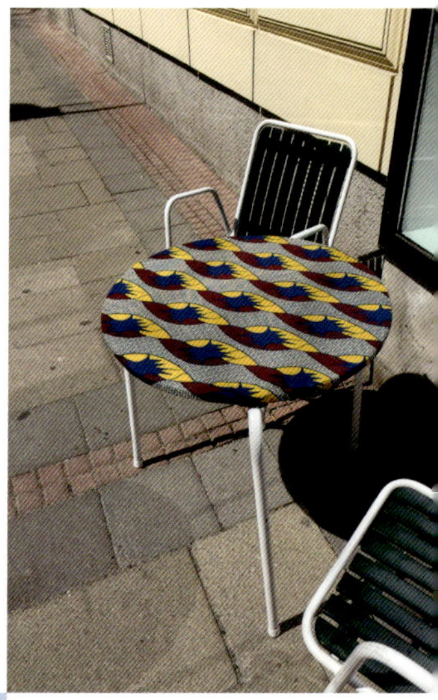

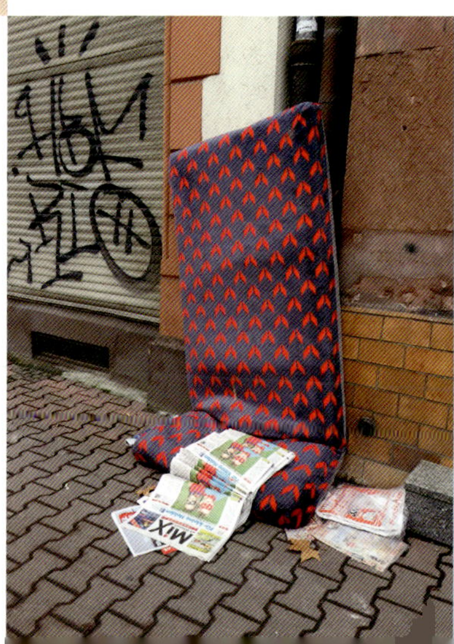

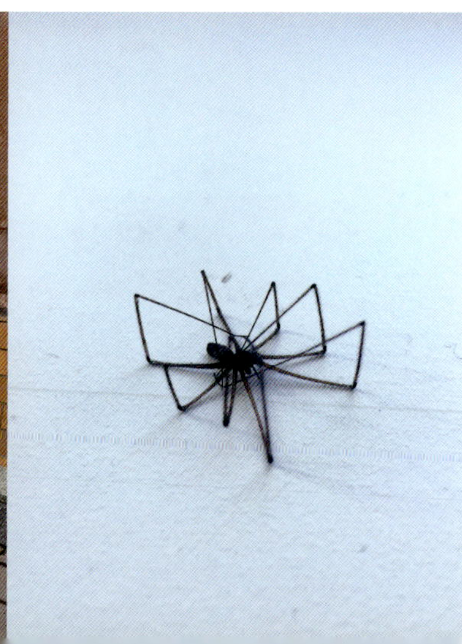

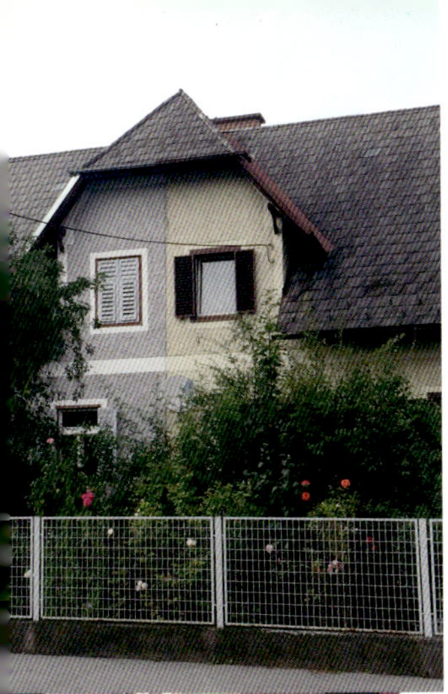
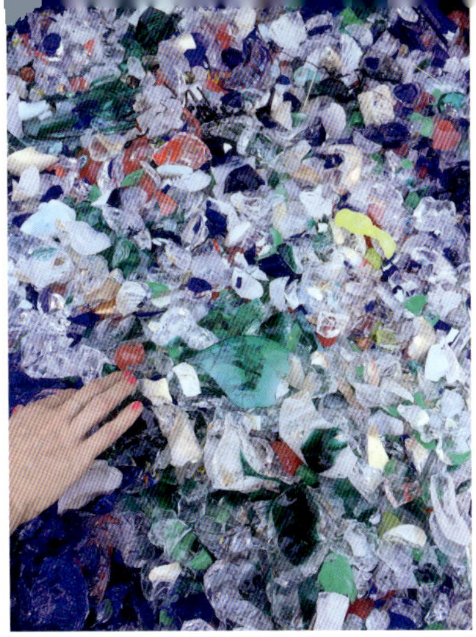
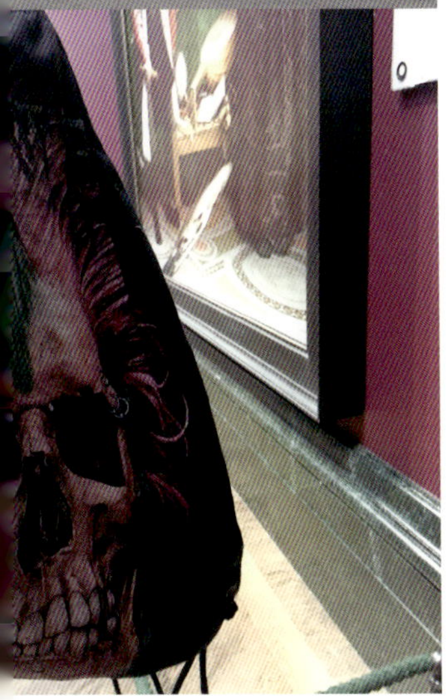
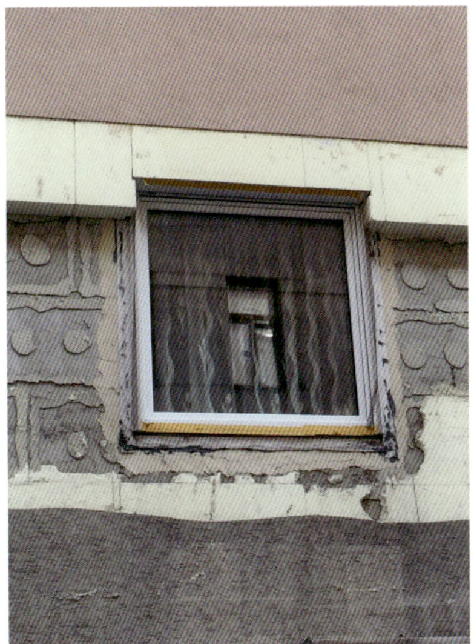
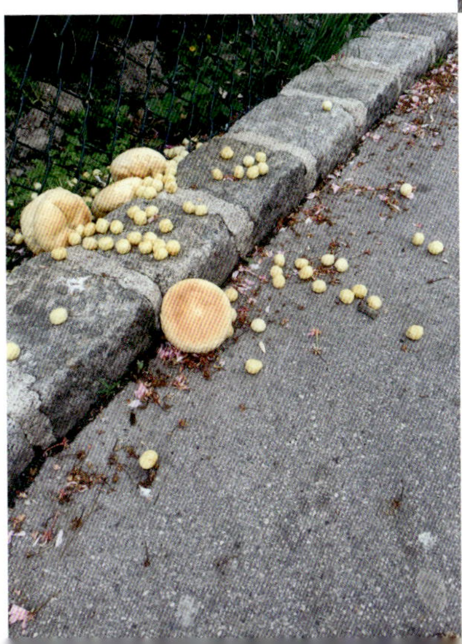
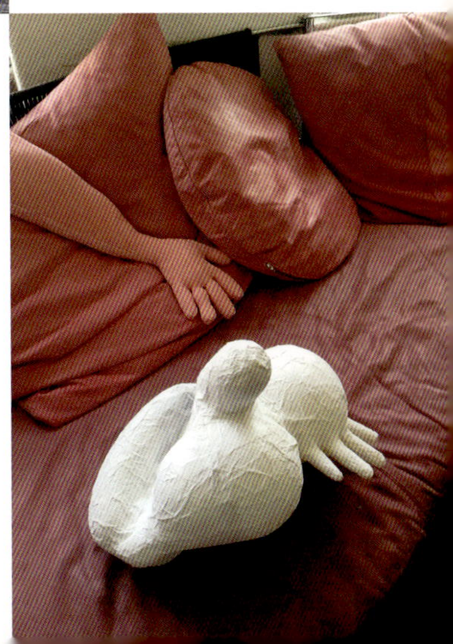

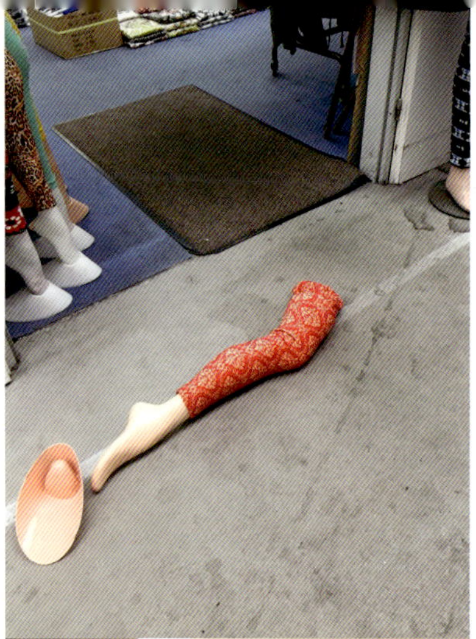

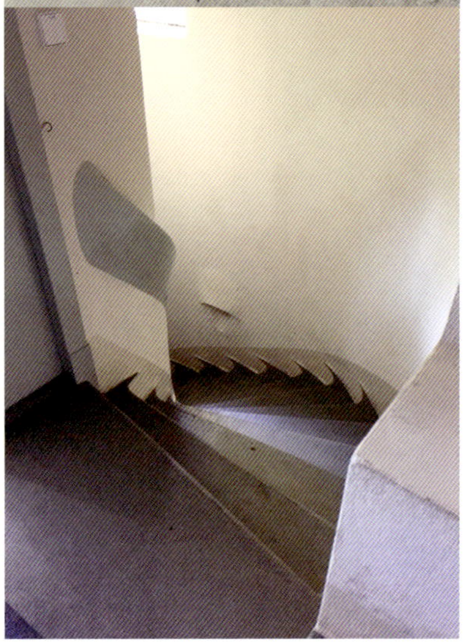

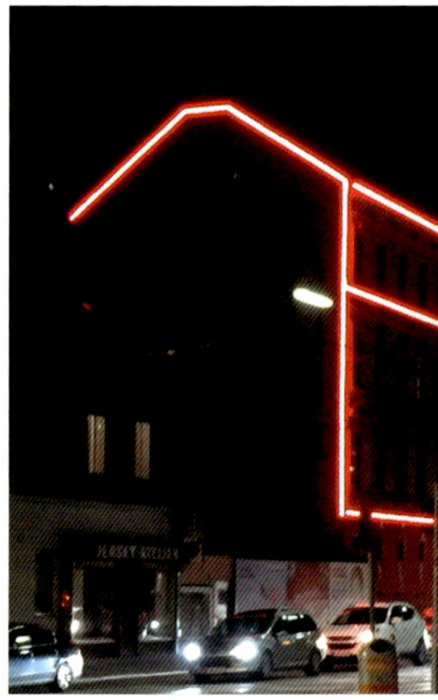

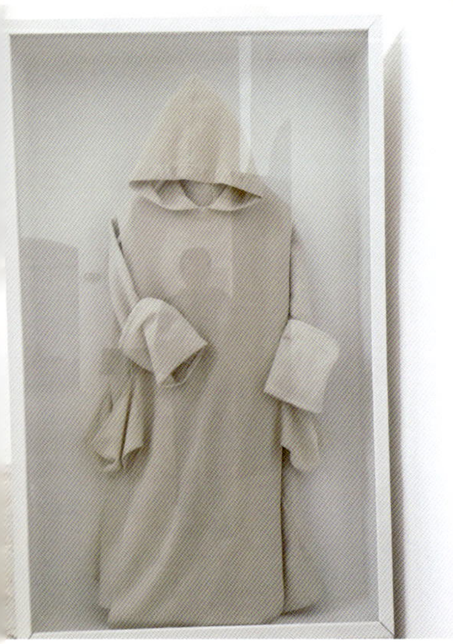

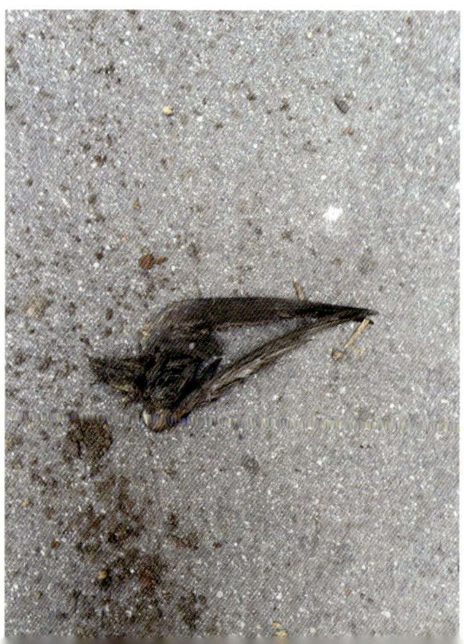

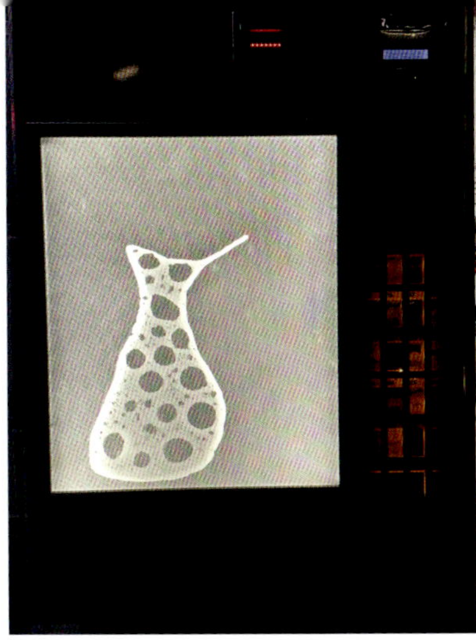

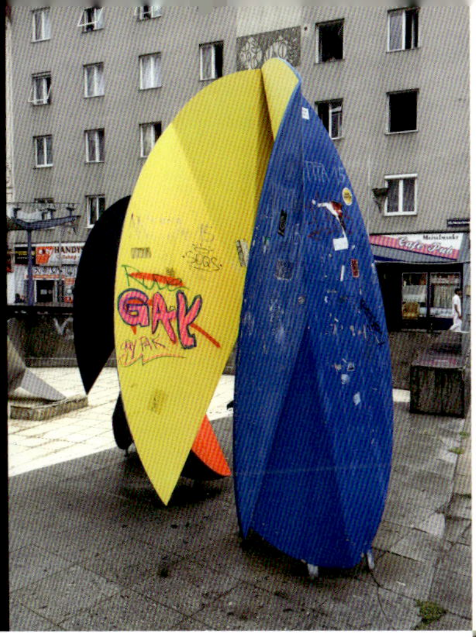

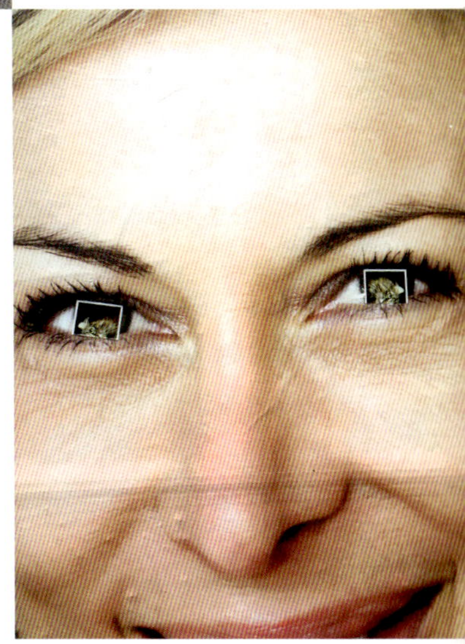

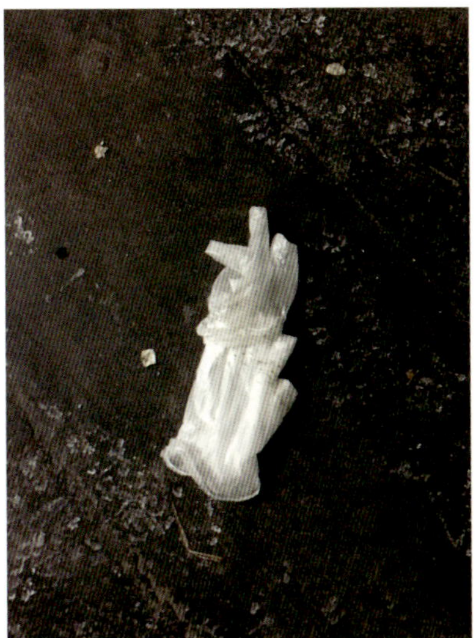

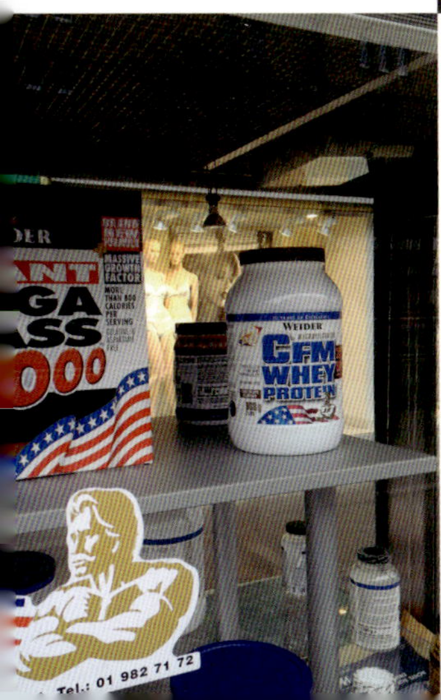
MASSIVE GROWTH FACTOR
MORE THAN 800 CALORIES PER SERVING
WEIDER
CFM WHEY PROTEIN
Tel.: 01 982 71 72

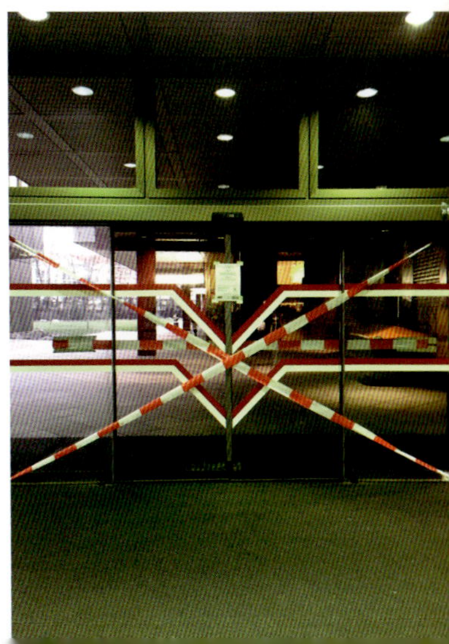

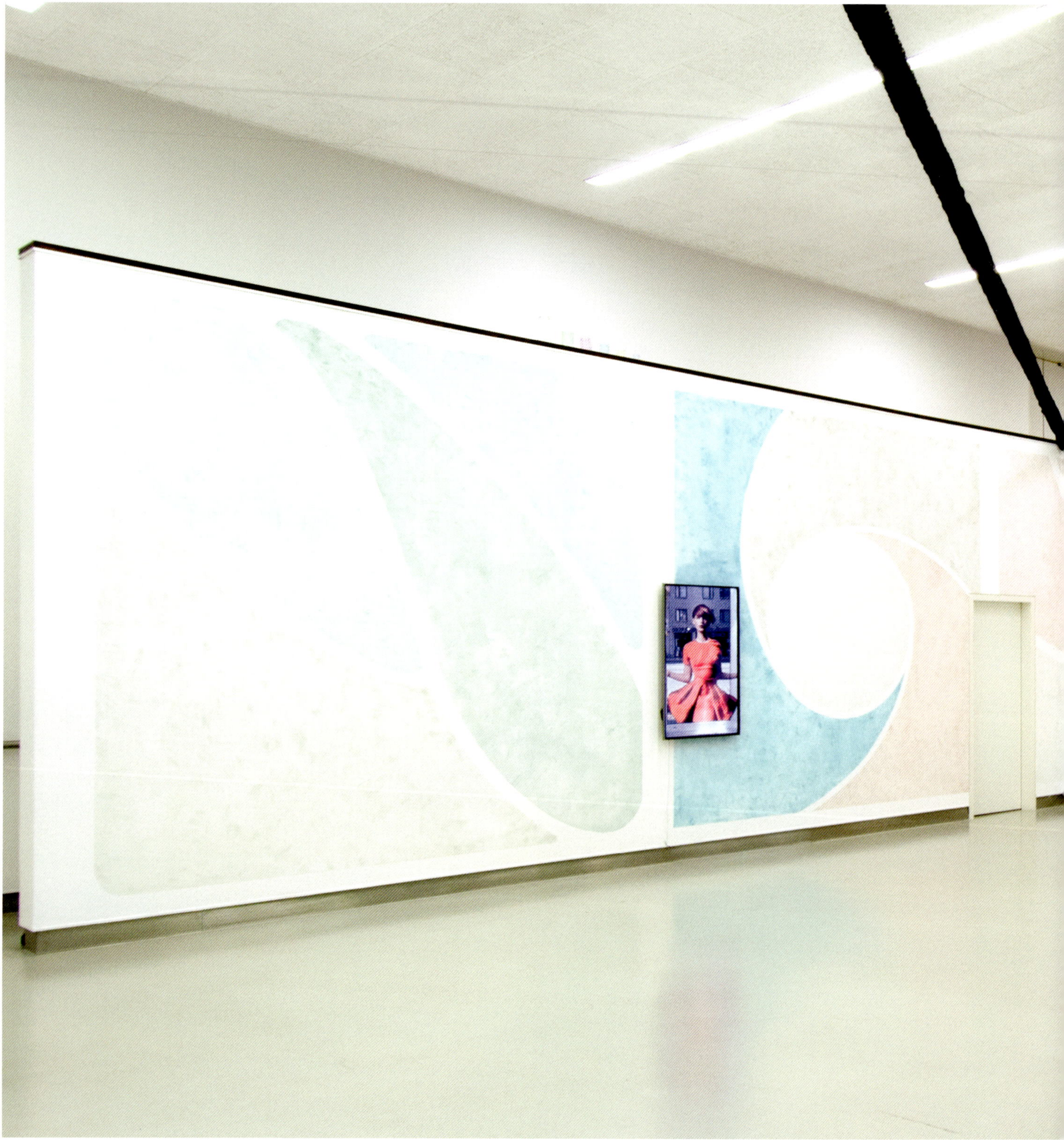

Kunsthalle Nexus, Saalfelden, 2016

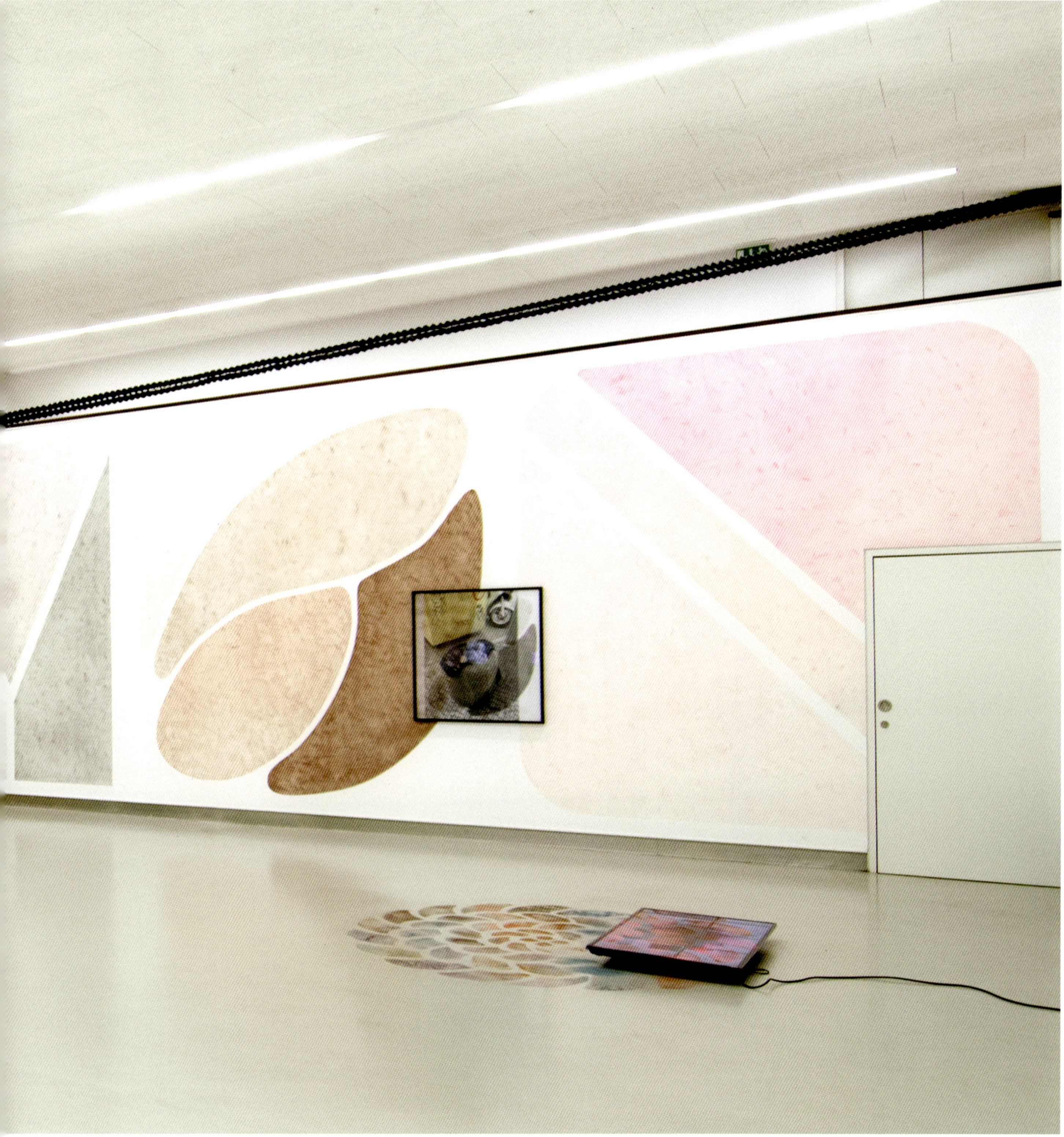

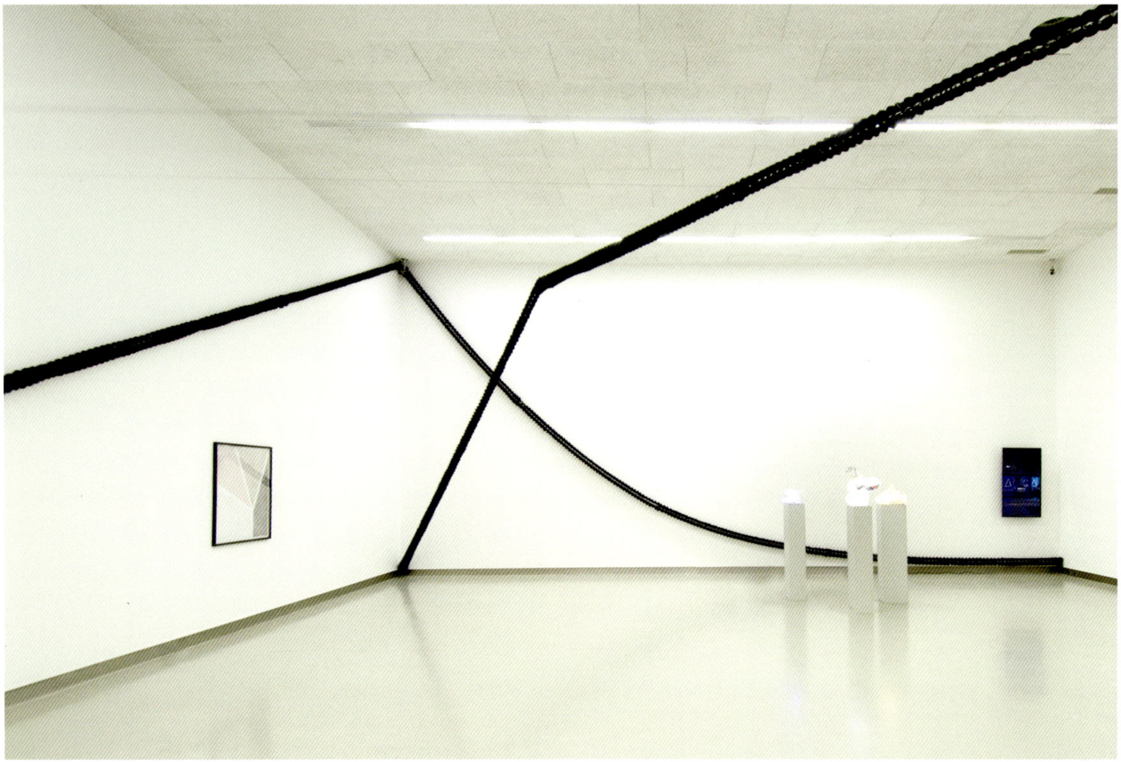

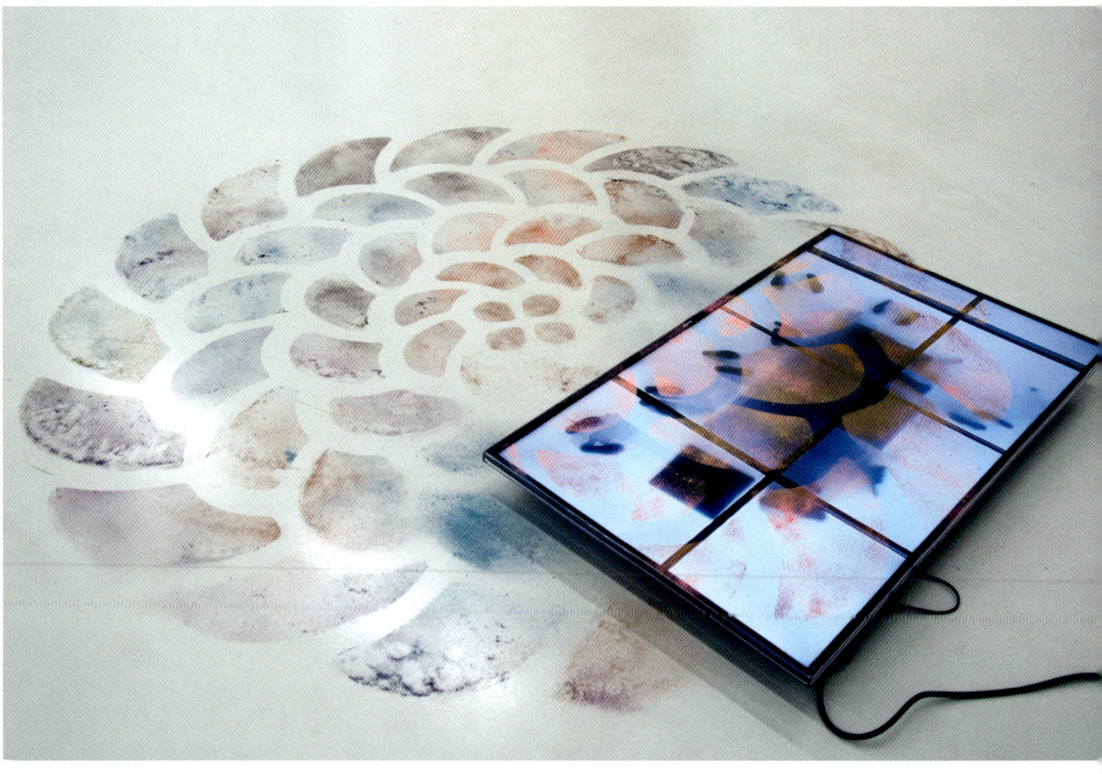

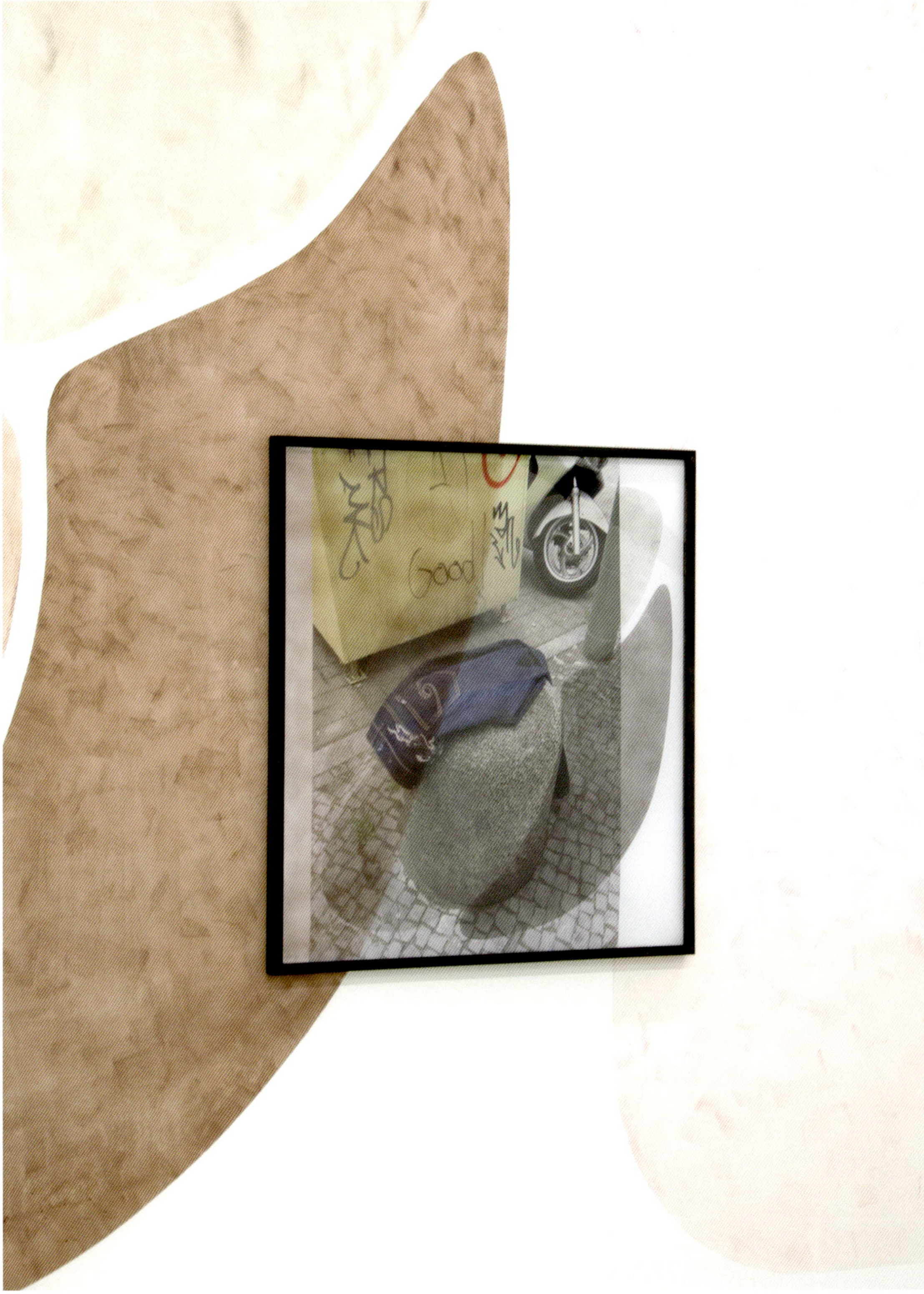

Untitled (Velours Noir), 100 x 100 cm, make-up und skin cream on inkjet print and glass, 2015/16
left page top: installation view
left page bottom:Untitled, ca. 200 x 200 cm, make-up on monitor and floor,
video (3:55 min, loop, sound) 2015/16

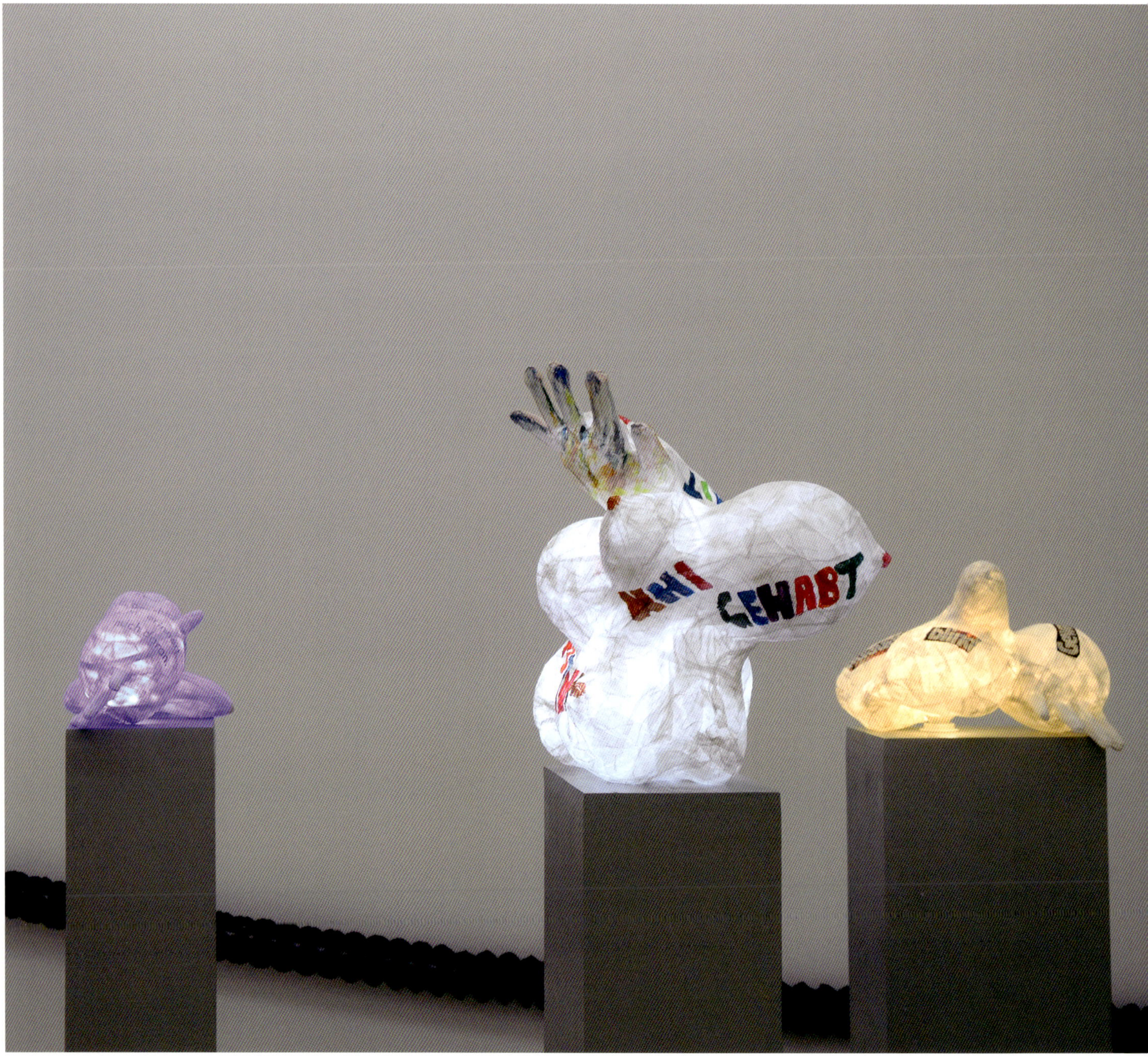
GEHABT

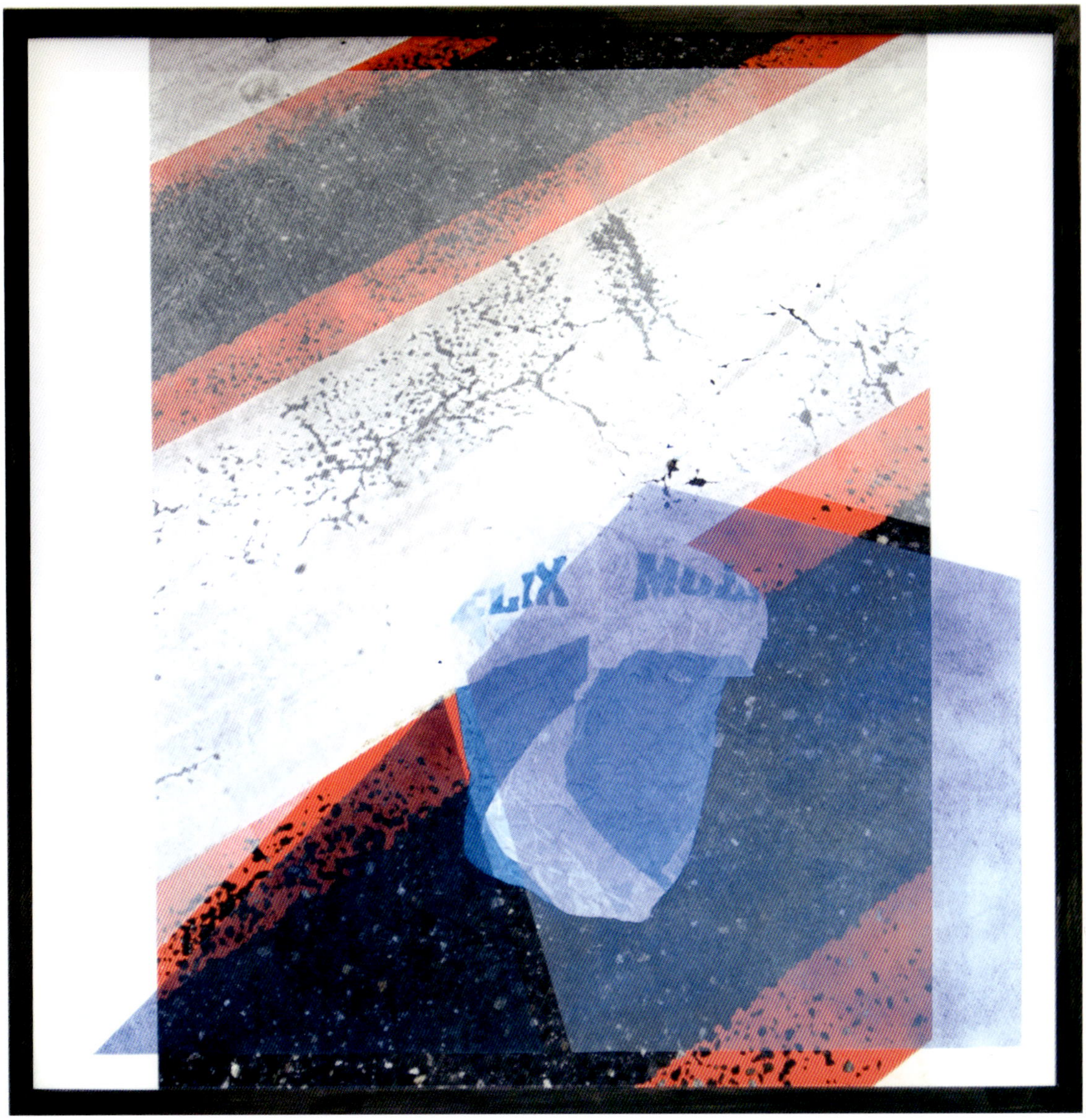

left page:
Antonia Low and Manuel Gorkiewicz: "A.M. wie Agnes Martin"
ca. 20 x 30 x 50 cm, acrylic on paper, LED, 2015/16
Kerstin Cmelka and Manuel Gorkiewicz: "Du hast noch niemand gehabt zum Schlafen mit ihm"
ca. 60 x 30 x 40 cm, gouache on paper, LED, 2015/16
Marten Frerichs and Manuel Gorkiewicz: "o.T. (geiler EUTER)"
ca. 30 x 30 x 40 cm, news paper, paper, LED, 2015/16
this page:
Untitled (Marine Girl), 80 x 80 cm, make-up and skin cream on inkjet print, 2016

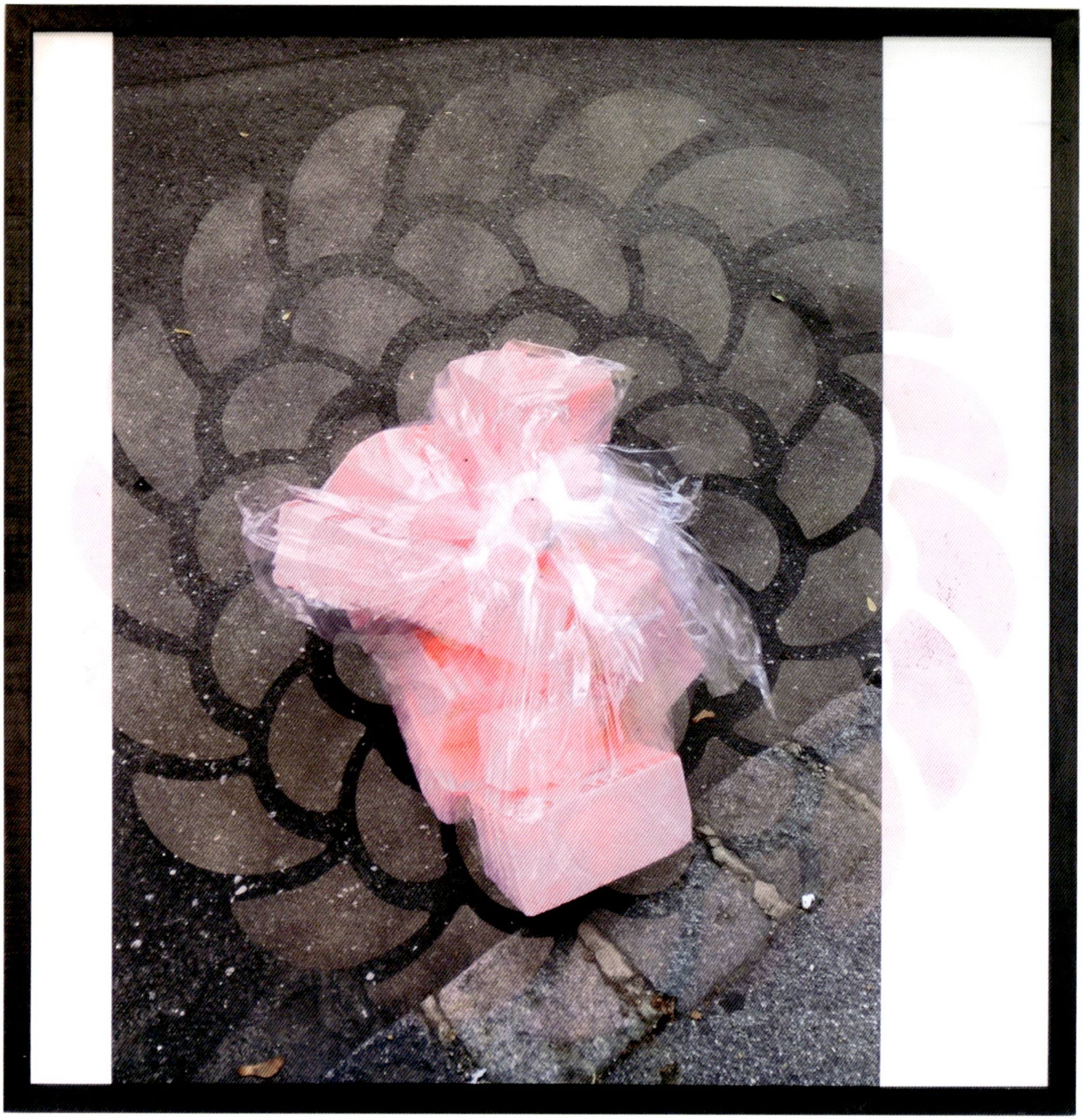

Untitled (Météorites), 80 x 80 cm,
make-up and skin cream on inkjet print, 2016

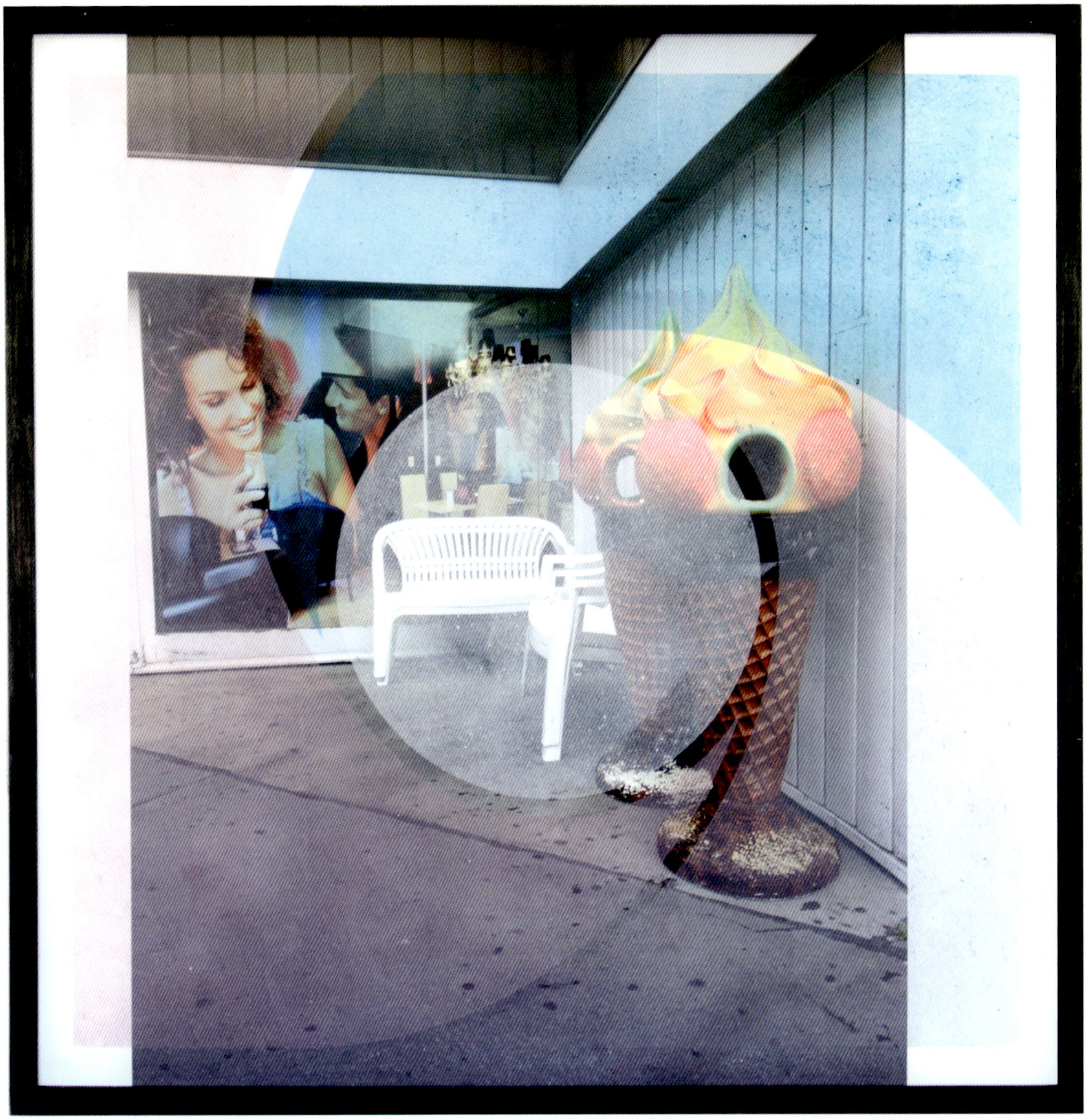

Untitled (Luminous Turquoise), 80 x 80 cm,
make-up and skin cream on inkjet print, 2016

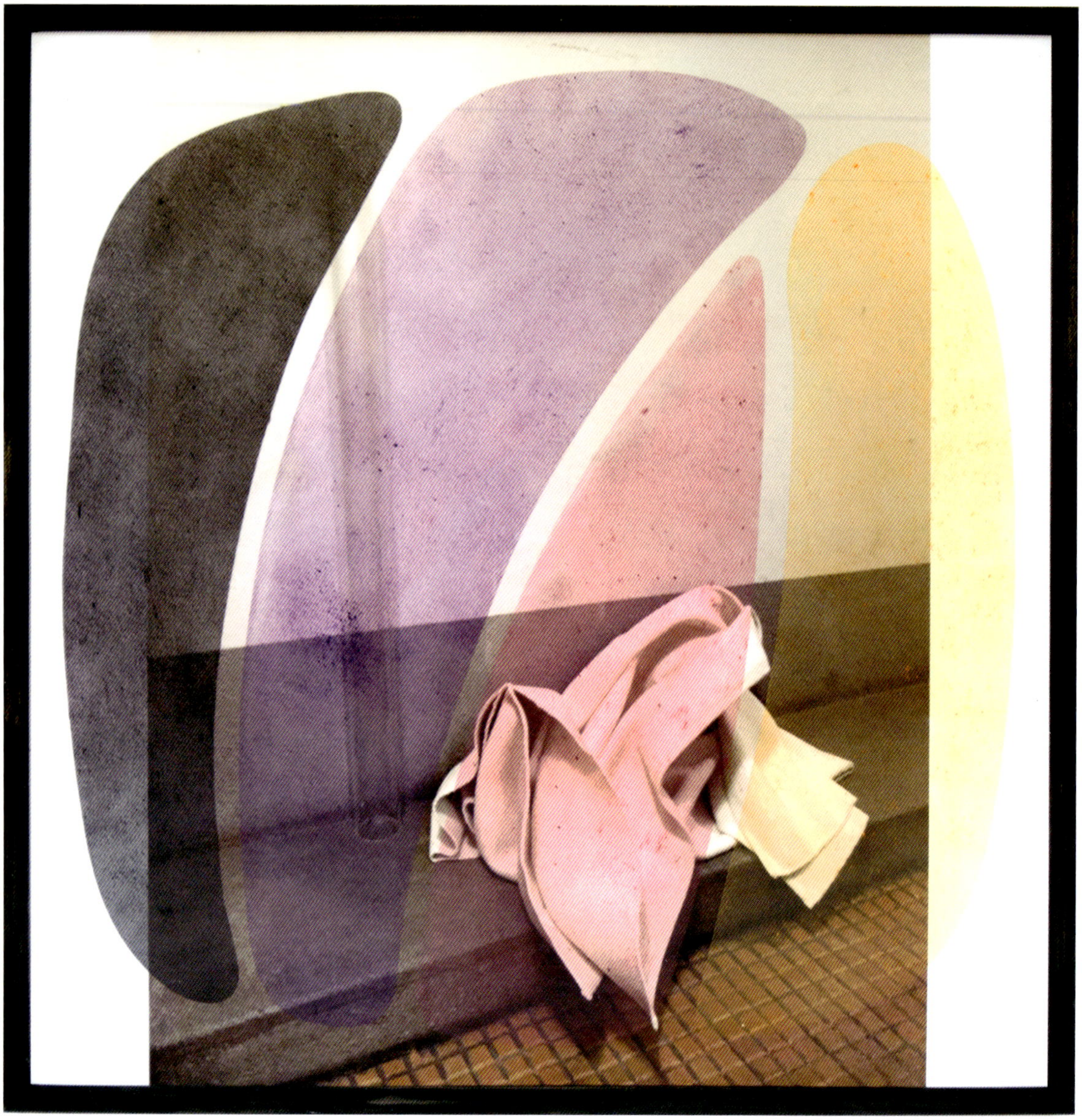

Untitled (Disco Smoking), 80 x 80 cm,
make-up and skin cream on inkjet print, 2016

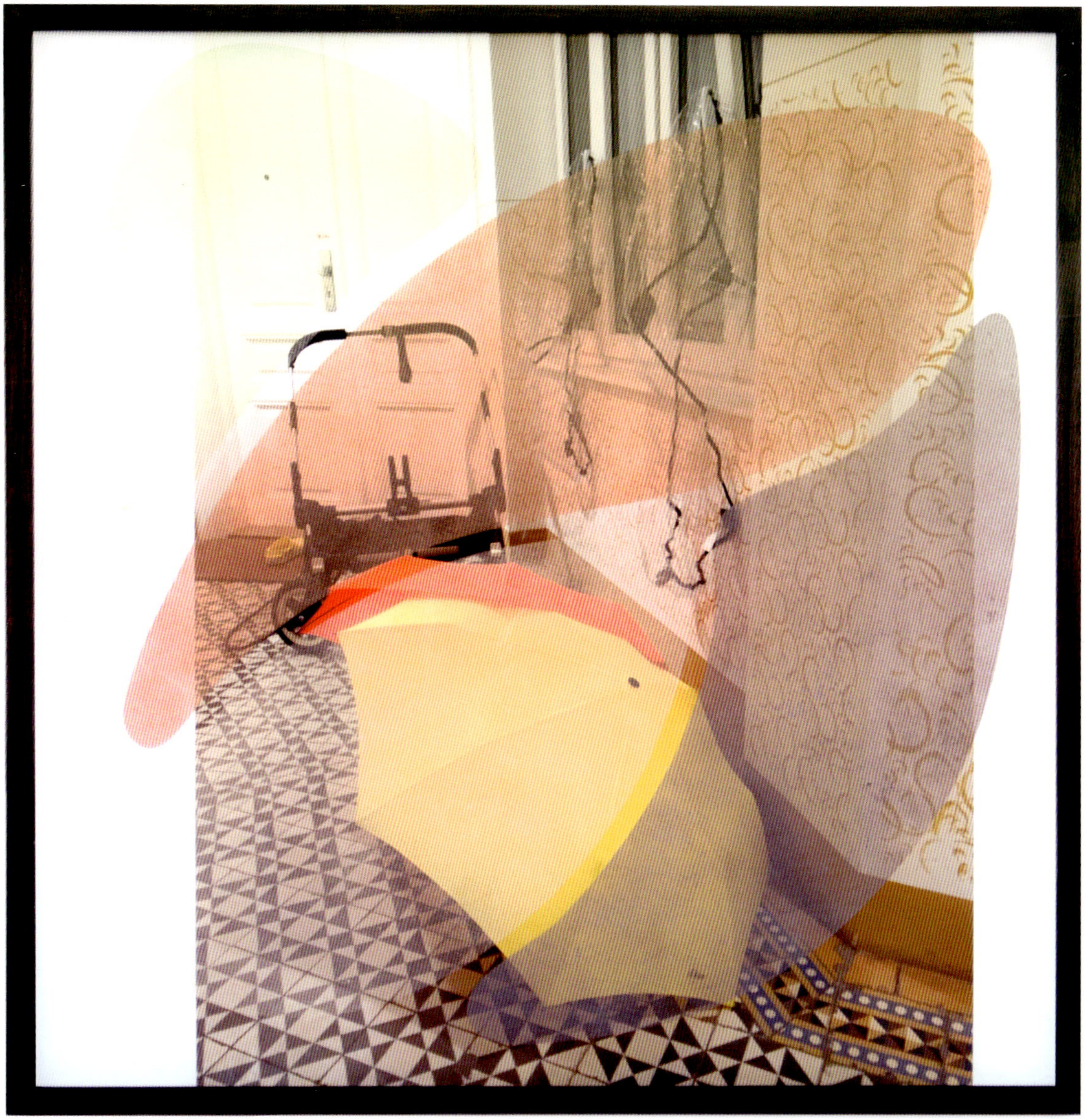

Untitled (Beige Trench), 80 x 80 cm,
make-up and skin cream on inkjet print, 2016

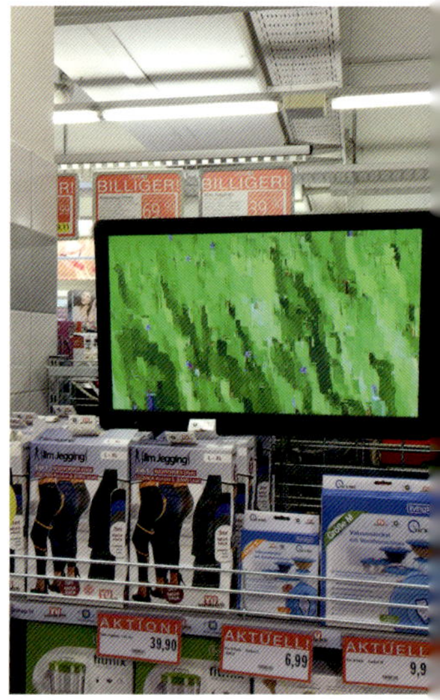
BILLIGER!
BILLIGER!
AKTION!
39,90
AKTUELL!
6,99
AKTUELL!

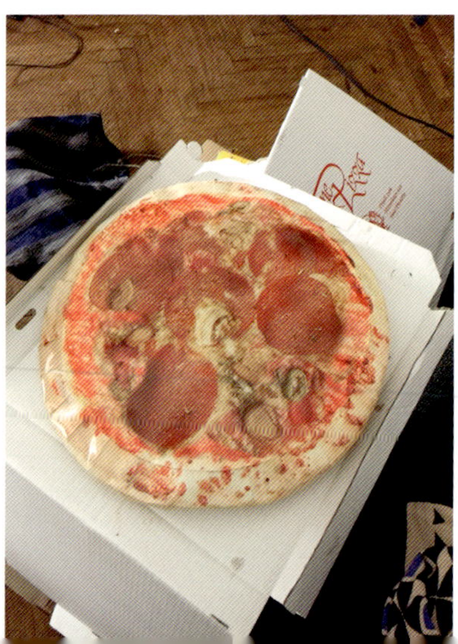

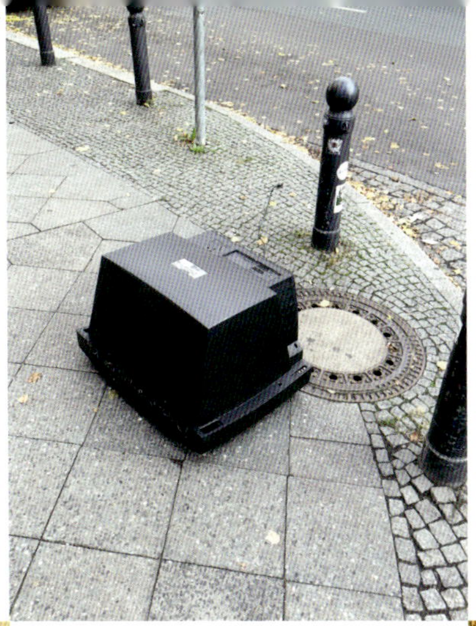

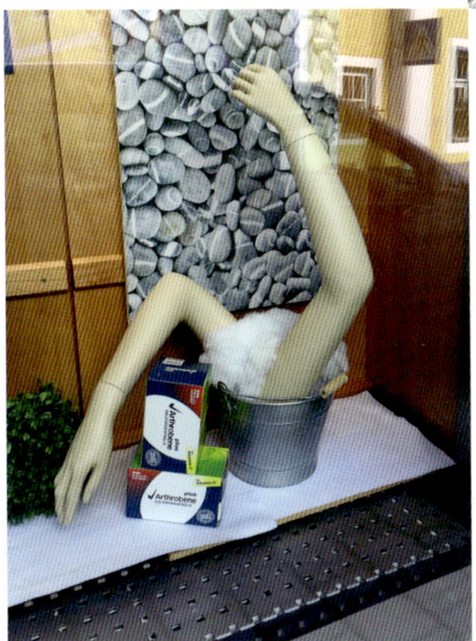

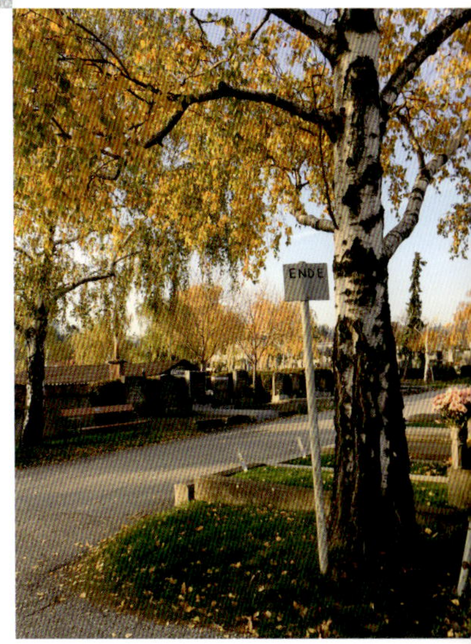
ENDE

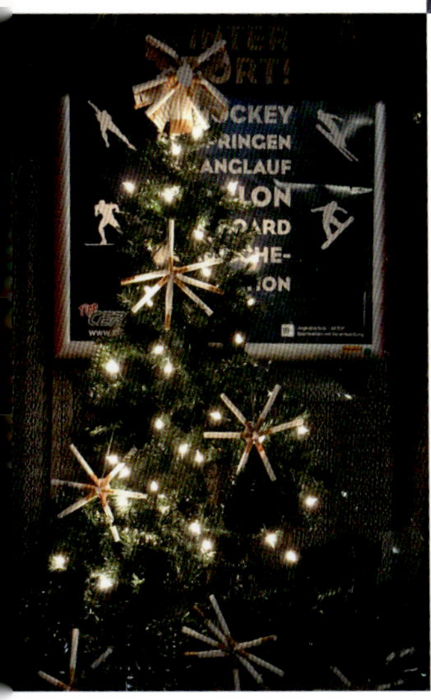

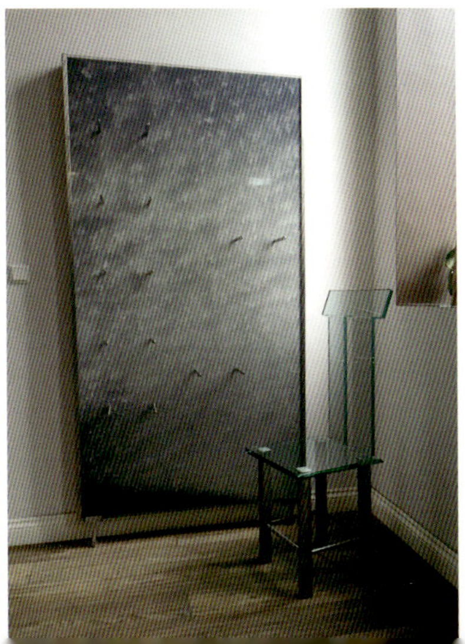

Manuel Gorkiewicz
born 1976 in Graz, lives and works in Vienna

Solo Exhibitions (selected):

2016
Kunsthalle Nexus, Saalfelden
2015
“Kerstin Cmelka mit Manuel Gorkiewicz, Mario Mentrup, Hanno Millesi und Mandla Reuter”
Badischer Kunstverein, Karlsruhe
2013
Galerie Johann Widauer, Innsbruck
2012
Galerie Perpétuel, Frankfurt am Main; Pro Choice, Vienna; “this time dressed”, Der Grieche, Berlin, 2012
with Marten Frerichs and Kerstin Cmelka 2010; Austrian Cultural Forum Prague
2009
“Regarding Branches of Shops and Trees”, skulpturiDK, Copenhagen, with Antonia Low;
Galerie Mezzanin, Vienna
2008
Neue Galerie am Landesmuseum Joanneum, Graz; Galerie Johann Widauer, Innsbruck, with Alexander Wolff
2006
Galerie Mezzanin, Vienna
2005
Antik, Berlin; “Manuel Gorkiewicz, Anna Jermolaewa, Alexander Wolff”, Wiensowski & Harbord, Berlin;
“Performance” Flaca, London, with Alice Chauchat, Christian Egger, Christian Mayer, Yves Mettler,
Magta Tothova, Ruth Weismann, Alexander Wolff
2004
Kunstraum Johann Widauer, Innsbruck; “Manuel Gorkiewicz / Christian Mayer”, Atelier Mandla Reuter, Dresden;
“Offspace, Ass Peep and Champagne”, Musterraum, Pinakothek der Moderne, München
with Anna Jermolaewa and Christian Mayer

Group Exhibitions (selected):

2016
“The Animals” Kunstverein Langenhagen
2015
“It’s all underneath the floor it’s all between the walls”, Heistinger Atelier, Vienna;
“Semperdepot” Near my Desc - Art Space, Vienna, with Christian Mayer; “inside / Outside”, Quadrart Dornbirn;
“Was die Wange rötet, kann übel nicht seyn”, Kerstin Engholm Gallery, Vienna
2014
urbanglass, New York; Ve.Sch, Vienna with Axel Koschier and Robert Müller
“Vogelsbergeriana”, Galerie der Stadt Schwaz; “Arsenale”, Sonnenhaus, Vienna;
“Hic & Nunc”, Stift Klosterneuburg
2013
“Der Schein” kestnergesellschaft, Hannover; “Chat JetPainting ‹Beyond› The Medium” Künstlerhaus, Halle für
Kunst & Medien (KM–), Graz
2012
“Der Grieche at Flutgraben”, Berlin; “Increasingly Colorfol – Current painting from Austria”, Galerie im Taxispalais,
Innsbruck; “Sculpturegarden” Strombad Kritzendorf; “Spazi Aperti X”, Accademia di Romania, Rome;
“Die Sammlung”, 21er Haus, Österreichische Galerie Belvedere, Vienna; “BOBOEGGOHOJOKRLEPIPOSTWI”,
Blattgasse 6, Vienna; “Die illustrierte Ausstellung”, Künstlerhaus Klagenfurt
2011
“Don’t Eat the Yellow Snow”, Wiensowski & Harbord, Berlin; “SLEEP: Performing Statistics”, Bar 17,
Black Door Istanbul; Parkfair, Vienna; “Stolen from my subconscious”, Kunstwerke Berlin
2010
“Georg Eisler Award 2010”, BA Kunstforum, Vienna; “Editionen”, Artelier Contemporary, Graz;
“Project Eisengasse 3” Artelier Collection, Graz; “Fahrenheit” Kunstraum, Schattendorf;
“Multiplex”, Sun Gallery, Munich
2009
“Sleepwalking”, Temporary Gallery, Cologne; Videogalerie Künstlerhaus Wien, Vienna;
“Bulletinboard Blvd.”, Pro Choice, Vienna
2008
“Open Sky”, regionale08, Ilz; Fabrikken for Art and Design, Copenhagen;
“Freunde und Bekannte”, sparwasser hq, Berlin
2007
Preisausstellung der Diözese Graz-Seckau für bildende Kunst, Graz;
“Pimp my Walls”, Apartment Stefan Schuster, Berlin; “Fresh Trips”, Kunstraum Innsbruck;
“Lange Tage”, Galerie Jan Wentrup, Berlin; “Your Latest Trick”, Jet, Berlin; “Øeen Group Show, Copenhagen

2006
"Extension Turn 2", Eastlink Gallery, Shanghai; "Förderungspreisaustellung des Landes Steiermark", Neue Galerie, Graz; "Societé des nationes factice et scindée en elle-même", Circuit, Lausanne; "mehr nicht", Auto, Vienna; "Vista Point" Kunstverein Medienturm, Graz; Austrian Cultural Forum Prague
2005
"Computerprints of whales / too", imPAVILLON, Wels; "Qui Vive", National Center for contemporary Art Moskow; "α β γ" Manuel Gorkiewicz, Marlene Haring, Christian Mayer, Galerie Mezzanin, Vienna; "Entdecken und Besitzen", Mumok, Vienna; "The European Design Show 2005", London Design Museum
2004
"In between spaces", Art Moscow; "Papierarbeiten 2", Studio Tilmann Baumgärtel, Berlin; "Papierarbeiten von Männern", Sudio Olliver Croy, Berlin; "Just what it is... #1", medien.kunst.tirol, Innsbruck; "See you later curator, or how to draw the fine line between high and low", Lassie, Vienna
2003
"Kontext, Form, Troja", Secession, Vienna; "Cadvre Exquis", Steirischer Herbst, Graz; "Office for Temporary Information Work", Medienturm, Graz; "Artkliazma", Moscow; Galerie 422, Gmunden
"Inscribing the Temporal", Kunsthalle Exnergasse, Vienna
2002
"Office for Temporary Information Work", A.T.O.M, Vienna; "Ho-Chi-Mon-Chi-Chi", Buryzone Gallerie, Bratislava; "Doubleheart", Kunsthalle Exnergasse, Vienna

2002–2011 co-editor of the magazine:
"Chicago", "Times", "Plotter", "Helvetica", "DIN", "Techno", "Löhfelm", "RR_02*", "Univers", "Tiffany", "Circuit", "Memphis", "Gringo", "Zeus", "The Mix", "Princess Lulu", "Pigiarniq", "Paper", "Libertine", and "Trixie"
http://www.ztscrpt.net

www.gorkiewicz.net

Kerstin Cmelka, artist, 1999–2005 studied at the Staatliche Hochschule für Bildende Künste – Städelschule, Frankfurt am Main under Peter Kubelka, Monika Schwitte, Thomas Bayrle, and Simon Starling. Lives and works in Berlin.

Christian Egger, artist and curator, studied at Academy of Fine Arts in Vienna. Since 2013 he has been curator at Künstlerhaus, Halle für Kunst und Medien (KM–) in Graz.
Lives and works in Vienna and Graz.

Martin Guttmann, artist and professor of Art and Photography at the Academy of Fine Arts Vienna.
Since 1980, he has worked together with Michael Clegg in the artist duo Clegg&Guttmann.
His works have been shown at international exhibitions such as documenta VIII or the Venice Biennale and are in the collections of: Whitney Museum, Stadtgalerie Stuttgart, Centre George Pompidou, and the Federal Art Collection of Germany in Bonn. Lives and works in Vienna.

About this Publication:

Manuel Gorkiewicz
Therapy
Make-Up Works
Voluptuous U-Turns on the Street of Style, Beauty, and Greed

Translation: George Schreiner

German copyediting: Anna Mirfattahi

English copyediting: Scott Evans

Design, layout, and typesetting: Manuel Gorkiewicz

Published by:
Vfmk Verlag für moderne Kunst GmbH
Salmgasse 4a
A-1030 Wien
hello@vfmk.org
www.vfmk.org

ISBN 978-3-903131-02-6

Printed in Austria

Distribution
D, A, and Europe: LKG, www.lkg-va.de
CH: AVA, www.ava.ch
UK: Cornerhouse Publications, www.cornerhousepublications.org
USA: D.A.P., www.artbook.com

Bibliographic information published by Die Deutsche Nationalbibliothek
Die Deutsche Bibliothek lists this publication in the Deutsche Nationalbibliografie; detailed bibliographic data is available in the Internet at http://dnb.ddb.de.

Edition: 500 copies

Fonts: Various faces of "Helvetica" used as system fonts of iOS from 2009 to 2016.

Mobile phone photos:
Nokia 3120classic (Apr. 2009–Nov. 2011) p.: 2, 4, 6, 7, 12, 13, 18, 22–26,
Samsung SGH-F480 (Nov. 2011–Feb. 2012) p.: 27 – 30
iphone4S (Mar. 2012–Nov. 2014) p.: 31, 34, 35, 42 – 44, 47 – 51, 54, 55, 58, 60, 65 – 67, 71, 72, 78, 79, 83–85, 92, 93, 96, 97
iphone6 (Nov. 2014–Apr. 2016) p.: 98, 101, 104, 103, 105, 108, 109, 114, 116–119, 130, 131, 134–136, 138

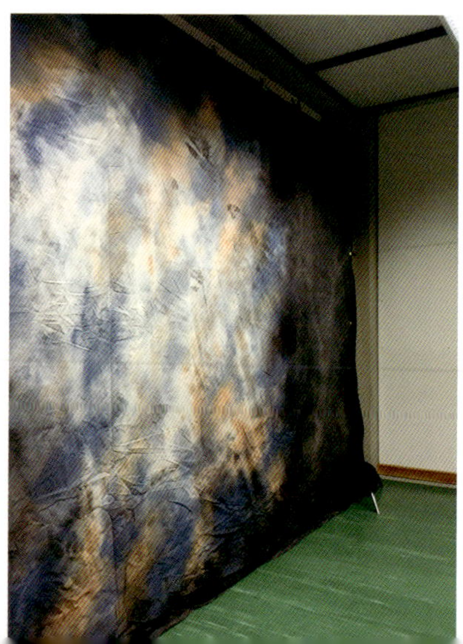

Photo Credits installation shots:
If not otherwise indicated © by Manuel Gorkiewicz
p. 19–21: Ondřej Polák, p. 32: Kerstin Cmelka; p. 38: Catrin Bold, p. 40, 41: Ulrich Dertschei;
p. 64: Markus Krottendorfer; p. 77 top: Nikolaus Schletterer; p. 82: Elena Valdrè; p. 90: Stefan Lux;
p. 102, 103: WEST.Fotostudio; p. 110, 111: Stephan Baumann, bild_raum

Special thanks to:
Svenja Deininger, Anna Jermolaewa, Alina Kolar, Christian Mayer, and Stefanie Seufert

and to the authors:
Kerstin Cmelka, Christian Egger, Martin Guttmann

Printed by Holzhausen www.holzhausen.at

Sponsored by:
Bundeskanzleramt Österreich Kunst und Kultur, Kulturamt der Stadt Graz, Kulturamt des Landes Steiermark,
Galerie Johann Widauer Innsbruck

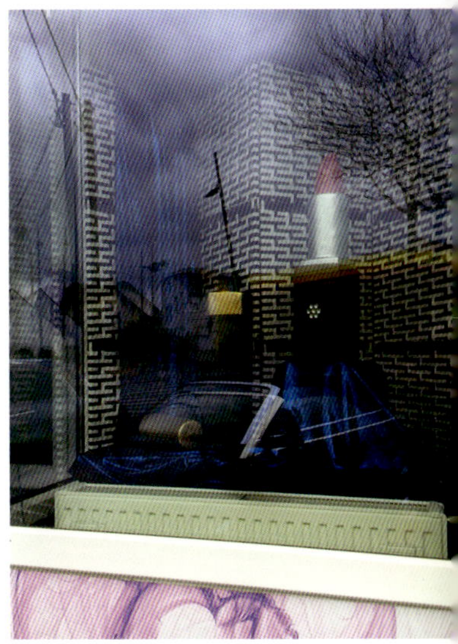

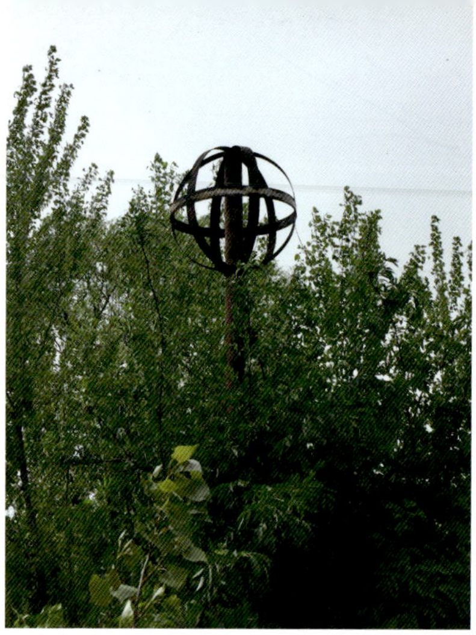

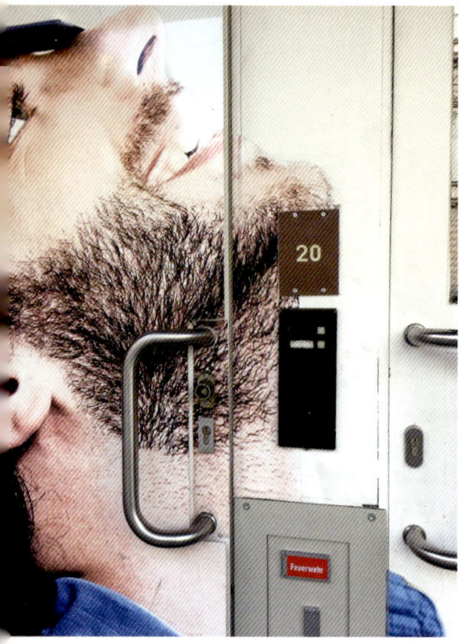
20

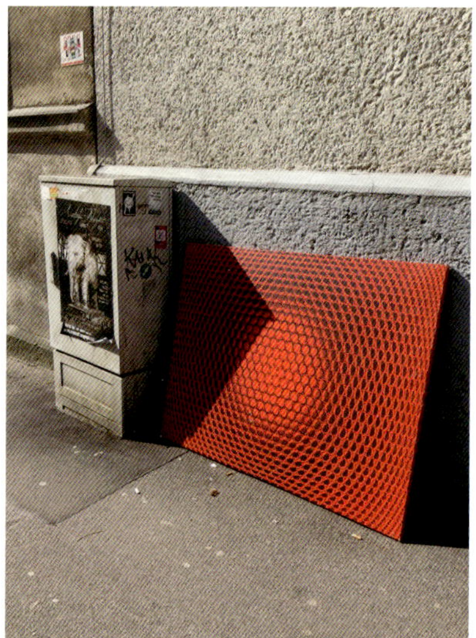

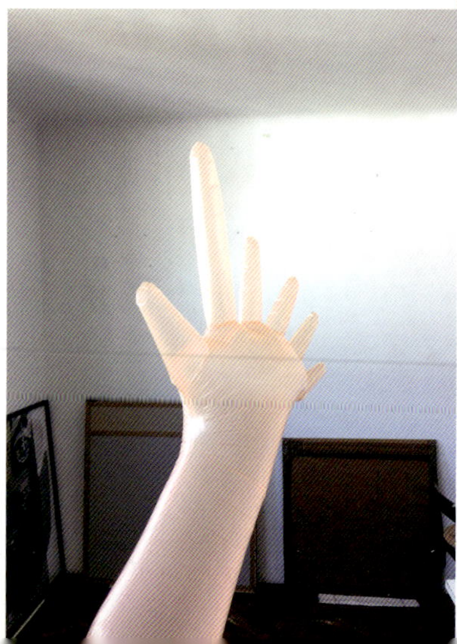